INSECT HISTORIES
OF EAST ASIA

Edited by David A. Bello

and Daniel Burton-Rose

INSECT

HISTORIES

of

EAST ASIA

UNIVERSITY OF WASHINGTON PRESS

SEATTLE

Insect Histories of East Asia was made possible in part by a grant
from the Samuel and Althea Stroum Endowed Book Fund.

UNIVERSITY OF WASHINGTON PRESS *uwapress.uw.edu*

LIBRARY OF CONGRESS CONTROL NUMBER: 2023933099
ISBN: 978-0-295-75178-8 (hardcover)
ISBN: 978-0-295-75180-1 (paperback)
ISBN: 978-0-295-75179-5 (ebook)

♾ This paper meets the requirements of ANSI/NISO Z39.48-1992
(Permanence of Paper).

DAVID A. BELLO   *In memory of my mentor, John E. Wills Jr.*

DANIEL BURTON-ROSE   *To Benjamin A. Elman, for emphasizing the internal coherence of the early modern Sinosphere, and Susan Naquin, for welcoming new perspectives without sacrificing attention to detail.*

CONTENTS

PART THREE THE INSTITUTIONALIZATION
OF ENTOMOLOGY IN TWENTIETH-CENTURY CHINA

ACKNOWLEDGMENTS

This collection grew out of "Accounting for Uncertainty: Prediction and Planning in Asia's History," a two-summer interdisciplinary collaboration organized by the Max Planck Institute for the History of Science (MPIWG) in Berlin and the International Consortium for Research in the Humanities' "Fate, Freedom and Prognostication" project at the University of Erlangen-Nuremburg. Our first thanks are due to Dagmar Schäfer and Michael Lackner, the coconveners of the "Accounting" project. Contributors Mårten Söderblom Saarela and Kerry Smith also shared affiliations with MPIWG; extended face-to-face collaboration between multiple contributors has enable a greater integration of concerns and topics than is often possible in a conference-derived anthology.

We also wish to express our thanks to fellow participants in the panel titled "Insects Histories: Contested Boundaries in Human-Insect Interfaces, 1700s–1950s" at the 2018 Annual Meeting of the American Historical Association. Our commentator Nancy Jacobs shared her perspectives on the global field of environmental history and animal studies, while Diogo de Carvalho Cabral and Frederico Freitas provided valuable insight into a different area studies approach to insect humanities with their expertise as environmental historians of Latin America.

Kjell Ericson and C. Pierce Salguero generously shared expertise and contacts. Susie Yue Wu contributed to our thinking on Chinese literature, mosquitoes, and metaphors. Anna Andreeva gave us confidence that our line of inquiry could prove fruitful in medieval Japan. Sue Naquin provided general encouragement. In addition to thanks that appear in several individual contributions, the editors also wish to express our gratitude to the following readers of individual pieces or the entire manuscript: Nicole Barnes, Lin Hsiu-ling, Tyler Feezell, and Setoguchi Akihisa. Three anonymous reviews commissioned by the University of Washington Press provided valuable suggestions for improving the overall coherency of this collection. We would also like to thank Annie Xi Wang, the curatorial assistant for the special collections at the Harvard-Yenching Library, for going above and beyond in making rare materials available to us during the pandemic. Daniel Burton-Rose would like to express his gratitude to his colleagues in the History Department at Wake Forest University and the librarians of Z. Smith Reynolds Library who provided a felicitous environment in which to complete this collection. David A. Bello would like to extend special thanks to friend and colleague C. Michele Thompson for her graceful and judicious interventions.

At the University of Washington Press we wish to thank Lorri Hagman, executive editor, for her enthusiasm for the project and consistent engagement with conceptual challenges and logistical hurdles, as well as Marcella Landri, assistant editor, and Joeth Zucco, senior project editor, for seeing the manuscript into production. Elizabeth Mathews provided the invaluable service of careful copyediting.

A NOTE ON TERMS AND CONVENTIONS

Dates in the lunar calendar are formatted with the abbreviated reign name for Chinese emperors, or full reign names for Chosŏn kings, followed by year/month/day (e.g., QL 52/9/2 for the second day of the ninth month of the fifty-second year of the Qianlong reign, Chŏngjo 5/3/21 for the twenty-first day of the third month of the fifth year of Chŏngjo's reign).

Chinese characters are provided in the text when they are necessary to illustrate a linguistic point. Other characters, such as those for personal names and titles of literary works mentioned in the text, are included in the glossary.

When unclear from the context, the linguistic origin of terminology is indicated with the initials C (Chinese), J (Japanese), K (Korean), and M (Manchu).

CHRONOLOGY OF DYNASTIES, REIGN PERIODS, AND COUNTRIES

Early China
Shang (ca. 1600–1046 BCE)
Zhou (1046–256 BCE)
    Western Zhou (1046–771 BCE)
    Eastern Zhou (771–256 BCE)
Spring and Autumn period
    (ca. 770–476 BCE)
Warring States (ca. 453–221 BCE)

Imperial China
Han 202 BCE–220 CE
    Western Han (202 BCE–8 CE)
    Eastern Han (25–220 CE)
Six Dynasties (220–589)
    Jin (266–420)
Tang (618–907)
Song (960–1279)
    Northern Song (960–1127)
    Southern Song (1127–1279)
Yuan (1271–1368)
Ming (1368–1644)
Qing (1644–1912)
    Kangxi (r. 1661–1722)
    Yongzheng (r. 1723–35)
    Qianlong (r. 1736–95)
    Jiaqing (r. 1796–1820)

Modern China
Republic of China (1912–49)
People's Republic of China
    (1949–present)

Japan
    Edo period (1600–1868)
    Meiji period (1868–1912)

Korea
    Chosŏn dynasty (1392–1897)
    Korean Empire (1897–1910)
    Japanese colonial period
    (1910–45)

FIGURE I.1. The filial paragon Wu Meng, offering his own flesh to mosquitoes in order to keep them from feeding on his parents, who were too poor to afford a protective net. From *Ershisi xiao tuzan* (Twenty-four filial paragons, with images and encomiums). Shanghai: Yihua Tang, 1873. Courtesy of the Harvard-Yenching Library.

Introduction

David A. Bello and Daniel Burton-Rose

From the cry of a tiny insect,
one can hear the sound of a vast world.
—Zhang Daye, *The World of a Tiny Insect*

Consider two images printed in China seventy years apart. The first features mosquitoes hovering over a dozing child reclining on a cot in a humble open-air building (fig. 1.1); beyond the area depicted, the parents for whom he sacrifices himself rest peacefully. In the second, a skeleton personifying Death rides a giant mosquito over an urban area, invoking the war planes that rained down destruction from the sky (fig. 1.2). These primary sources provide windows into cultural phenomena and political events, prompting lines of inquiry into filial praxis in popular ethics and the bitterly fought Sino-Japanese War (1937–45). In each image, mosquitoes embody a cultural message concerning the oversized place of tiny insects as metaphors.

This volume follows insects to explore the complex interactions of human societies and their embedded ecologies in Chinese, Japanese, and Korean history. The time span covered is vast—from the earliest written records to the mid-twentieth century—as is the geographical range: Manchuria and the Korean Peninsula in Northeast Asia, the Japanese archipelago in the east, and mainland China, occupying huge swaths of continental southeastern Asia. We make no pretensions of comprehensive coverage; our goal is to look more closely.

In working through a historical record created by literate people, we critically employ biological knowledge about insect species as a means of filling in information often unavailable to those who created the primary source record. We recognize the inevitable cultural qualifications on the aspiration for objectivity in scientific discourse and appreciate the technological and analytical means now developed for observing empir-

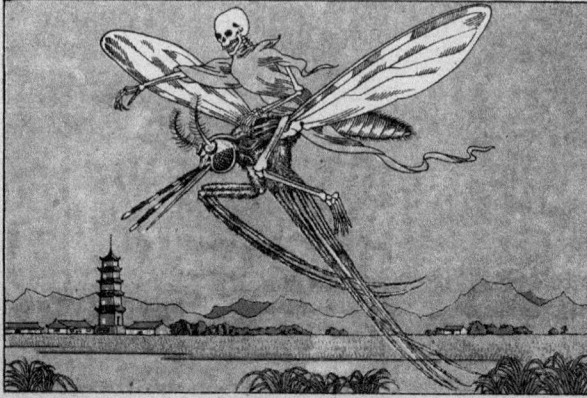

FIGURE I.2. Combating malaria through mosquito eradication. From a public health calendar produced by the National Institute of Health of the Republic of China, July 1943. Courtesy of the History of Medicine Division, US National Library of Medicine.

ical reality. In the terminology developed in the long-running dialogue between the fields of history of science and environmental history, our project is constructivist in its historicization and contextualization of all systems created by humans that claim objectivity, and it is materialist in insisting on a concrete reality underlying potentially infinite representational regimes.[1] The more materialist chapters in this volume align with scholars in animal studies interested in moving beyond human representations of the nonhuman to find new ways to explore nonhuman agency historically.[2] Other chapters examine how human historical actors attempted to perceive insects as a totality and as specific species. This project thus combines humanistic methodology with a measured reading of present-day biological scholarship to triangulate an ecologically dynamic picture of the past. We call this analytical approach insect humanities and employ it in East Asia, our area of expertise. In this we are using methodology to pursue lines of inquiry in tandem with scholars of colonial ecologies in Korea under Japanese imperialism, South Asia under British rule, and Brazil.[3]

A perspective altered by placing insects at the center of inquiry is exemplified in figure 1.1, which depicts a young boy with his hair in a topknot wearing only a bib. He lies at apparent ease on a platform in an open-walled structure within a fenced enclosure. Aside from some tufts of grass in the yard, the only other living creatures are eleven winged specks. In the rough woodblock carving, they could pass for a range of creatures, from wasps to moths. The accompanying text clarifies what the viewer is intended to see. Titled *Unrestrainedly Mosquitoes Drink Their Fill of Blood* (Ziwen bao xue) and attributed to the literati-official Zhu Youran (1836–1882), it reads:

> Jin [dynasty (266–420)]. Wu Meng. Eight years of age; by nature of utmost filiality.
>
> As his family was poor, its sleeping divan had no netting. Every summer night the mosquitoes swarmed on his skin to eat their fill of blood and gore with abandon. Although there were many, he did not swat them off because he feared if he did so, they would leave him to bite his parents. Such is the utmost love in mind and body for one's parents!

The encomium perorates:

On summer nights without [mosquito] netting
Mosquitos amass, but [he] daren't shoo them away
They eat their fill of blood and gore with abandon
Thus avoiding being sent forth through his parents' bed curtain[4]

In the *Twenty-Four Filial Paragons,* Wu Meng is the only one who proves his filial devotion through a relationship with bugs. The systematization of filial paragons, which began in the Han dynasty (202 BCE–220 CE), is often regarded as portraying the moral quintessence of Sinitic culture embodied in the most essential of human relationships. In Wu's case, it is the biological imperatives of mosquitoes that make his filial act possible: they serve as a catalyst for the tempering of this foundational human link.

Mosquito behavior inspired agendas beyond those of the immediate family order. Unrestrainable appetite for blood offered ample occasions for extended Confucian moralism: as contributor Olivia Milburn has documented elsewhere, medieval Chinese poets frequently allegorized these bloodsuckers to corrupt officials.[5] A similar voracity—and intimidating strength in numbers—shown by locusts inspired their use in the same allegorical manner in premodern Chinese literature.[6] In both cases, literati zoomorphically naturalized insect behavior as a distinctively pejorative characteristic of a particularly distasteful demographic. This social resonance of insect-inspired metaphors was not limited to the vast area known as China: it radiated out to diverse cultural groups intertwined through their mutual use of Sinitic characters—an area we refer to as the Sinosphere. The case of Manchu-language sources discussed in this volume shows that even neighboring cultural groups that developed non-Sinitic writing systems were still compelled to engage with tropes developed in the early Chinese corpus.[7]

While the cultural import of such human constructs is apparent, their power as synecdoches originates in insect behavior, such as blood sucking or crop munching. A central contention of this volume is that the influence of insects on human societies cannot be reduced to these constructs. Historians, philologists, and literature specialists may proceed to diversify the inherently anthropomorphic source base produced by human cultures using the detailed knowledge of insect behavior available to us through current entomological literature. This volume offers such a nuanced and integrated understanding of human-insect interrelations, thereby expanding on animal studies work through a focus on less charismatic insect species in the previously marginal context of East Asia.[8]

In this understanding, anthropocentric frameworks—simply defined as semiconscious "natural" assumptions of human priority in any given relationship—are increasingly unsustainable. What gets historically "done" is more plausibly driven by a mutually conditioning network that is an emergent property of people and their surroundings.[9] Thus, female mosquitoes, in following their reproductive cycle, must first be inclined to bite rapaciously before a dutiful child can sacrifice his blood in an attempt to protect his parents from similar predation. The filial result becomes a distinguishing cultural norm of Sinosphere word and deed, constituted by a particular human-insect relation. Humans are thus put in our proper place as part of the larger, interdependent biodiversity that underlies all life on earth, without prioritizing insects over people. *Insect Histories* resituates both species, reconsidering not only how human institutions have influenced insects but also how insect behavior has influenced humans, often without explicit acknowledgment or conscious awareness.

These multispecies significances are exemplified in figure I.2. In this case, the public health propaganda of the Chinese Nationalist Party (Guomindang) employed syncretic Christian and indigenous Chinese iconography. One of the Four Horsemen of the Apocalypse is mounted on a mosquito-bomber, glossed with the slogan "In Order to Protect Against Malaria We Must Eradicate Mosquitoes."[10] There is a double demonization in play, of both human and insect actors: neither the Japanese militarists nor pathogen-spreading mosquitoes can be accommodated as coinhabitants of Chinese territory. Such use of "vermin" to demonize combatant and noncombatant social groups during World War II was hardly limited to the Asia-Pacific theater. This particular image was a product not only of wartime exigencies but also of the Chinese Nationalist indigenization of a hygienic regime that was initiated by Euro-American powers in the late nineteenth century in order to exploit the treaty-port system.[11] Such campaigns against pests were duly extended by the Japanese in their concurrent domestic consolidation and imperial expansion, as well as by the authorities of the technocratic developmentalist Republic of China (1912–49).[12]

Humanity's direct and quotidian contact with insects is the historical formative experience empowering socially mobilizing appeals, from the moving Confucian ideal of filiality to the numbing death toll of World War II. Nevertheless, the historical consequences of this prolonged, intimate integration have yet to be taken systematically into account to accommodate a field of view encompassing more than one species—many more than one in the case of insects. These consequences have become easier to perceive—and all the more imperative to comprehend—in the pallid light of the mass extinction event that defines our current moment.

INSECT HUMANITIES IN THE ANTHROPOCENE

Insect in our title is a compromise necessary in addressing an English-language audience whose taxonomic consciousness is conditioned by the present-day life sciences. The precise physical referent of the term *insect* is a problem of translingual practice across both space and time: the transliteration *chong* in the Chinese Pinyin romanization system represents pronunciation of the Sinograph 蟲 only as it is spoken in Standard Chinese (Mandarin) and not in other Chinese dialects or in other languages that employ Sinographs.

The character to which we refer by *chong* has a vast semantic range, which plausibly includes the general sense of "creature," traceable back to the Han period. A key passage in *The Book of Rites of the Elder Dai* (Da Dai Liji), attributed to Dai De (active 48–33 BCE), declared, "As for feathered *chong*, there are 360 with the phoenix as their paragon; as for furred *chong*, there are 360 with the *qilin* as their paragon; as for shelled *chong*, there are 360, with the divine turtle as their paragon; as for scaled *chong*, there are 360 with the flood dragon as their paragon; as for naked *chong*, there are 360 with the sage as their paragon. These are the Ideal Kinds of *Qian* and *Kun* and the proper enumeration of birds, beasts, and the myriad things."[13] In the early modern period, *chong* included bugs, worms, snakes, and insect products such as wasp nests.[14] Although the category included many venomous creatures, the connotations of the term were by no means exclusively negative, with silkworms being particularly favored as key partners in the multispecies coconstruction of the civilizational ideal in East Asia. As the pioneering natural historian and physician Li Shizhen (1518–1593) put it in his *Comprehensive Materia Medica* (Bencao gangmu, 1596), some *chong* "have merit" (*you gong*), while others are "toxic" (*you du*): it is the work of people to distinguish the difference.[15]

In the early twenty-first century, we necessarily conceive of our mandate somewhat differently. Under current pressures of habitat destruction and climate change, the significance of human connections with insects has never been more apparent. Like many works written in the Anthropocene, *Insect Histories* is motivated in part by the pressing issues of catastrophic climate change and massive species loss.[16] Long-entrenched habits of mind that lump insects into beneficial or harmful categories, depending on the perceived impacts on human communities, tend to overlook the role that insects play more broadly in the webs of interaction upon which we humans depend for our continued survival. A cultural concession that grants insects an inherent value free from their individual or collective utility to humans is even more elusive.

In the global present, the pressure on insect species to endure ecologically unprecedented changes presents a mortal threat to myriad forms of life on earth. It is now a truism that "charismatic megafauna"—iconic and mainly mammalian species—have largely cornered the market for human cross-species sympathy. As one ecologist put it, "We have a pretty good track record of ignoring most noncharismatic species."[17] The existential tie between humans and insects—only now in the process of roping more than a handful of photogenic species into general public discourse— likewise constitutes an intellectual mandate for an altered interspecies practice of insect humanities.

However, there is a growing popular and specialized literature—most recently converging in a scientific paper stressing an urgency to "popularize" insects in order to "future-proof" their diversity—concerned with a supporting cast of what might be termed "minifauna" whose behavior delivers critical ecosystem services, particularly pollination.[18] Indeed, both the honey bee (*Apis mellifera*) and monarch butterflies (*Danaus plexippus*) have secured roles alongside these melancholy mammals as poster hatchlings for the "Sixth Extinction."[19]

Some of this new attention has been tied to leaps in the optical technologies for perceiving insects. In his introduction to the pathbreaking BBC documentary series *Life in the Undergrowth* (2005), secular saint of naturalists David Attenborough observed, "We've only recently had the tiny lenses and electronic cameras that we need to explore this miniature world." In Western Europe, China, and Japan, insects and other "microorganisms" were among the first objects upon which new optical technologies were tested.[20]

Such attention, however, is not yet commensurate with the sheer scale of insects' biological footprint. Estimates of the number of insect species range from 2.5 to 10 million, with "only" around a million described so far—a figure that still accounts for about 80 percent of all known species. These numbers far outweigh the diversity of any other group of organisms and are literally heavier collectively in terms of biomass than any other terrestrial animal category. There may be as many as ten quintillion individual insects alive at any given time. Other distinctive characteristics, generally termed "sociality," have allowed select insect species to attain degrees of specialized cooperative behavior that exceed human efficiencies—dramatically embodied in some of nature's most elaborate constructions, huge climate-controlled termite nests and ant-cultivated fungus farms. Indeed, it has even been argued that if all vertebrates were removed from the earth, "ecosystems would" continue to "function flawlessly." In contrast, if just ants, bees, and termites were removed, most green plants (angiosperms) would die and "terrestrial life would probably collapse."[21] Humans would quickly find their agency catastrophically constrained, at best, in the absence of this foundational biodiversity that human institutions have blithely and arbitrarily judged beneficial or harmful.

Scale may be a more measured category through which to appreciate the fundamental contrast between some insect-human relations and those of other animal-human interactions. No megafauna predators managed to dispatch hundreds of thousands of humans in 2017–18. However, for the same period, malaria-bearing mosquitoes—using human bodies as reproductive hosts rather than as food—caused an estimated 435,000 fatalities out of 219 million infections globally.[22] Indeed, pandemic insect vectors have probably affected humans more than any other animal, with just six accounting for tens of millions of human casualties in historic times.[23]

Insect-borne disease, as an emergent property, has presented enormous human challenges right up to the present. Currently, for example, complete eradication of the mosquito is proving to be an elusive oversimplification of more complex environmental relationships. These relationships can themselves be understood in broad terms as a "natural selection" that promotes adaptations between the malarial vectors of mosquitoes and blood parasites. A mutually influential interaction between mosquito DNA code sequences (genotype), mosquitoes' consequent physical and behavioral features (phenotype), and the surrounding environment has allowed the insects to evolve a resistance to the main type of insecticides most effectively used against them since the 1960s: pyrethroids.[24] There is also evidence of malarial blood parasite (*Plasmodium falciparum*) resistance—again based on selective variation and mutation of this protozoan—to antimalarial drugs.[25] Disease control is furthermore hampered by more purely human socioeconomic limitations to a country's public health and educational infrastructure. Although malarial control has been effective in many regions of the globe, it has stalled or even declined in others—particularly sub-Saharan Africa—for interlinked reasons of biology and society. The elimination of malaria remains a possibility, especially with the deployment of insect vectors genetically modified to die young or inoculated against parasites and with combining several antimalarial drugs to impede the emergence of resistance.[26] However, this possibility is a much-qualified one dependent on not entirely predictable ongoing interactions between social and ecological (or, together, environmental) factors, including politics.

The complexities of emergent properties of insect-human relations have not always been apparent and remain yet to be fully understood. Ominously, there are too many signs that the existential import of insects has come into human view just as their vital habitats are disappearing from sight. One 2019 study found 98 percent of insects in a rainforest had disappeared in the last thirty-five years; by 2020, specialists had issued "a Warning to Humanity on Insect Extinctions."[27] Pesticides are certainly a major problem, but they are synergistically related to other more fundamental dangers like loss of habitat connectivity.[28] Serious engagement with human-insect interactions is complicated by the fact that both are embedded in larger ecologies. These are themselves incompletely understood complex systems that are not entirely predictable and liable to exhibit newly emergent properties with dynamics not directly attributable to the sum of their previous, constituent parts. Complexities also arise from differences of time and culture that can change the meaning of categories as basic as those of "insect." Hence, we begin with a Confucian "rectification of names" (*zhengming*), accordingly adapted for Anthropocene times and insect humanities concerns.[29]

OVERVIEW OF THE CONTRIBUTIONS

Insect Histories is organized thematically into three parts. Part 1 opens with a consideration of the semantic range of *chong* in the earliest available sources. It then proceeds to examine the fraught relationship between the biological and discursive manifestations of two of the insect groups placed within that pliable taxonomic container—honeybees and locusts, respectively—over the course of the imperial period.

Part 2 provides case studies of the way in which the biological imperatives of several groups of insects have either gummed up or lubricated the works of state planners. The state agents in the three contributions are officials of the Qing Empire (1644–1912) in the eighteenth and nineteenth centuries, Japanese colonial authorities in early twentieth-century Korea, and bureaucrats in Japan directly after World War II.

Part 3 analyzes the way in which formal academic disciplines that took insect behavior and taxonomy as their primary focus of attention came into being. The contributions are cognizant of the rich corpus of Sinitic texts on insect identification, morphology, and distribution. Euro-American imperial expansion subsequently disrupted this corpus, which then reemerged as a hybrid nationalist Chinese entomology that accepted the imported epistemology while mining the Chinese-language historical record for indigenous content. These two studies of the resulting apparatus that made insects legible to people demonstrate the importance of historicizing culturally specific knowledge production and tracking its subsequent circulation, whether it be Linnaean taxonomy or Soviet genetics.

In addressing terminological issues that are basic to an understanding of the written record of human-insect interaction in the premodern period, part 1 begins with Federico Valenti's investigation of the meaning of *chong* in Warring States (ca. 453–221 BCE) texts that became canonical and the earliest treatises that traced the meaning and origin of individual Sinographs. He finds that the range of usages is remarkably broad: *chong* was both a rubric for all fauna and the remnant "other" category for creatures that did not fit into the established categories of quadrupeds (*shou*), birds (*niao*), and fish (*yu*). In documenting the fluidity and complexity of *chong* at its earliest point of systematization, Valenti cautions against impulses to read early modern or modern taxonomy backward, and he also makes a persuasive case for the centrality of *chong* in the conceptualization of nonhuman animals more generally. His findings provide deep background on the continuing taxonomic dynamism of the phylum Arthropoda and related categories, especially in light of the dramatic categorical changes prompted by phylogenetics and the ever-increasing fossil record.

Mårten Söderblom Saarela extends discussion of the conceptual range of *chong* into the late imperial period through a study of the process of Manchu translation of *The Classic of Poetry* (Shijing) and several Manchu dictionaries produced in the first century of Qing rule. Manchu scholars relied on Zhu Xi's (1130–1200) glosses to elucidate terms that rarely appeared outside of *The Classic of Poetry* and which lacked a clear relationship to known species. Translation, in this case, was not a mere academic exercise: Söderblom Saarela's account of contemporary Qing management of locust outbreaks in multilingual terminological perspective shows how definitional matters had a material impact on how these outbreaks were standardized in a multiethnic context typical of Qing administration.

In chapter 2, Olivia Milburn offers an entomologically informed evaluation of the tropes relating to honeybees in medieval Chinese literature. This contribution is a model of what might be termed a multispecies translation, evaluating the way in which gender norms were projected onto nonhuman species in order to naturalize them among people. Milburn shows that elite constructs of honeybees generally reveal more about elites themselves—male gender anxieties in this case—than about insects. She does not, however, simply abandon the discursive field to the literati but includes the "voice" of the honeybee to the extent possible through a thorough discussion of its biology centered on the fact that "any binary distinction between male and female is not helpful for understanding honeybee society." The result is a reading of the obsession in Chinese literature with inverted coding of honeybee hierarchy as male-dominated by augmenting a gender perspective with an adverse biological one to produce a genuine insect humanities analysis. Milburn reveals just how male-constructed this process was by showing that even biological facts about superior female roles in honeybee relations known to premodern China did not deter the transformation of queen bees into literal and literary "king bees" (*fengwang*). Overall, the chapters in part 1 show inevitable terminological inconsistencies, oversights, and outright negations of insect realities in the process of human understanding.

Part 2 takes up the application of this understanding—by no means always in error—of insects in the practice of managing state and society in Qing China, Chosŏn Korea (1392–1897), and imperial and postwar Japan. Despite the many and obvious differences separating the centuries covered, the efficacy of the East Asian state and its commitment to environmental governance of social and economic relations is strikingly persistent throughout. One comparative conclusion that may be drawn

xxvi DAVID A. BELLO AND DANIEL BURTON-ROSE

here is that modern technology may not be a prerequisite for a viable level of insect control; another is the striking adaptability of insects even to human assault, industrial or otherwise.

David A. Bello's contribution reframes scholarly interest in locust management as an issue in Qing statecraft literature through an application of modern entomological work in a way similar to that of Milburn, but within a larger environmental context of land use. He examines environmental dynamics of how biological changes necessary to transform grasshoppers into agriculturally devastating swarms were stimulated and complicated by the vast transformation of landscapes into cereal production. Cognizant of how the agricultural foundation of Chinese society was itself a precondition for the "natural disaster" of locust depredations, Bello homes in on some of the administrative contradictions arising from locust behavior. These contradictions, in turn, resulted in enhanced—and generally effective—state mobilization of peasant society. Nevertheless, the basic tempo of environmental governance was substantially set by insect behavior.

Sang-ho Ro's contribution explores how modernization of agriculture and industry on the Korean Peninsula under Japanese colonialism displaced indigenous silk moth strains. The Japanese colonial state imported strains from the archipelago belonging to what is currently designated Japanese *Bombyx mandarina*, to the eventual effective disappearance of wild Korean species. Species replacement included the implementation of large-scale "Chinese" mulberry (primarily *Morus alba*) cultivation to feed the imported strains. Japanese imperialism thus led to a terraformed Korean silkworm habitat closer to the ideal landscapes depicted in Chinese sericulture texts. This overall transformation was a result of "the functional alliance between Korean farmers and the empire," effected by *Bombyx mandarina*, which complicates, without denying, Korean resistance to Japanese imperialism.

Kerry Smith's chapter shows the greater complexities of this governance within more intricate modern relational webs, interwoven with more systematized technological, social, administrative, and economic threads. Centered on the "Campaign for Lives without Mosquitoes and Flies," which was carried out amid the built environment in Japan from 1952 to the late 1960s, Smith's account conveys just how much human organization is required to respond to the disruptive effects of insect behavior to achieve the hygienic modernity so central to displays of mid-twentieth-century state power. The state alone, however, was insufficient for success of the campaign. Public health and medical entomology experts in Tokyo had to depend on local volunteers in rural (mostly) villages and towns for effective implementation. These mutually dependent state-society relations were not only reminiscent of those driving many voluntarist mass campaigns in Maoist China; they also recapitulate a similar degree of Qing administrative reliance on peasant implementation of locust eradication policies. One significant continuity between these diverse human historical experiences emerges as an insect resilience that is largely indifferent to political nuances between capitalism, communism, and monarchism. In the Japanese case, this resilience also proved formidable, if not decisive, in the face of modern eradication procedures that replaced traditional methods.

Part 3 returns, in a modern scientific mode, to some of the classification issues raised in part 1. Characteristic of China in the early to mid-twentieth century is its loss of pride of place as the paradigmatic fount of classical practice and its conversion into a laboratory of hybrid modernity. The scientific nationalism of post-"Liberation" Maoist China had been emerging from transnational practice since the 1910s, as a hybrid form of perceiving the natural world first developed in early modern Europe intermixed with a culturalist drive to assert a dominant place for China as a modern global power.

Daniel Burton-Rose examines the self-conscious establishment of biology and entomology as academic disciplines in the Republic of China in the 1920s and '30s. He argues that there were two relevant bodies of knowledge on insects in this period: a Chinese-language one and a Euro-American one, with the latter largely ignoring the former. The Chinese-language corpus, however, did not permanently disappear. Making a distinction between institution building and cultural indigenization, Burton-Rose follows the first generation of Chinese biologists trained in the United States up to the point when they once again picked up the questions raised by their Ming (1368–1644) and Qing exegetical counterparts regarding species identifications in the early China textual corpus.

Lijing Jiang follows the institutionalization of entomology as a discipline in the tumultuous period from the late 1930s to the 1950s. Through the career trajectory of insect taxonomist Chen Shixiang (1905–1988), Jiang shows how the peripatetic nature of science during the Sino-Japanese War actually enabled the collection of insect specimens in a manner inadvertently beneficial to the field. If anything, wartime conditions benefited entomology *vis-à-vis* the study of large mammals, as it required less capital-intensive commitment. Jiang closes with a demonstration of the pressures on China's modern scientific insect consensus that arose from the influence of Soviet taxonomical orthodoxies in the 1950s as they related to the development of entomology as a field in the People's Republic of China.

Taken together, these contributions constitute a basis for extending the insect humanities analytical framework in new directions in and beyond East Asia. These include expanding the span of historical and spatial coverage of insect species and of cultural practices and tropes, as well as devoting more attention to the perspectives of nondominant East Asian cultural groups.

EAST ASIAN INSECT HISTORIES
IN THE CONTEMPORARY BIODIVERSITY CRISIS

Given their degree of imbrication with humans, it is unsurprising that insects in East Asia have not been able to avoid the consequences of global contact any more than people have. Sheer insect diversity, nevertheless, continues to present a challenge to even the most basic measurements of the crisis these species are undergoing. Invertebrates rank among the most "data deficient" species in contemporary conservation biology—an almost literal oversight related to general human limitations in perceiving size and quantity that is exacerbated, in the East Asian context, by the cultural dominance of English in bioscience.[30]

Deficits in attention to insects in East Asia have now reached a crisis point that is categorically different from past controversies over the exact membership of *chong*. *Insect Histories* addresses this sensory shortcoming by attuning a wider audience to the rhythms of a human existence that has been progressing in accompaniment with chirping, buzzing, humming, crepitating, and stridulating. These sounds have not been mere background noise but have resonated throughout the human experience on earth. We currently have the means to hear them more clearly than at any previous moment. These means are not purely technological but also include the historical and spatial depth of the textual corpus produced in East Asia over the last two and a half millennia.

NOTES

Epigraph: Zhang Daye, *Weichong shijie*, preface 1a. Translation from Zhang Daye, *The World of a Tiny Insect*, 35.

1. For a cogent summary of these debates, see Hersy and Vetter, "Shared Ground," 412–16.

2. For a thoughtful overview of trends in animal studies, see Domańska, "Animal History."

3. Moon, "Becoming a Biologist in Colonial Korea"; Deb Roy, "White Ants, Empire, and Entomo-politics in South Asia"; de Carvalho Cabral, "Into the Bowels of Tropical Earth" and "Meaningful Clearings."

4. Wu Meng (fl. 270–310) was a historical personage, for whom a biography survives in the official history of the Jin dynasty (*Jin shu*, 2482–83). Wu Meng was not the only figure associated with the filial tale of feeding mosquitoes with his own body: see Knapp, *Selfless Offspring*, 31–32, who also documents how widely this tale circulated.

5. Milburn, "The Chinese Mosquito."

6. For an instructive allegory of locusts as corrupt officials, see the conversation in verse with a locust swarm by the Northern Song statesman Wang Ling (1032–1059), available in translations by Jonathan Pease and Wilt Idema. See: Wang Ling, "I Dreamed of Locusts," 216–17, and Idema, *Insects in Chinese Literature*, 94–97, respectively.

7. The scope of the region defined by engagement with the Sinitic corpus is cogently defined in Kornicki, *Languages, Scripts, and Chinese Texts in East Asia*, 1–21.

8. For a description of existing scholarship from an insect humanities perspective, see Burton-Rose, "Towards a Sinophone Insect Humanities." Even important recent anthologies on human-animal relations tend to focus on human constructions of mammals, such as those that include the following insect-centered articles: Few, "Killing Locusts in Colonial Guatemala"; Lurie, "Orientomology"; and Pattinson, "Bees in China." Animal studies book series evince varying proportions of insect-related material. Among Reaktion Books' Animals, Penn State University Press's Animalibus: Of Animals and Cultures, and Brill's Human-Animal Studies, insects are best represented in the Reaktion Books series.

9. Concepts informing the human-insect relations central to this volume range from actor-network theory in the social sciences to the basic concept of "emergent properties" in the complex systems (including environmental) sciences. For further discussion, see Taylor, "Anthropomorphism and the Animal Subject" and New England Complex Systems Institute, "Concepts: Emergence."

10. Barnes, *Intimate Communities*, xvi–xvii.

11. From the perspective of the inclusive category of *chong* (discussed below), these public health campaigns include those against schistosomiasis through

efforts to eradicate parasitic flatworms, discussed in Gross, *Farewell to the God of Plague.*

12. For a nuanced account of sanitation reforms under Japanese colonialism—in the imperial capital of Korea (present-day Seoul) and Taiwan, respectively—see Henry, *Assimilating Seoul*, 130–67; Liu, *Prescribing Colonization*. On developments in China in this period, see Lei, *Neither Donkey nor Horse.*

13. Kong Guangsen, *Da Dai Liji buzhu*, 13.22a–b. For a discussion of this passage in relation to other early taxonomic schema, see Zou, "Guanyu woguo gudai dongwu fenleixue," 328–29. The number 360 is a cosmogonic figure—here corresponding to Heaven and Earth—derived from the foundational divination text *The Classic of Changes* (*Zhouyi* or *Yijing*).

14. Nappi, *The Monkey and the Inkpot*, 96–98.

15. For the Chinese original and a full translation of the quoted section, see Unschuld, *Ben Cao Gang Mu*, 8:131–32.

16. The Anthropocene may be simply defined as the epoch in which humans have become a measurable geological force. For a more authoritative formulation, see Anthropocene Working Group, "Working Group on the 'Anthropocene.'" On insects and the Anthropocene, see Wagner et al., "Insect Decline in the Anthropocene."

17. Joe Nocera, of the University of New Brunswick in Canada, quoted in Vogel, "Where Have All the Insects Gone?" See also Dirzo et al., "Defaunation in the Anthropocene."

18. Samways et al., "Solutions for Humanity."

19. This phrase was popularized in Kolbert, *The Sixth Extinction.*

20. Screech, *The Lens within the Heart*, 196.

21. Grimaldi and Engel, *Evolution of the Insects*, 3–5; Department of Systematic Biology, "Numbers of Insects." Angiosperms (flowering, seed-bearing plants) currently compose 80 percent of all known green plants in existence. There is strong evidence that insects coevolved with angiosperms: see Grimaldi and Engel, *Evolution of the Insects*, 4–5.

22. World Health Organization, "This Year's World Malaria Report at a Glance."

23. Grimaldi and Engel, *Evolution of the Insects*, 5.

24. For a more nuanced understanding of genotypic and phenotypic interactions, see Kirschner and Gerhart, *The Plausibility of Life*, 12, 29–37. Pyrethroids are synthetic compounds developed from natural pyrethrins, a basic component of plant resistance to insect pests, that are found in species of the *Chrysanthemum* genus. On the history of pyrethroid development as a pesticide, see Davis, *Banned.*

25. White et al., "Averting a Malaria Disaster."

26. Sriskantharajah, "Malaria Elimination."

27. Carrington, "Insect Collapse"; Cardoso et al., "Scientists' Warning to Humanity."

28. Cardoso et al., "Scientists' Warning to Humanity."

29. In East Asian intellectual discourse, this Confucian term came to refer to the periodic need to recalibrate language as it drifted semantically from that which it originally indicated.

30. Amano et al., "Tapping into Non-English-Language Science"; Borgelt et al., "More than Half of Data Deficient Species."

PART ONE

Conceptual Categorization and the Philology of *Chong*

ONE

What Did It Take to Be a *Chong*?

PROFILE OF A
POLYSEMOUS CHARACTER
IN EARLY CHINA

Federico Valenti

When a human child explores the variegated animal world, the correspondence between a living being and its name is a fundamental tool for understanding the natural environment. Because cultures develop in different habitats, the animals they encounter represent different species. Every culture identifies some archetypal animals whose prominent physical characteristics inspire specific terminology. The most paradigmatic creatures are the domestic animals that have shared their lives with humans since the beginning of farming. Some nondomesticated animals occupy an archetypal cultural role due to their proximity to humans. For instance, a kangaroo has distinctive features that prevent it from being assigned to a generic category of miscellaneous Australian creatures; the same is true of lions in the African savannah and sloths in Central and South American rainforests. But what about the myriad of "lesser" creatures with which our planet teems? How can they be understood and integrated into a coherent scheme?

A vast array of nonhuman animals was described and catalogued in premodern Chinese sources. Zoological classification worked in a very different way than it does in modern taxonomy: the ambiguity in early Chinese sources was not a flaw but a resource employed in classification. *Chong*—"creature"—had a more comprehensive meaning in the past than it does in the present: most likely it encompassed all animals. Animal terms are abundant in lexicographic works such as dictionaries and glossaries; they also occur in the canonical and ritualistic texts that came to be the core curricula of scholars and aspiring officials. Examination of these sources reveals that the concept of "assembled creatures" (*kun chong*) began as an all-encompassing zoological placeholder and only over time developed its current meaning of "insect" in Modern Standard Chinese (Mandarin).

The animals that nowadays are called "insects" are easily classified by stating that they have six legs. If we go deeper into the etymology, we discover that the word *insect* describes an animal whose body is segmented in different parts: the Latin word *insecti* is a direct calque from the Ancient Greek lexeme *entomon*, with the same exact meaning. This is a hint regarding how the perception of the natural word shifted over time. It is a challenge to analyze hypothetical categories of animals in a remote civilization without any comparison to modern taxonomy. Not only is the reference material completely different from the classical Greco-Roman encyclopedic works but it is mandatory to travel back in time and investigate these particular "biological classifications" excluding any correspondence with our methods of classifying living beings.[1]

Taxonomies in early Chinese society were not necessarily related to a better understanding of the biological world: they represented a process relating principally to a global and standardizing nomenclature. The only and fundamental element necessary to recognize and categorize animals was their common name and eventually their local names. In addition, any other relevant distinctions were the ones between big and small, male and female, carnivorous and herbivorous; not those between fish, reptile, invertebrate, or other contemporary biological and taxonomical nomenclature—such as classes, phyla, and families—employed by contemporary zoologists.

Despite the difficulty of outlining a uniform zoological system in ancient China, animals are abundantly attested in early Chinese culture. In addition to the vast iconographic repertoire of zoological depictions from the Shang (ca. 1600–1046 BCE) to Han dynasties (202 BCE–220 CE), references to the animal world survive in early Chinese scripts.[2] The modern Chinese script still preserves pictographs that represent a stylized image of an animal, the so-called characters that "represent a form" (*xiang xing*): graphs with purely iconographic origins that are still evocative and meaningful.[3] The graph that is written in contemporary "traditional" Chinese script as *chong* 蟲 (*C.lruŋ) is a "conjoining meaning" (*huiyi*) character: a character composed of two or more characters that determine semantically its meaning with no phonetic elements.[4] The conjoining characters, in this case, are three *hui* 虫 (*[r̥]u[j]ʔ), which is a character that "represents a form."[5]

While the former character is attested only from the Warring States period (ca. 453–221 BCE) onward, the latter has a more ancient origin dating back to the Shang dynasty Oracle Bone Script (*jiaguwen*, ca. 1200–1000 BCE). It depicts a curled creature with a small head and a long, hooked tail as if it is represented in the act of slithering; hence the direct affinity with snakes and not insects. As the dictionary *Le Grand Ricci* points out, there is no proof that the ancient Oracle Bone Script graph represented the word *snake* or had any semantic connection to the animal world: among the various definitions, it can be related to the concept of "damaging," especially in a religious context; it can be a variant of the character "the others" (*tuo/ta*), and can also be a proper noun or a personal pronoun.[6] If we exclude its use as a proper noun and its pronominal value, the Oracle Bone Script graph only implied the meaning "causing damage, harm," something that could be seen as a characteristic of particular animals: certain kinds of snakes are harmful to human beings, and certain kinds of invertebrates are noxious both to humans and to crops.

Another fascinating character that is related to the graphic forms of *chong* is *kun* 虫 (*[k]ˤu[n]), an evident duplication of the character *hui*. It is attested from the Oracle Bone Script corpus onward, but even in this case there is no evidence of a zoological use of this graph because it is only implied as a proper noun.[7] In order to evaluate and identify this graph, we need to examine another character that developed separately from a strict logographic point of view: *kun* 昆 (*[k]ˤu[n])—the semantic range of which includes "elder brother," "offspring," "multitude," and "alike"—is a graph that "represents a form"; it originally depicted an invertebrate, maybe a scorpion-like creature. The renowned historian and paleographer Li Xueqin (1933–2019) comments on its graphic evolution: "Its early depiction was the form of an insect; later its body was erroneously transcribed as 'the Sun' (*ri* 日) and its two legs were erroneously transcribed as 'to compare' (*bi* 比)."[8]

This character has been glossed with several different meanings: for example, as "same; alike" (*tong*) in Xu Shen's (58–147) *Explaining Graphs and Discerning Characters* (Shuowen jiezi), as "elder brother" (*xiong*) in the Mao recension of *The Classic of Poetry* (Shijing), and as "following" or "later" (*hou*) in *Approaching Elegance* (Erya), a glossary-like work traditionally dated to the third century BCE but which reached its present form as late as the mid-second century BCE.[9] There are other instances, however, in which *kun* appears as a modifier of the character *chong*. For example, in *The Book of Rites* (Liji) chapter "The Conveyance of Rites" (Li yun), there is a sentence that reads: "There were no floods, droughts, or plagues caused by the myriad of creatures (*kun chong*)."[10]

Comparing this passage with one from *The Book of Rites of the Elder Dai* (Da Dai Liji) of Dai De (active 48–33 BCE), it is possible to delineate another possible meaning of the character *kun*: "A *myriad* of small *creatures* hatches from their eggs. A myriad (*kun*) is a multitude (*zhong*)."[11] This text makes clear that *kun* is another way to say "multitude" (*zhong* *tuŋ-s). This is corroborated by the commentary on a passage in *The History of the [Former] Han* (Hanshu), which was composed by Ban Gu (32–92) and covers the years of the Western Han dynasty (202 BCE–8 CE), by the Tang period commentator Yan Shigu (581–654): "*Kun* is a multitude. *Kun chong* [a myriad of creatures] can also be written as *zhong chong* [a multitude of creatures]."[12] Finally, there is a quote directly from *Explaining Graphs and Discerning Characters* in which it is possible to rediscover the "doubled *hui*" *kun* character as an independent semantic classifier that generates as many as twenty-four different characters. Its gloss also validates the interpretation of *kun* as "myriad, multitude": "*Kun* is a collective/general noun for *chong*."[13]

There are at least two, if not three, different characters that are currently read and understood as *chong* that developed independently and only came to overlap in meaning over a long period of time: *chong* 蟲 and its single-*chong* form 虫, pronounced *hui*. While the latter is used today as the simplified version of the former, there is some evidence that the two characters coexisted to some extent until the triple-*chong* form assimilated the semantic value of the single-*chong* form.[14] As Li Shizhen (1518–1593) wrote in his *Comprehensive Materia Medica* (Bencao gangmu), "Bugs are the smallest of living things, and there are many different kinds, so the character for 'bug' comes from three individual bugs taken together."[15] It cannot be ignored that by Li's time the character *chong* had already the meaning of "petty/inferior creatures," a semantic value probably influenced by the use of *chong* as a placeholder for all the animals that could not be classified otherwise: it indicated the "leftovers" of the animal world, a basic element for a "non-inclusive" taxonomy.[16] Later sources focus more on the lexicographic value of the term *chong*, leaving aside the biological value of the character. *Explaining Graphs and Discerning Characters* commentator Duan Yucai (1735–1815) simply indicated that the conjoined meaning of the triple-*chong* character follows the one of the character "crowd" (*zhong*

眾/众): "The character 'person' (*ren* 人) tripled becomes the character 'crowd' (*zhong*); the character 'snake/worm' (*hui* 虫) tripled becomes the character 'creature' (*chong* 蟲)."[17]

How did such a general concept become an explicit category marker in early Chinese thought? The *Approaching Elegance* chapter "Glosses on Creatures" (Shi chong) provides a vast array of animals classified under the *chong* label, a category that has been translated in several ways in order to subsume the different genres and species that are included in it. One scholar observed that the category includes "insects, worms, spiders, reptiles, etc.," while another characterizes it as referring to "zoo-entomoid creatures."[18] There is no evidence in the received *Approaching Elegance* of a different use of *chong* and its *hui* form: the character appears only four times in the whole text (five if we count the title of the chapter "Glosses on Creatures") and each instance presents a triple-*chong* form. The only gloss that aims at describing the characteristic of the *chong* category is the last one in the chapter "Glosses on Creatures": "Those that have legs are called *chong*, those without legs are called *zhi* 豸."[19] No further information is given regarding animals that belong to the *chong* category; for instance, their aspect, the number of their legs, the features of their skin, and their habitat or behavior are unknown.

There is no evident explanation about any other characteristic of this category of animal, such as its aspect or the features of the skin. The category that in this case is juxtaposed to *chong* is *zhi* and not, for example, "fish" (*yu*), which also does not have a categorical antonym; the dichotomous element of this gloss is the presence or absence of legs. The use of legs as distinguishing taxonomic element is relevant in the description of the animal kingdom; for example, the word *shou* and the word *qin* are glossed in *Approaching Elegance* as a contrastive lexical pair: "The ones with two legs and feathers are called 'wildfowl' (*qin*); the ones with four legs and fur are called 'quadrupeds' (*shou*)."[20]

In this case, there is an explicit reference to the correlative classification, as the terms "feathers" (*yu*) and "fur" (*mao*) are indicated as a supplementary feature of the *qin* and *shou* categories. Moreover, there is some evidence of a quasi-homophonic with a related meaning (paronomastic) correspondence between "wildfowl" (*qin* 禽) and "to catch with a net" (*qin* 擒) and between "quadrupeds" (*shou* 獸) and "to hunt" (*shou* 狩): animals that can be caught with nets and traps (*qin* 擒) are classified as *qin* 禽, while animals that can be hunted (*shou* 狩) are classified as *shou* 獸.[21]

Proceeding to another lexicographical source, *Explaining Graphs and Discerning Characters* dedicates two separated sections to either character: in chapter 14 it is possible to find separate *hui* and *chong* sections. According to *Explaining Graphs and Discerning Characters*, the *hui* form represents "a[nother] name for the viper (*fu*), three inches long, its head as big as a human thumb. It is depicted lying down."[22]

Therefore, it is highly probable that the original meaning of the *hui* form was the representation of a certain kind of snake: the *Hanyu da zidian* (published 1979–89) reports that there are at least three different forms of the single-*chong* (*hui*) character that are attested in the ancient Oracle Bone Script and Bronze Script, each one depicting a different shape of the "head" of the snake.[23] Nevertheless, the *Explaining Graphs and Discerning Characters* definition of the *hui* form continues in more generic terms: "Small and minute among the living beings, some of them walk, some have fur, some are naked, some have shells, some have scales; by means of [the graph] *hui* they are represented."[24]

While this could be an array of the differences that exist between distinct species of invertebrates, there are some hints of the use of the *hui* form as a universal term for different types of animals. In his commentary on *Explaining Graphs and Discerning Characters*, Duan writes: "*The scaled and armored [animals] by means of *hui* are given form. This is the case of *chi* dragons, hornless dragons, clams and mussels. The ones that fly by means of *hui* are given form. This is the case of bats. The ones that have fur or are naked by means of *hui* are given form. This is the case of the ape (*yuan*) and the monkey (*wei*)."[25]

All the characters in this passage used as examples for different categories of animals present the *hui* form in the radical position. They all appear in the *hui* section of *Explaining Graphs and Discerning Characters*, which is composed of 159 glosses in total. From this statement by Duan, it is possible to draw two conclusions: firstly, the *hui* semantic classifier is principally used to represent animals that belong to four out of the five different categories identified by the correlative classification method implied in works such as *The Book of Rites* and *The Rites of Zhou* (Zhouli): namely scaly, armored, furred, and naked animals.[26] While the feathered animal category is apparently omitted, there is a reference to "flying ones" (*fei zhe*) which evidently completes the correlative classification picture. Secondly, we must underline the strong relation with the pure logographic classification since *Explaining Graphs and Discerning Characters* must be considered as a text that presents a list of graphs, rather than a text that presents a list of words.[27] It is not surprising that all the different animals from the five correlative categories considered as *chong* are represented by characters with the *hui* semantic classifier. However, these animals are classified elsewhere under a different category; for instance, *Approaching Elegance* categorizes "bats" (*bianfu*) as a "flying animal" (*niao*) and the monkeys *yuan* and *wei* as "quadrupeds/wild beasts" (*shou*).[28] These elements exacerbate the differences between a pure logographic classification in which different graphs are classified based on their semantic classifiers and a more empirical and naturalistic classification that is focused on the meaning transmitted by graph (i.e., the animal) rather than its graphic representation.

The triple-*chong* section, on the other hand, is very small if compared to the *hui* section since it presents only six characters (five if we exclude the first one, *chong*). Moreover, this first gloss quotes entirely the *Approaching Elegance* passage about the juxtaposition between *chong* and *zhi*, without giving any further clarification. In *Explaining Graphs and Discerning Characters*, on the other hand, Xu Shen does not avoid citing the reference to *chong* versus *zhi* in *Approaching Elegance*, but he dedicates a whole section to the semantic classifier *zhi,* which is implied in characters related to the feline semantic field: "[The character] *zhi* [indicates] wild beasts with elongated backbones that move flexibly, [when they] desire to kill their prey, they patiently wait and stalk [them]."[29] Duan noted that the reference of this character to legless invertebrates is due to their body length: "As a matter of principle, the body of legless creatures is very long; for example, the ones akin to snakes or earthworms."[30]

The translation of *chong* here is clearly "creature, animal," since a snake is not an invertebrate. However, due to the reference of the *Approaching Elegance* gloss *chong* versus *zhi*, Duan appears to have used *chong* in the way it is used in the "Glosses on Creatures" chapter, hence with the meaning of "zoo-entomoid, invertebrate."[31] He also points out that the use of the word "backbone" (*ji*) is simply an extended meaning (*yinshen*) and not a reference to vertebrates only. Nevertheless, the characters that follow this section of *Explaining Graphs and Discerning Characters* are mainly mammal predators (especially felines such as wildcats and leopards) marking the difference between the semantic value of this *zhi* and the one found in *Approaching Elegance* and in the *chong* section of *Explaining Graphs and Discerning Characters*.[32] While there could be a paronomastic link between *zhi* (*[d]re?) and the character that means "walking hesitatingly" (*chi* *[d]re), this does not exclude the ambiguity of the graph in describing two completely different categories of animals.[33]

The historical linguist Michael Carr elucidates this semantic expansion of *chong* with the relative semantic contraction of *zhi* by stating that there were two semantic shifts. In the first one, *chong* originally meant "animals," then it came to mean "animals with feet," and then to mean "insects, reptiles, etc." On the other hand, *zhi* originally meant "insects," then came to mean "animals without feet" or "animals that stalk or crawl," and then came to mean "reptiles without feet." For Carr, these two semantic shifts are the key to demonstrating that in early Chinese vocabulary there was a lexical equilibrium in which the semantic expansion of one term is conversely linked to the semantic contraction of another term.[34]

Carr's theory is based on older phonetic reconstructions and errs from the outset: if we check older scripts such as the Oracle Bone Script and Bronze Script, it is possible to discern that the graph *zhi* does indeed "represent a form" of an animal, depicted vertically and sideways.[35] There are sources that identify this animal as "a feline, a head with whiskers, paws, backbone" or a "carnivorous animal, with a large body, big mouth and sharp teeth," yet neither *Le Grand Ricci* nor Li Xueqin speculates as to the species of animal represented by the Oracle Bone Script form of *zhi*.[36] Nevertheless, I contend that *zhi* originally depicted a feline, then expanded in semantic value by including the meaning of legless invertebrates: while the graphic representation of *zhi* maintained some characteristics that we can identify as "paws," "whiskers," and "mouth," the description of *zhi* in *Explaining Graphs and Discerning Characters* focuses on other characteristics, such as possessing an "elongated spine" (*chang ji*) or the tautological feature of "moving like a *zhi*" (*xing zhi zhi ran*). Such characteristics are not exclusive to the animal originally represented by the character that "represents a form," but they are compatible with legless animals with elongated bodies like snakes, centipedes, or earthworms. After all, the graph that originally represented a fish underwent a similar semantic expansion: the character *yu* ("fish") started as a pictograph that depicted the body of a nonspecific fish, but it later became the categorical marker for any kind of animal that lives in water, including mollusks, crustaceans, tortoises, cetaceans, newts, and salamanders.[37]

In order to expand the semantic boundaries of the concept of *chong*, it is necessary to retrieve instances of the use of this character in earlier *loci classici*, mainly in three texts that are related to the sphere of rituals:

TABLE 1.1. The use of *chong* in the "Monthly Regulations" (Yue ling) chapter of *The Book of Rites* (Liji)

昆蟲	蟄蟲	孩蟲	蟲螟	蝗蟲	介蟲	鷙蟲
kun chong (myriad creatures)	zhe chong (hibernating creatures)	hai chong (hatchlings)	chong ming (caterpillar-like crea- tures)	huang chong (locusts and other creatures)	jie chong (armored creatures)	zhi chong (predatory creatures)

The Rites of Zhou, The Book of Rites, and *The Book of Rites of the Elder Dai.* In these texts, the zoological terminology is presented without any direct reference to the entomological world. In fact, the use of the term *chong* in these works is not related to the concept of insect or invertebrate, but it is generally implied as a common *descriptum* for the five phases (*wu xing*). Table 1.1 illustrates the use of *chong* in the "Monthly Regulations" (Yue ling) chapter of *The Book of Rites*.[38]

A partially identical scheme is retrievable also in *The Book of Rites of the Elder Dai*: from this scheme, we can deduce that there are at least five different kinds of *chong*, each with a different typology of skin (with scales, feathers, short hair, fur, or a shell) and a different affinity with a period of the year.[39] If we add to this scheme the legendary four animals related to the four seasons and to the four cardinal points mentioned in the "Summary of the Rules of Propriety" (Qu li), the first chapter of *The Book of Rites*, we can see a clearer picture of the semantic value of *chong* as a collective noun for any kind of "creature" with no relations to insects or invertebrates.[40]

Even if these are unmistakable hints of the use of *chong* as a general term for "animal," *The Book of Rites* presents the word *chong* in combination with other lexemes that stand outside of the correlative classification use of this polysemous character. They are as follows:

1. "Myriad creatures" (*kun chong*). This expression is the standard disyl-lable for "insect" in Modern Standard Chinese (Mandarin). How-ever, in *The Book of Rites*, this expression is present with the hyper-nymic meaning of "a high number of different creatures." Examples include:

   a. "Only after all the vegetation withers and drops its leaves, [is it possible] to enter forests in the hills [in order to cut trees]. Until all the animals withdraw into their burrows, [it is not possible] to fire the fields [to fertilize them]."[41]

Even though the conventional translation by James Legge (1815–1897) renders *kun chong* as "insects," I speculate that in this case, the semantic value of this disyllable is "all the animals."[42] The verb "to hide, to hibernate" (*zhe*), as we will see, is often related to the noun *chong* in a relation "descriptor-*descriptum*," thus hibernating creatures. Nevertheless, the disyllable is parallel with "all the vegetation" (*cao mu*), which is a less ambiguous generic term that encompasses all flora, so we can cautiously say that *kun chong*, in this case, is a generic term that encompasses all fauna. In fact, the verb *zhe* is not exclusively linked with the hibernation of insects, but could simply mean "to hide," "to retire," and thus can be related to a wider array of animals.[43] Moreover, the following lines describe the offspring of different kinds of animals, so the implication of *kun chong* as mere "insects" would be limiting.

b. "Therefore there were no plagues of flood, drought, or caused by a multitude of insects."[44]

In this case, the disyllable stands for a multitude of harmful insects, so it is to be understood as "the myriad of insects" rather than "creatures." The commentary of Zheng Xuan (127–200) states that they belong to the category of locusts and caterpillars (*ming zhong zhi shu ye*), the quintessential noxious invertebrates.

c. "[May the] ground dikes stay in their place, [may the] water flow in its channels, [may harmful] creatures not rise and appear, [may harmful] plants return to swamps."[45] This passage represents another occasion in which there is a correspondence between "fauna" (*kun chong*) and "flora" (*cao mu*). For this reason, I speculate once again that the semantic range of this compound is not restricted to the world of insects but rather subsumes the entirety of fauna. In addition, the previous line contains a parallel passage in which the two initial subjects are "ground" (*tu*) and "water" (*shui*), making the discourse logical and coherent: ground to water to animals (not only insects) to plants.

d. "The different [species of] animals, the fruits of plants, the entities of light and shade (*yin yang*), were all made ready."[46]

Even in this last example, the term "fauna" (*kun chong*) is parallel to "flora" (*cao mu*) and also to the "entities of light and shade" (*yin yang zhi wu*), another lexeme that subsumes a vast number of beings. This is another hint of the hypernymic nature of *kun chong* in *The Book of Rites*. A divergent opinion is retrievable in Zheng Xuan's commentary, which describes *kun chong* as "creatures (*chong*) that are born with the warm season and die at the arrival of winter." This description fits the category of insects; however, this is a later interpretation.

There are other fascinating references to this disyllable in other *loci classici,* such as *Xunzi,* of the third century BCE, *The Book of Rites of the Elder Dai, The History of the Han,* and the *Huainanzi,* presumably composed by Liu An (179–22 BCE). Here are some examples:

e. "Consequently, the myriad creatures are born accordingly to their own time and space."[47]

f. "The hundreds of grains and the vegetation are planted according to the seasons, therefore the transformations of all animals are harmonized," and "Human beings, wildfowl, wild beasts and the other myriad of creatures and so on, have all their means of birth."[48]

g. "When the Way to be a Lord is reached, then both the flora and fauna each one reaches his own proper place."[49]

h. "Even birds, beasts and the other myriad of creatures were refined and transformed by them."[50]

In all these instances, the binomial expression always has the value of "myriad creatures" and not necessarily just "insects." In fact, the term *kun chong* is on another occasion in correlation with the expressions "myriad entities" (*wan wu*; hypernym for both flora and fauna), "herbs and plants" (*cao mu*; hypernym for flora), or "bipeds [wildfowl] and quadrupeds [wild beasts]" (*qin shou* or *niao shou*; hypernym for fauna). I am quite sure that between *kun chong* there are other animals, such as the ones belonging to the "fish" (*yu*) category: it is surprising that fish and other aquatic animals were omitted from this kind of enunciation; it is more plausible that *kun chong* had the same value of what is nowadays "et cetera."

2. "Hibernating creatures" (*zhe chong*). Even in this case, conventional translations of *chong* are often related to the insect realm. However, the text simply states that these "*chong*" perform specific actions that are common to every kind of animal that slumbers or hibernates during the winter. If the translation "creatures" is substituted for the translation "insects," a greater internal consistency appears:

a. "Creatures that have been torpid during the winter begin to move."[51]

b. "Hibernated creatures in their burrows are all in motion, opening their doors and beginning to come forth."[52]

c. "Creatures that hibernate stop up the entrances to their burrows."[53]

d. "Creatures that need to hibernate would not retire to their burrows."[54]

e. "All the hibernating creatures curl up in slumber from within [their burrows]."[55]

f. "Creatures that have been torpid during the winter would come forth again [from their burrows]."[56]

g. "Hibernated creatures will manifest themselves and come back to active life."[57]

3. "Hatchlings" (*hai chong*). There is only one instance of this expression in *The Book of Rites,* and it states the prohibition on killing birds at any stage of their life: "Nests should not be thrown down; hatchlings should not be killed, nor embryos, very young or [already] flying birds."[58]

Even in this case, Legge's translation of *chong* as "insects" is problematic since the binomial expression *hai chong* stands together with two other characters ("fetus" [*tai*] and "young animal" [*ao*]) that do not identify a specific class of animals, so there is no point in considering *hai chong* "unformed insects." It is, rather, probably a term for bird hatchlings or fecundated eggs since the passage discusses damaging nests or birds.

4. "Caterpillar-like creatures" (*chong ming*). This single instance in *The Book of Rites* refers to the incorrect performance of summer rituals during springtime: "If summer rituals were observed, there would be

great droughts in the country; the warm winds would come too early, and noxious creatures like caterpillars would harm the grain."[59]

In this case, *chong* is in a rather ambiguous position: it can be seen as a hypernym for *ming* so that the sentence may be translated as "creatures like caterpillars" without gaining the semantic meaning of "insect," but it is rather a generic reference to animals.

5. "Locusts and other creatures" (*huang chong*). There are two instances of this expression in the "Monthly Regulations," and they are strictly related to the previous passage. In this case, "locusts and other creatures" will appear if the spring rituals are performed at the wrong time of the year: "If spring proceedings were observed, then there would be the calamity of locusts and other creatures, strong gusts would come, plants in full bloom would not bear fruits."[60]

And again: "If spring proceedings were observed, then locusts and other creatures would destroy [the crops]; the streams and springs would all become dry, and the majority of the common folk would suffer from scabies and ulcers."[61]

Legge decided not to translate *chong* and considers it as a coda for the character "locust" (*huang*). From my understanding of this passage, *chong* might be considered the generic term "creatures" and it could imply that not only locusts will harm the fields but also other creatures less paradigmatic than the locust.

6. "Armored creatures" (*jie chong*). Following the previous scheme of disasters that happen on an incorrect implementation of the seasonal government proceedings, the two instances of "armored creatures" are retrievable in a similar context: "If in this first month of autumn, the proceedings of government proper to winter were observed, then the negative energy of life would greatly prevail; the armored creatures would destroy the grain, and warlike operations would be called for."[62]

And again: "If in the last month of winter, the governmental proceedings proper to autumn were observed, the white dews would descend too early; the armored creatures would appear in monstrous forms; throughout the four borders people would have to seek their places of shelter."[63]

Legge first translates *chong* as "insects" and then as "creatures." The commentary by Zheng Xuan identifies *jie chong* in the first instance as a kind of crab that eats cereals (*dao xie*) and the second instance as "creatures that belong to the species of soft-shell turtles or crabs" (*chou wei bie xie*). This is conforming to the correlative classification where "armored creatures" are shellfish and turtles.

7. "Predatory creatures" (*zhi chong*). This is a curious instance in which the animals described are undoubtedly related to the class of birds: "[he would face] birds and beasts of prey with their talons and wings without regard to their fierceness."[64]

A final remark regarding the taxonomies in *The Rites of Zhou*: while the correlative classification method is implied more or less identically, the term used to represent generic animals is not *chong*, but the disyllable *dong wu*, which literally means "moving entity," a word that in Modern Standard Chinese identifies the general term for "animal." It is difficult to establish why the compilers of *The Rites of Zhou* were inclined to use this lexeme instead of *chong*. Carr proposed that *dong wu* was implied in *The Rites of Zhou* due to its phonetic resemblance to *chong*, but new phonetic reconstructions point away from this interpretation.[65] The use of *dong wu* as a generic term for "animals" is justified by the comparison with the generic term for plants *zhi wu*, with the meaning of "immobile entity," and not by phonetic connections.

To corroborate this hypothesis, the passage of *The Rites of Zhou* in the chapter "Earth Ministry of the Official Education" (Di guan situ) implies *dong wu* only as a generic term. Every time a class of animal is announced, the generic term shifts to a more specific one: that is, "furred entities" (*mao wu*), "feathered entities" (*yu wu*), "scaly entities" (*lin wu*), "naked entities" (*luo wu*), and "armored entities" (*jie wu*). The substitute lexeme for *chong* is *wu* and not *dong wu*. In addition, the term *chong* is indeed present in *The Rites of Zhou* in three passages of the chapter "Autumn Ministry of the Punishments" (Qiu guan sikou) and in two passages of the chapter "Winter Ministry of the Artificer's Records" (Dong guan kaogongji).[66] In the first case, *chong* appears in two disyllables, namely *mai chong* and *shui chong*. The former is identified by the commentary of Zheng Xuan and the subcommentary of Jia Gongyan (fl. Tang dynasty) as "a noxious invertebrate that hides inside the house," while the latter is probably a generic term for amphibian: the two officials cited in the passage are in charge of frogs (*guo* 蟈 and *yu* 蛙, which here is a probably graphic variant of *guo*). In the second case, *chong* is used as the name of a decoration of a bell or is a common term to indicate "small creatures" (*xiao chong*), an expression that is retrievable in the *Explaining Graphs and Discerning Characters* definition of *chong*.[67]

This extreme "generalization" of the term *chong* could radically change the perceived structure of early Chinese taxonomies: even if it is the common understanding that *chong* is polysemous and can mean both "invertebrate" *and* "creature" (of any species), one meaning does not preclude the other. In fact, early Chinese categorization is not very concerned with internal anatomical differences, which is instead a critical distinction from modern practice. The "diachronic semantic shift" from "animal" to "insect" that Carr evokes could be a giant misunderstanding caused by the incommensurability of our present categories and the ones present in early China.[68]

CONCLUSION

The early Chinese term *chong* indicated any kind of creature that did not have characteristics that would have assigned it to another category, hence it could be the outermost and featureless element in a noninclusive taxonomical system. Nevertheless, thanks to this open-ended system, creatures such as insects and invertebrates in general were systematically labelled *chong* because no other categorical marker could subsume them as featureless animals in the zoological world. Since animals such as birds, fish, and mammals had a more specific terminology that defined them more accurately (the so-called categorical markers), insects were recursively identified simply as *chong*, and as more categorically belonging to the "myriad of creatures"— *kun chong*—that could not be easily taxonomized in the multifaceted early Chinese worldview.

NOTES

1. As Christoph Harbsmeier observed, we should be particularly careful when addressing categories and taxonomies in premodern society as "the Chinese tended to be interested in definitions not in a Socratic way and for their own sake as descriptions of the essence of things, and they were very rarely interested in definition as an abstract art in the Aristotelian manner." Harbsmeier, *Science and Civilisation in China*, 54.

2. See Sterckx, "Ritual, Mimesis, and the Nonhuman Animal World," 269.

3. See Boltz, "Liù shū."

4. This is one of the six categories (*liu shu*): that is, the six traditionally recognized types of Chinese character structures or usages. The *huiyi* characters are also called "syssematic" characters; see Behr, "'Homosomatic juxtaposition.'" If not otherwise specified, the Old Chinese reconstructions are from Baxter and Sagart, *Old Chinese.* "(Sch.)" indicates the reconstruction in Schuessler, *Minimal Old Chinese and Later Han Chinese.*

5. In order to properly distinguish the two "forms" of *chong*, from now on this form (*hui*) will be identified either as "*hui* form" or "single-*chong*" form. *Hui* is an alternative pronunciation of the character because it is considered as an early depiction of another character *hui* 虺 that represents a kind of snake. The fourth-century dictionary *Yu pian* points out that "*Hui* 虫 is the old script for the character *hui* 虺." Gu, *Yupian jiaoshi*, 4:4927.

6. The Oracle Bone Script graph is the same that generated the graph *ta*. Nowadays it is implied to represent the neuter third-person singular pronoun ("it"), but originally it depicted a kind of snake. See Li Xueqin, *Ziyuan*, 1172.

7. "Name of a Spirit or of an ancestor to whom the Shang offered sacrifices. It could bring misfortune upon the king." Another instance of *kun* identifies "the name of a tribe and of its territory." See *Le Grand Ricci Online.* (All translations by author unless otherwise noted.)

8. Li Xueqin, *Ziyuan*, 608.

9. The title of Xu Shen's dictionary is of fundamental importance in the history of early Chinese texts, since it is one of the few instances when the author of the text gives it a certain title. See Bottéro, "Revisiting," 20. The datings of *Erya* and its relation to other texts are contested; the meaning of its title is also opaque. See Valenti, "Biological Classification," 10–14.

10. *Liji zhengyi*, 832.

11. *Da Dai Liji jinzhu jinyi*, 71

12. Ban, *Hanshu*, 307.

13. Duan Yucai, *Shuowen jiezi zhu*, 674.

14. In the simplified script of the People's Republic of China (*jiantizi*), the *hui* character is used with the exact same meaning of *chong* (tripled *hui*), which is considered its variant in the traditional script (*fantizi*).

15. Li Shizhen, *Bencao gangmu*, 39 *mulu*.1a; translation by Nappi, *The Monkey and the Inkpot*, 97.

16. Valenti, "Biological Classification," 156–59.

17. Duan Yucai, *Shuowen jiezi zhu*, 676.

18. Carr, "A Linguistic Study,'" 65; Boltz, *The Origin and Early Development of the Chinese Writing System*, 137.

19. *Erya zhushu*, 326.

20. *Erya zhushu*, 358.

21. "[The animals categorized as] wildfowl are [the ones that can be] caught with nets and traps. It is said that birds' strength is feeble, they can be caught with

nets and then be captured. [The animals categorized as] wild beasts [quadrupeds] are [the ones that can be] hunted. It is said that their strength is vigorous, it is not possible to encounter and catch them with nets or traps; first they must be surrounded and then 'hunted' (*shou*), only then they are captured, that is why they are called 'wild beasts' (*shou*)." *Erya zhushu*, 358.

22. Duan Yucai, *Shuowen jiezi zhu*, 663. This animal is also present in the *Erya zhushu*, 337.

23. See *Hanyu da zidian*, 3025. Inscription in *yi* 乙 8718 depicts an "arrow-headed" snake, while the one in *tie* 鐵 46.2 depicts a "wedge-headed" snake. There is also an "eyed" snake in the Bronze Script on the tripod of Chang (*Chang ding*). All of these graphs can be correlated to *hui/chong*.

24. Duan Yucai, *Shuowen jiezi zhu*, 663.

25. Duan Yucai, *Shuowen jiezi zhu*, 663.

26. Carr, "A Linguistic Study"; Sterckx, *The Animal and the Daemon*, and Valenti, "Biological Classification."

27. As Harbsmeier put it: "Hsü Shen [Xu Shen] is not explaining words, he is explaining graphs in terms of the meaning relevant for a satisfactory explanation of the graph." Harbsmeier, *Science and Civilisation in China*, 73.

28. *Erya zhushu*, 352, 368–69.

29. Duan Yucai, *Shuowen jiezi zhu*, 457.

30. Duan Yucai, *Shuowen jiezi zhu*, 457.

31. See Boltz, *The Origin and Early Development of the Chinese Writing System*.

32. Duan Yucai, *Shuowen jiezi zhu*, 457–58.

33. For further discussion, see Carr, "A Linguistic Study" 69.

34. Carr, "A Linguistic Study," 72.

35. The vast majority of animals are, in fact, represented vertically and sideways. Older phonetic reconstructions include, for example, Karlgren's *Grammata Serica recensa*, as opposed to the more recent Schuessler, *Minimal Old Chinese*, and Baxter and Sagart, *Old Chinese*.

36. Wieger, *Chinese Characters*, 332; Gu, *Hanzi tujie zidian*, 257. *Le Grand Ricci* asserts that, in its ancient usage, *zhi* is "the name of a tribe and its territory that used the name of an unidentified animal in order to designate itself" (*Le Grand Ricci Online*). Li Xueqin states, "It is a character that represents a form. It looks like a species of animal, but actually it is impossible to know which one" (*Ziyuan*, 848–49).

37. The chapter "Glosses on Fish" (*Shi yu*) of the *Erya* includes all the above-mentioned fauna.

38. *Liji zhengyi*, 550–652.

39. *Da Dai Liji jinzhu jinyi*, 209–10, 478–79.

40. On these four animals, see *Liji zhengyi*, 818, and the discussion in Sterckx, *The Animal and the Daemon*.

41. *Liji zhengyi*, 437.

42. For example, Legge, *The Lî Kî*, I–X, 221.

43. *Le Grand Ricci Online*; *Hanyu da zidian*,3078.

44. *Liji zhengyi*, 832.

45. *Liji zhengyi*, 936.

46. *Liji zhengyi*, 1572.

47. Hutton, *Xunzi*, 318. Both Knoblock and Hutton translate *kun chong* as "swarming insects" (Knoblock, *Xunzi*, 128) or simply "insects." I suggest amending the text by removing the reference to insects, because *kun chong wan wu* is a "wrap-up" formula, rather than a taxonomic evaluation.

48. *Da Dai Liji jinzhu jinyi*, 236, 471. It would be strange to say first "the myriad of entities" and then "insects." The formula *wan wu kun chong* could be another way to encompass all the living things.

49. Ban, *Hanshu*, 307.

50. Major et al., *The Huainanzi*, 302. Once again, the translation of *kun chong* as "insect" would be misleading. Since wildfowl and wild beasts are already cited, I would suggest translating *kun chong* as "and all the multitude of the remaining creatures."

51. *Liji zhengyi*, 531.

52. *Liji zhengyi*, 556.

53. *Liji zhengyi*, 618.

54. *Liji zhengyi*, 620.

55. *Liji zhengyi*, 631.

56. *Liji zhengyi*, 644.

57. *Liji zhengyi*, 1302.

58. *Liji zhengyi*, 545.

59. *Liji zhengyi*, 562.

60. *Liji zhengyi*, 581.

61. *Liji zhengyi*, 651.

62. *Liji zhengyi*, 610.

63. *Liji zhengyi*, 659.

64. *Liji zhengyi*, 1843.

65. Here is a comparison between some of the Old Chinese reconstruction systems: Karlgren's *Grammata Serica recensa* (1957) has *dong wu* as **d'ung-miwət* and *chong* as **diông*; Schuessler's *Minimal Old Chinese* (2009) has **dôŋ?-mət* versus **druŋ*; Baxter and Sagart's *Old Chinese* (2014) has **[Cə-m-]tˤoŋ?-C.mut* versus **C.lruŋ*. While Karlgren's reconstruction of both words might have indicated that *chong* could have been a derivative contraction of *dong wu*, later reconstructions diverge substantially.

66. *Zhouli zhushu*, 1156–8 (Qiu guan sikou); *Zhouli zhushu*, 1292, 1330 (Dong guan kaogongji).

67. Duan Yucai, *Shuowen jiezi zhu*, 663. As the name of a decoration of a bell, in the form of a reptile, see Biot, *Le Tcheou-li*, 270, 470.

68. Carr, "A Linguistic Study," 67.

TWO

The Masculine Bee

GENDERING INSECTS
IN CHINESE IMPERIAL-ERA
LITERATURE

Olivia Milburn

Honeybees (*Apis cerana*) were of great economic importance in early imperial China, thanks to their role in producing both wax and honey, and because of this they were the subject of intense interest to people.[1] Beeswax was in demand for use in lighting, as well as in various industrial and artisanal processes; honey was utilized as a sweetener and as the base for a wide variety of medical preparations.[2] However, as literature from the Han dynasty (202 BCE–220 CE) onward attests, this interest in bees was not accompanied by either exact observation or accurate reporting of honeybee behavior. All honeybees were gendered masculine in these texts, whether queens, drones, or workers. Queen bees were characterized as kings, ruling nests or hives from their central throne rooms; drones were described as "generals" or "prime ministers" in constant attendance on their monarchs; while worker bees were also depicted as male, probing feminine flowers alongside their equally masculine butterfly companions. At the same time, bee societies were consistently described in approving terms by male members of the literati elite for the strong hierarchies supposedly maintained between "ruling" and "servile" members of the nest, and they were further masculinized by military metaphors, in which the worker bees were portrayed as a well-armed, regimented corps obeying the orders of their kings. By gendering honeybees in this way and endowing them with masculine traits, poets and writers found themselves promulgating a vision of an extraordinary society, in which male king bees gave birth to eggs, which hatched into further manly insects that grew up to be ever-vigilant warriors on the defensive against any threat to their royal progenitor.

The honeybee in Chinese literature exemplifies ideas about gender that conjure an image of the ultimate patriarchal society.[3] Human projections onto insect subjects have resulted in many misunderstandings from an entomological point of view, but they can serve to highlight major cultural concepts and deep-seated concerns.[4] The masculinized honeybee is no exception. Unlike some of the insects considered in other chapters of this book, such as flies, mosquitoes, or locusts, honeybees were always bound to be presented positively, not least because their products are of enormous significance to humans—benefits that significantly outweigh the unpleasantness of being stung. However, by consistently gendering honeybees as masculine, Chinese literati throughout the imperial era revealed deep underlying fears about women and femininity, as they constructed the vision of a society that reproduced sexually yet without any need for female involvement.

HONEYBEE SOCIETY AND GENDER:
THE STATE OF THE FIELD

In many societies, honeybees have been the subject of projections about gender and hierarchy, with the result that some extremely peculiar theories about their biology and social organization have been developed.[5] China is far from unique in having gendered honeybees as masculine, and ancient literature from a wide variety of civilizations gendered the queen bee as male. Although some of these ideas were based upon careful observation of these eusocial insects, people often seem to have struggled to understand this kind of society.[6] Perhaps as a result of this bafflement, there are numerous instances of other concerns—most notably worries about women in positions of political power—being projected onto bees.[7] In spite of the enormous amount of research produced on honeybees, there remains a great deal that is unknown about their evolution and social organizations, but the basic parameters have been established by modern scientific studies. Since traditional understandings of gender play no useful part in analyzing honeybee societies, this discussion will revolve around caste and genetics, both of which are significantly more helpful in explaining the roles played by different kinds of bee within each colony. There are three main castes of honeybee: queens, drones, and workers. Each performs a very specific function in the nest or hive, and bee society is strongly geared toward ensuring the reproductive success of the queen.[8] Since queen bees are the only bees in each colony that are physically capable of mating, it is crucial that this event should take place successfully in order to ensure the birth of the next generation of honeybees.[9] In situations where mating is disrupted, both queens and worker bees will produce unfertilized eggs, which can only hatch out into drone bees, and this will ensure the eventual collapse of the entire colony.[10] As in any eusocial insect society, all castes need to be present for the group as a whole to survive.

Speaking from the perspective of genetics, each bee colony is made up of close relatives. Fertile queen bees and infertile worker bees (which can lay eggs but not mate) are not genetically distinct from each other, since the difference in size and function within the colony is set by feeding at the larval stage.[11] Eggs destined to become queen bees are placed in larger "queen cups" and fed exclusively on royal jelly; eggs destined to become workers are placed in regular larval cells and fed first on royal jelly and then on a mix of honey and pollen.[12] The crucial role played by juvenile feeding in the creation of queen bees is confirmed by what happens in the event of the sudden death of the queen bee, in which case workers will build larger extensions onto some of the standard-size larval cells and begin feeding the larvae with royal jelly exclusively with a view to creating emergency queens.[13] These emergency queens will, however, remain smaller and less fertile than normal queens thanks to the difference in early nutrition. Drones are genetically quite distinct from the other bees in the colony because they are created by arrhenotokous parthenogenesis: the usual form of reproduction among living and ancestral Hymenoptera.[14] Hence, these bees are born from unfertilized eggs laid by the queen and have sixteen chromosomes. By contrast, queens and worker bees, born from fertilized eggs, have thirty-two chromosomes. Since all drone bees born to an individual queen produce genetically identical sperm, queens and worker bees produced from the same batch of fertilized eggs will be exceptionally closely related to each other.[15] This genetic relationship is crucial for encouraging individual insects to subsume their own interests in favor of the reproductive success of the colony as a whole (one of the definitive characteristics of eusociality). As a result of their eusocial organization, any binary distinction between male and female is not helpful for understanding honeybee society. However, as will be demonstrated below, members of the literati elite in China would insist on viewing honeybees through the prism of patriarchal attitudes, with the result that all too often literature about bees tells us more about people than it does about insects.

THE MASCULINE HONEYBEE

As previous studies have demonstrated, the development of specific nomenclature for honeybees that would distinguish them from other bees and wasps (Hymenoptera/*feng*) occurred relatively late in China.[16] Because *feng* is an umbrella term, in this chapter only literature in which the production of honey is specifically mentioned will be considered, in order to be quite sure that the honeybee is in fact the insect under discussion. The inclusion of the bee within the general class of *feng* is significant, because the association between Hymenoptera and masculinity was established extremely early on: thus the Han dynasty book of aphorisms entitled *Exemplary Figures* (Fayan) develops on a line found in *The Classic of Poetry* (Shijing) ode "Petty and Small" (Xiaowan) to suggest that wasps were all male and reproduced entirely through the adoption and assimilation of the larvae of other insects.[17] In the light of this commonality in vocabulary to describe Hymenoptera, it is not surprising that from their earliest appearance in Chinese literature, honeybees were also gendered male.[18] The first reference to masculine honeybees is generally agreed to be that found in *Doctrines Weighed* (Lunheng) by Wang Chong (27–ca. 100 CE). Apparently by the first century CE, honeybees were already being associated with *yang*—the masculine principle—and this understanding would set the stage for further explorations of these insects as male: "Eating sweet foodstuffs is of no harm to people. But if you eat even slightly too much honey, it can poison you. Honey is the secretions of bees, and bees are *yang* creatures."[19]

This description is the first to indicate that honeybees would henceforth be regarded as male insects, as well as being an exceptionally early reference in Chinese literature to toxic honey—a problem that continues to periodically poison and kill people in situations where wild honey is consumed without pollen analysis.[20] Little other early literature on the honeybee survives, until Guo Pu (276–324 CE) produced the first rhapsody on the subject in the medieval period: the "Rhapsody on a Honeybee" (Mifeng fu), also known as the "Rhapsody on Honey" (Mi fu). This piece

was part of an important contemporary literary trend, since during the
early Age of Disunion numerous rhapsodies were produced on the subject of insects, and many of these texts focused specifically on providing
literary representations of insect behavior.[21] Unfortunately, only fifty-five
lines of Guo Pu's rhapsody survive to the present day, preserved in quotations in other medieval texts. The textual relationship between these
fragments, and how much of the rhapsody has been lost, is not at all clear.
When quoted today, the rhapsody is usually given in approximately the
form found in the *Complete Prose of the Jin Dynasty (Quan Jin wen)* compiled
by Yan Kejun (1762–1843); however, various other arrangements for this
material have been proposed.[22] Given that the transmitted text is so corrupt and disputed, any translation of this rhapsody can only be tentative.
In all of the proposed reconstructions, the rhapsody opens with a strong
assertion of the superiority of honeybees over other kinds of insects,
before moving into a lyrical description of bees spreading out across the
landscape, which is expressed in rhymed couplets:

I bewail the stupidity of the myriad life-forms:[23]
Apart from the enlightened family of chaste insects.[24]
Even the tiniest of bees found amid thickets and weeds,
Have also inscribed their names in this winged tribe.
Here, they float through gardens and plantations,
There, they fly high above forests and valleys.
Now soaring, now gathering,
Spinning about, they whirl through the air.
In confusion, like snowflakes swirling,
Chaotic, like clouds scattering [across the sky].
Their shadows darkening the sun,
And the sound of their flight resonating like thunder.[25]

The rhapsody then moves on to describe the collection of nectar from
a variety of plants and the creation of honey within the comb. The poetic terminology used in this particular section would prove enormously
influential; for example, two literary terms for honeycomb—"golden
chambers" (*jinfang*) and "jade cells" (*yushi*)—are both derived from this
particular piece.[26] In the conclusion, Guo Pu turns his attention to the
subject of bee society. Here, for the first time in Chinese literature, there
is a reference to scout bees going forth and locating a new nest site, prior
to the bees leaving the site of their previous habitation in a swarm. This

rhapsody also provides a very early description of the role of guard bees, who protect the entrance to the hive or nest by patrolling and stinging any intruder.[27] However, unlike real life, where guard bees represent a tiny fraction of the total colony and perform these activities for an extremely short period of time in between much longer stints as nurses or queen attendants (inside the nest) and forager bees (outside the hive), the portrayal of honeybee social behavior found in this rhapsody suggests that protection was a major part of their daily routine. This may represent a misunderstanding of bee activities, or an intrusion of human values into Chinese views of insect lives, whereby a soldier's role was prized more highly than either the performance of domestic duties or agricultural labor. Thus, the many different occupations undertaken by worker bees during their short lives were condensed and simplified to present a highly militarized and authoritarian view of honeybee society:

> They investigate where they could live at peace,
> Checking out where they could be at rest.
> They fix on a location where they can prepare for troubles,
> They settle in green backwoods, where they can make a home.
> They proclaim their enlightenment within the winged tribe,
> They guard their kingdom as if with locks.[28]
> Their punishments are as severe as if they used sword and axe,
> They go on campaign as fast as if they received a military dispatch.[29]
> They gather without planning, and yet they keep to their time,
> They move constantly, and yet with coordination.
> The great ruler accordingly leads [his] people,
> And lives in peace with the *lingque* bird.[30]
> Every time he is the first to emerge and soar into the sky,
> Circling round to bring new order to these cliffs and caves.[31]

This rhapsody is extremely important in the history of writing about honeybees in China, forming a cornerstone of the literary tradition that would see bees henceforth being described as an army of highly disciplined male insects. In particular, the reference to the "great ruler" is indicative of the way in which Chinese literati would consistently gender the queen bee as male, and the authoritarian image given here of the honeybees' monarch would prove highly influential. Guo Pu's rhapsody shows considerable interest in the social structures found in bee society, most notably their ability to maintain good order and cooperate while living together in large communities. It would appear that from the early medieval period onward scholars and philosophers in China were already beginning to use bee social organization to posit a model for human society, though as later literature on the honeybee will attest, it was a very strange, single-gender vision that they espoused.

THE MASCULINE KING BEE

Early references in Chinese literature to the queen bee always use masculine terminology: this is the king bee (*fengwang*), and this term continues to be used right up to the present day. In spite of this masculine phraseology, the role of the king bee in giving birth to other members of the nest was well understood and clearly not regarded as contradictory. Chinese models of ideal human societies have traditionally stressed the correlation between family and state and have equated the role of the monarch with that of both parents, as in the locution "The ruler of the country is the father and mother of his people" (*Guojun min zhi fumu*) or "The Son of Heaven is the father and mother of the people, and thus he can act as monarch of All-Under-Heaven" (*Tianzi zuo min fumu yiwei Tianxia wang*).[32] In this instance, where king bees were known to literally be the parent of many (if not all) of the other honeybees in the nest, their social organization could be considered merely an extension of this familial model.[33] King bees were thought to reside in a particular space in the comb—the "king bee platform" (*fengwang tai*)—and from this location would announce their orders to the populace. It is likely that the king bee platform is the term referring to brood comb: in natural honeybee nests constructed inside rock cavities, the comb is divided in three with honeycomb at the top, pollen storage in the center, and brood comb at the lowermost level. In the classic description of the king bee platform given in the essay entitled "Recording Bees" (Ji feng) by Wang Yucheng (954–1001), the author writes, "The king [bee] has no sting. . . . When the nest is first colonized, [honeybees] will always first build a platform, as large as a chestnut: this is commonly known as the king's platform. The king lives on top, and gives birth to offspring inside it: sometimes three and sometimes five [at a time], for there is no regular number. The king's children will all in turn become kings themselves. Annually, they will divide their clan and depart [in a swarm]."[34]

Many aspects of this description are entomologically incorrect: queen bees do have stings and use them to kill rival queens on first emerging into the nest.[35] The eggs laid by queen bees produce all the different castes within the hive, so not all offspring will become queens in their turn. Furthermore, should a queen become old or ill, she will be killed by the worker bees in order to allow a new queen to take over.[36] However, in this entomological fantasy, interest in accurately reporting bee behavior was limited, because this essay was intended at least partly as a critique of human actions. In much of Chinese literature on the subject of honeybees, the virtues of bees form a powerful contrast with the unpleasant activities of human beings, who are not only morally inferior but actively disrupt this ideal society out of sheer greed.[37] Some scholars view this theme as a critique of the elite, who form a parasitic burden upon peasant communities. Others suggest that it reflects a genuine environmental concern, since prior to the development of sustainable apiculture, taking honey was an extremely destructive procedure that would result in the demise of many honeybees, and overexploitation would thus threaten the future supply of a highly desirable range of bee products. Accordingly, in the remarkable poem "Bees" (Feng'er) by Yang Wanli (1127–1206), the poet begins with a description of bees making honey inside the comb, but in the last three couplets he voices the complaints of the king bee himself. The malignancy of human intervention in bee life is here laid bare by characterizing the person ordering all this death and ruination as a glutton (laotao). Honey is not a necessity, so the wanton destruction wrought by humans is caused by pure greed. Having this judgment expressed in the voice of the king bee who is watching his home being wrecked and his offspring murdered is very powerful:

> Honeybees do not eat from human stores,
> For dew is their wine and flowers their food.
> In making honey there is no need for speed, but choosing flowers
>   must be done fast,
> Thus when the honey is formed, it still contains the perfume of a myriad
>   flowers.
> Once the honey is formed, the tens of thousands of bees dare not taste it,
> For they will transport it to their honey kingdom and offer it to their
>   king bee.
> But the king bee has no time to enjoy it,
> For humans are already cutting into the honeycomb.

Where the old honey has become wax,[38]
But the fresh honey remains delicious.
"The honeycomb and wax plaques once cut become useless,[39]
But the glutton's minions now able to raid my home.
The old bees are ignored, they are just scum,
The young bees are newly pupated and have not yet hatched.
Yet the glutton attacks with fire, not knowing when to stop,
Even as he destroys my home and captures my children."[40]

The same strong idealization of bee society, which was clearly envisioned as an "all-for-one" supportive state in which the mass of ordinary members would ever flock to defend the monarch-parent, would remain extraordinarily emotive throughout imperial-era literature. It is a very popular theme in entomological literature and poetry and is perhaps best epitomized by the Ming dynasty poem entitled "Lament on the Grave of the Honeybees" (Fengzhong tan) by Shao Bao (1440–1523). In this most peculiar piece, the poet seems to be bewailing an instance of colony collapse following the death of the king bee—here termed yifeng (the one bee), which would be equivalent to yiren (the one man), a very ancient term for the ruler.[41] This literary representation of honeybee social behavior is explicitly framed, yet again, as a critique of human actions:

When the one bee lives, the masses stay.
When the one bee is killed, the masses die.
Their graves are piled high, how can it be like this . . . ?
The one bee is the ruler, the masses are his vassals.
So who can say that bees are inferior to human beings?[42]

To a certain extent, this kind of poem does reflect the reality of the lives of eusocial insects, which are utterly dependent on each other and where individuals make significant sacrifices in order to ensure the success of the society as a whole. However, instead of accepting that all castes need to be present for the colony to survive—and the crucial role of workers in particular should have been readily observable—Chinese literati focused instead on the hierarchical ruler-vassal relationship and divided bees into royal and servile classes. This in turn ties in to a very ancient discourse that argued that a subject should lay down his life to protect his lord from the slightest difficulty: "When the ruler suffers humiliation, his vassals should die" (Jun ru ze chen si).[43] Since this tradition of equating loyalty with a willingness to die for the monarch was already well established in antiquity, it is not surprising that the deaths of bees in the context of a colony collapse would be regarded as an instance of insects showing superior virtue to human beings.

THE MASCULINE DRONE

There are relatively few references specifically to drones in Chinese literature. Once such references do begin to appear, they describe drones in military or official terms: these are "general bees" (*jiangfeng*) or "prime minister bees" (*xiangfeng*). This terminology appears to be derived ultimately from one text, *A Record of the Transformations of Yin and Yang* (*Yinyang bianhua lu*), which is of unknown date and authorship and is today known only from quotations about the passages concerning bees.[44] The description found in *A Record of the Transformations of Yin and Yang* is generally correct in the timing of the birth of drones and their ejection from the nest, as well as noting their lack of participation in nectar collection, but is wrong in suggesting that they play a key role in making honey. Since the main purpose of drones is to fertilize queen bees, their function in maintaining the honeycomb is limited to fanning it in the event of overheating or shivering to reduce the cold. The section of *A Record of the Transformations of Yin and Yang* that deals with drones is quoted in slightly differing forms in various sources, but the Ming dynasty *Extended Investigations from the Mountain Hermitage* (*Shantang sikao*) version of the text reads:

> Bees every year in the third or fourth lunar months give birth to black-colored bees, which are called "general bees" or also "prime minister bees." The king bee is then born from the prime minister bee. Prime minister bees cannot collect [nectar from] flowers; they can only make honey. Probably without these bees it would be impossible to make honey. In the seventh or eighth month the prime minister bees all die. If the prime minister bees do not die then the rest of the bee population will starve. There is a common saying: "If prime minister bees survive the winter, then the honeycombs will be empty."[45]

The crucial evidence for demonstrating that these "generals" and "prime ministers" must be drones is the reference to their deaths in autumn. Since worker bees are produced only from fertilized eggs, the queen must mate with as many drones as possible in the autumn to ensure an ongoing supply of new bees born in the hive, and drones are killed by the act of mating, in which their bodies are explosively separated from their endophallus.[46] Even in the event of a failure to mate, honeybee drones will still live only about ninety days. However, by far the most interesting aspect of this description is the line about how "the king bee is born from the prime minister bee," which is suggestive of a very remarkable view of honeybee reproduction. Given that numerous accounts indicate that king bees were known to produce eggs, and "prime minister bees" were apparently involved in the process, we can only assume that the author of *A Record of the Transformations of Yin and Yang* had in mind a vision of sexual reproduction involving two male partners, which would in turn produce more masculine bees.

THE MASCULINE WORKER BEE

In honeybee society, given that drones and queens perform only reproductive tasks, all other functions are carried out by workers. They build the comb and fill it with honey and pollen for which they have foraged far and wide; they care for larvae and the queen bee, as well as performing cleaning, guarding, and temperature regulating activities in and around the nest. Some literary representations of worker bees (which can be explicitly designated as "bee vassals" [*fengchen*] in the monarchical terminology employed in such representations) do focus specifically on these roles; thus, for example, the poem "Spring Days" (Chunri) by Qin Guan (1049–ca. 1110) includes the line "For the honeycomb to be kept fresh and neat relies on the bee vassals" (*Mipi xin cai lai feng chen*).[47] However, it is generally the case that when worker bees appear in Chinese literature, they are represented not merely as masculine gendered but also as highly sexualized creatures. Worker bees, foraging for pollen and nectar, were considered very explicitly male because the movement of thrusting their mandibles into flowers was equated with the sex act. In very much the same way and for the same reason, butterflies were also coded as masculine, and bees and butterflies appeared together in a wide range of metaphors for sexual activity. Examples of this include "bee madness and butterfly mania" (*fengkuang dieluan*) or "bee fixations and butterfly love" (*fengmi dielian*), both of which are terms for sex. In addition, the emotions of men longing for a girlfriend were termed "bee fixations and butterfly imaginings" (*fengmi diecai*) or "bee imaginings and butterfly visions" (*fengcai diequ*).[48] Men who were noted for their sexual experience were also often compared to bees and butterflies (*fengdie*).[49] Finally, "bee go-betweens and butterfly messengers" (*fengmei dieshi*) is a locution popular from the Song dynasty to describe those taking letters arranging secret meetings between lovers.[50] All of these examples go to demonstrate the strong association maintained in traditional Chinese literature between worker bees and masculinity.

Workers were the kind of honeybee that people were most likely to come across, and therefore the vast majority of literature about bees must be assumed to describe the oldest members of this caste, when they were performing foraging activities away from the hive. Younger nest-bound bees would be described only when the honeycomb is itself the topic of discussion. It is now well understood that part of the complexity of honeybee society is the result of caste specialization, which means that without all the different members of the colony being present and at a range of ages and functions, it is impossible for any of the remainder to survive.[51] An understanding of bee interdependence seems to have been held back within Chinese literature in favor of focusing on a strongly hierarchical vision of honeybee society, which had been present since at least medieval times: this is summed up in the *Book of Transformation* (Huashu) in the aphorism "Bees observe the proper norms between lord and vassal" (*Feng you junchen zhi li*).[52] This division between monarch and subjects is found in numerous literary representations; for example, in his poem "Enjoying an Overgrown Garden All by Myself" (Xianyuan dushang), Bai Juyi (772–846) states, "When bees swarm you can distinguish lord and vassal" (*Feng fen jian jun chen*).[53] Furthermore, there was a tradition of praising honeybees for their industriousness, and this was combined with a belief that bees were carefully controlled by and obedient to their king. This understanding of honeybee colony dynamics can be seen in a wide variety of literary sources. For example, the seventh poem by Meng Jiao (751–814) in the series entitled *On the Cold Food Festival at Jiyuan* (Jiyuan Hanshi) emphasizes the success of the bees in managing their resources, while at the same time attributing this exclusively to the orders issued by their king. This suggests that without the strong rule of the bee king, the other members of the hive would be utterly improvident:

For their ruler's sake, honeybees all sharpen their mandibles,
Sucking dry the myriad flowers to be found around the village.
In their lord's home, every single cell is now full to bursting,
Their multicolored winter hive is indeed very deserving of praise.[54]

The same perspective on bee society can be seen in many other writings. There is a long-established tradition in writing about bees that stresses the supposedly authoritarian nature of their social organization and places all credit for the colony's survival on the king bee. Thus the opening couplet of the poem entitled "In Response to Zizhan's 'Song of Mead'" (He Zizhan "Mijiu ge") by Su Zhe (1039–1112) states, "The king bee supports his court [numbering] tens of thousands of mouths/ With beeswax as their grain and honey for their drink."[55] From this regimented and micromanaged vision of honeybee society, it seems to have been a short step to a militarized one, in which metaphors drawn from the army were regularly invoked.[56] This kind of rhetoric can be seen in writings such as the second of the three poems entitled "Honeybees" (Luofeng) by Yuan Zhen (779–831). In this piece, the poet explicitly evokes the image of bees as an army unit, marching out to find food:

The pear-blossom delights in the moon over the Qingdu [Monastery],
The bees frolic in the spring [breezes] around the Purple Hall.
At the honeycomb they divide into military units,
Nibbling at the flowers to feed their lord and parent.
They have wings much like similar species,
But their minds are hardened against other kinds [of insects].
How could they know that in the human world,
There is no one who can sting other people?[57]

The poet here praises the bees for their violent defense of their own nests, with intruders killed to prevent them gaining access to the hive. Apparently, human beings are inferior in their lack of interest in protecting their lord and ruler at all costs. The entwined relationship between family and state in honeybee colonies was clearly regarded as highly admirable, with the king-father acting as a benevolent despot that his armed and vigilant offspring were happy to protect. Given the dominant tradition in literati writings about honeybees drew on images of masculinity, militarization, and sexual promiscuity, it is not surprising that when women started producing poetry in large quantities in the Ming and Qing dynasties, they tended to seek alternative modes of discourse that would be less alienating. Rather than portraying bees as obedient soldiers loyally serving their royal father, they tended to write in a different tradition, associated with Buddhist images of honeybees, which saw making honey as a metaphor for gaining intellectual attainments.[58] This women's textual tradition can be exemplified by the poem "In Reply to the Young Girl Next Door" (Da linmei) by Shen Cai (b. 1752):

> I chant for a long time when the moon is facing the window,
> I recite quietly when the sun is at its zenith.
> The young girl next door said to me:
> "Reading books is just bringing pointless suffering on yourself."
> "Many thanks for your advice, girl next door,
> But in my heart I respect the past.
> It can be compared to bees making honey,
> It is the most important thing in my life.
> A thousand boxes of books will defeat one hundred walled cities,
> Worldly matters are as light as a feather.
> If only it could always be like this,
> In my next life, let me still be an old woman."[59]

This poem provides a sexless image of bees that is in its own way quite as remarkable as any of the hypermasculine representations considered above. The poet here sets aside gender as irrelevant and argues that productivity (whether of literature or honey) should be considered a more important measure of a successful life than reproduction. Whether she was aware of the entomological accuracy of her description or not, her comparison of the usefulness of nonlaying worker bees with that of postmenopausal women remains highly striking and original. Shen Cai's confident assertion of the value of work provides another layer in the rich tradition of Chinese writings about honeybees.

CONCLUSION

Chinese literature about honeybees has always been dominated by images of masculinity and authoritarianism and military metaphors. This has been so prevalent that there has been very little room for the development of alternative discourses, and at some level, real life observations of bees became curtailed: as beekeeping became popularized, people had more and more opportunities to actually watch what bees did, but neverthe-less members of the educated elite continued to prioritize deep-rooted cultural constructs in their writings. This masculine model of honeybee society became so ingrained that in the end, whether this was entirely conscious or not, Chinese literati men found themselves writing about a purely male society, in which masculine bees laid eggs which produced more male bees. In such a society, where all members belong to the same gender, gender becomes irrelevant: thus, members of the literati came to write of an idealized patriarchal family and state in which every member performed their tasks for the benefit of the monarch-father.

In gendering queen bees in particular as male, Chinese literati were participating in a pattern found in vast swathes of the world, where rul-ership and femininity were seen as incompatible. Studies of Western thinking on the queen bee have often argued that it was the presence of women monarchs on the throne that forced a reassessment of the gender of honeybees and allowed philosophers to accept that females could hold supreme power in both human and insect societies. However, since the queen bee was consistently gendered as male in Chinese thought, in spite of the presence of one female emperor and many women regents at dif-ferent times through the imperial era, a strict correlation between having women in positions of political power and accepting the existence of the queen bee is unlikely. Instead, it might be more useful to think of literary representations of honeybee colonies in China as a vision of a society in which the biological functions of the monarch were irrelevant when faced with the overwhelming majesty of their role.

NOTES

1. *Apis cerana* is commonly known as the Asian or Eastern honeybee, as opposed to *Apis mellifera*, the Western honeybee; see Dar et al., "The Classic Taxonomy of Asian and European Honey Bees." These two species of honeybee are the only ones known to have been farmed extensively since antiquity.

2. The economic importance of beeswax is often neglected in modern studies. For discussions of the early use of beeswax in candles and as a lamp-fuel, see Ma, Martinón-Torres, and Li, "Identification of Beeswax"; Zhang Lei, "Zhongguo gudai dengju xingzhi"; and Qin, "Yingguang shanshuo hua zhutai." Fan and Hu, "Qiantan Tangdai mifeng chanye," provides an overview of the economic signifi-cance of beeswax as documented in the official histories of the Tang dynasty. The

medical and culinary uses of honey are described in Milburn, "A Taste of Honey," 46–51.

3. Furth, *A Flourishing Yin*, argues for a more nuanced understanding of the yin-yang dichotomy in Chinese thought on gender, rather than a strongly binary interpretation. However, in some instances, even where this binary was clearly unsatisfactory, it was nevertheless strongly imposed. This can be seen for example in the treatment of intersex individuals, who were required to accept categorization as either male or female; see Milburn, "Bodily Transformations."

4. This point is also made with respect to Western representations of honeybees in Berenbaum, "Sons of Bees."

5. For studies of early Western ideas about honeybee social organization, see Mayhew, "King-Bees and Mother-Wasps," and Overmeire, "The Perfect King Bee."

6. Eusocial species, including some insects, mammals, and crustaceans, are characterized by a division between reproductive and nonreproductive individuals, overlapping generations within the colony, and cooperative care of juveniles. Eusocial species tend to caste specialization, with individuals losing the ability to perform activities carried out by members of other castes; see Nowak, Tarnita, and Wilson, "The Evolution of Eusociality," and Sherman et al., "The Eusociality Continuum."

7. The work of Charles Butler, *The Feminine Monarchie: or The Historie of Bees* (1634), was crucial for first popularizing the idea of the queen bee in the West. This resulted in considerable intellectual contortions as patriarchal and gender roles had to be reassigned within an "Amazonian" bee society; see Prete, "Can Females Rule the Hive?" and Merrick, "Royal Bees." Though usually associated with monarchical discourse and apologies for absolutist monarchical rule, bees were also pressed into service to promote Republican ideas; see Bourque, "'Tout est en desordre dans la ruche.'"

8. In academic literature about honeybees, nests refer to living sites constructed by the bees themselves, hives to human-built containers. Since in many cases imperial-era Chinese literature does not clearly specify whether the bees under discussion are wild or (semi-) domesticated, the two terms will be used interchangeably in this chapter.

9. Studies of worker bee egg-laying activities for *Apis cerana* consistently show a very poor rate of success, though in the absence of a queen they are quicker than the Western honeybee to begin laying eggs; see Oldroyd et al., "Worker Policing and Worker Reproduction in *Apis cerana*," and Holmes et al., "Why Acquiesce?"

10. *Apis cerana* is, however, capable of producing fertile queen bees not only through sexual reproduction but also through thelytoky, which means that for small and vulnerable bee populations, survival is possible even if the queen bee does not successfully mate; see Holmes et al., "Genetic Reincarnation of Workers as Queens."

11. As a caste, worker bees perform a wide variety of activities in and around

the hive; these are a function of age and will change as the honeybee grows older. Furthermore, not all worker bees perform the same duties, since certain functions require only a few bees at any one time to be active in carrying them out. For a detailed description of this process, see Winston, *The Biology of the Honey Bee*, 89–109.

12. Beetsma, "The Process of Queen-Worker Differentiation in the Honeybee."

13. Wongsiri et al., "Queen Rearing with *Apis cerana*."

14. Heimpel and Boer, "Sex Determination in the Hymenoptera."

15. So far, numerous studies suggest that worker bees do not show nepotism (which in this context refers to favoring eggs fertilized by the same drone and preferentially feeding the resultant juveniles), which is thought to be a result of just how closely genetically related they are; see Koyama et al., "Absence of Reproductive Conflict." The principles behind such altruism are considered in Ratnieks, Foster, and Wenseleers, "Conflict Resolution in Insect Societies."

16. Pattinson, "Bees in China," 99.

17. Wang Rongbao, *Fayan yishu*, 9 ("Xuexing" 學行). The description of wasps "adopting" other insects is found in Kong Yingda, *Mao Shi zhengyi*, 744 (Mao 196: "Xiaowan"). This concept is thought to be derived from people observing predation by the relevant wasps.

18. While the earliest surviving dictionary of the Chinese language, *Shuowen jiezi*, simply notes that Hymenoptera sting, the commentary on this line makes extensive reference to early traditions that associated wasps and other related insects with "pure masculinity" (*chunxiong*); see Duan Yucai, *Shuowen jiezi zhu*, 675.

19. Huang Hui, *Lunheng jiaoshi*, 951 ("Yandu" 言毒).

20. Cases of fatalities arising from naturally toxic honey in modern China are discussed in Q. Zhang et al., "Fatal Honey Poisoning Caused by *Tripterygium wilfordii* Hook F in Southwest China"; and Q. Zhang et al., "Fatal Honey Poisoning."

21. Zha, "Han Wei Liuchao niaoshouchong fu santi." Guo Pu was also the author of other early literature on insects, such as the "Pifu fu" (Rhapsody on ants).

22. Yan Kejun, *Quan Jin wen*, 120:2149. For alternative arrangements of the surviving fragments, see Zhang Pu, *Han Wei Liuchao baisanjia ji*, 56:544; Chen Yuanlong et al., *Yuding lidai fu hui*, 138:14a; and Li Sugen, "Jin Guo Pu 'Mifeng fu' jiaoyi."

23. This rhapsody uses an extremely unusual term for "myriad lifeforms" (*pinwu*) that originates in the *Yijing*; see Kong Yingda, *Zhouyi zhengyi*, 7 ("Qian" 乾).

24. "Chaste insects" (*zhenchong*) refers to Hymenoptera in general; see Sun, *Mozi xiangu*, 239 ("Minggui xia" 明鬼下). The use of such rare terms in the opening of Guo Pu's rhapsody stresses his erudition.

25. Yan Kejun, *Quan Jin wen*, 120:2149. This is a slightly revised version of the complete translation of this rhapsody, previously published in Milburn, "A Taste of Honey." For an alternative translation, see Idema, *Insects in Chinese Literature*, 72–73.

26. See for example, Yu, "Feng," 479:1a–1b.

27. For studies of guard bee activities, see Chapman et al., "Nestmate Recog-

nition"; Breed, Smith, and Torres, "Role of the Guard Honey Bees"; and Abrol, "Defensive Behaviour."

28. Both Chen et al., *Yuding lidai fu hui*, 138:14a, and Li Sugen, "Jin Guo Pu 'Mifeng fu' jiaoyi," 34, give this line as "They guard [the portals] as strictly as with locks" (*hunwei gu yu guanyao*).

29. A *yuxi* is a military dispatch to which a feather was attached to show its urgency; see Sima, *Shiji*, 93:2641.

30. The *lingque* bird is a highly mysterious creature, known only from this one reference. Some commentators identify this as the same as the *mimu* or "honey-mother" bird. The lost text entitled *Linhai yiwu zhi* (Record of the strange creatures of the coastal regions) by Shen Ying (d. 280 CE), quoted in Li Fang et al., *Taiping yulan*, 928:4125, says, "The *mimu* is a small bird, black in color. In the first lunar month at dawn it leads honeybees through the mountains, looking for a safe place, and the bees follow it. At dusk the *mimu* returns and enters [the hive] with the bees."

31. Yan Kejun, *Quan Jin wen*, 120:2149.

32. Ban, *Hanshu*, 27a:1322; and Kong Yingda, *Shangshu zhengyi*, 112 ("Hongfan" 洪範), respectively. The same idea is also mentioned in other texts; see for example Sun, *Mozi xiangu*, 60 ("Shangxian zhong" 尚賢中); and Huang, Zhang, and Tian, *Yi Zhoushu huijiao jizhu*, 9:1067 ("Rui Liangfu jie" 芮良夫解).

33. Since queen bees can remain productive for many years, over time, honeybee colonies will show less genetic variety as any sibling workers and drones die off; however, propensity to swarm among worker bees can apparently differ greatly depending on paternal lineage—a quality that appears to be present in both *Apis cerana* and *Apis mellifera* species; see Huang and Zeng, "Nepotism in Swarming Honeybees"; and Estoup, Solignac, and Cornuet, "Precise Assessment," respectively.

34. Wang Yucheng, *Xiaochu ji*, 14:199. Managing swarming behavior was a key development in beekeeping in China; see Pattinson, "Pre-modern Beekeeping in China."

35. There have been numerous studies about the competition between rival virgin queens for *Apis mellifera* to explore differing factors in why a particular individual queen bee is able to survive; see for example Gilley, "The Behavior of Honey Bees"; Harano and Obara, "The Role of Chemical and Acoustical Stimuli"; and Tarpy and Mayer, "The Effects of Size and Reproductive Quality." However, to date there has been virtually no research on this topic for *Apis cerana* queen bees.

36. The killing of old queens, known as supersedure, is not just a matter of the aging of an individual bee but also determined by climate and food supplies; see Chinh, Boot, and Sommeijer, "Production of Reproductives in the Honey Bee Species *Apis cerana* in Northern Vietnam"; and Hamdan, "Natural Supersedure of Queens in Honey Bee Colonies."

37. This literary trope is discussed in Lei Mingxia, "Wei shei xinku wei shei tian"; Wang Yonghou, "Yong feng shi hua"; and Li Lu, "Fengmi shici."

38. Beeswax is indeed synthesized by honeybees from honey, with the conversion rate being approximately eight kilos of honey for each kilo of wax secreted. For the history of different theories of beeswax production promulgated in the West, see Hepburn, *Honeybees and Wax*, 6–10.

39. The reference made here to wax plaques presumably refers to the hexagonal caps on the individual cells.

40. Yang Wanli, *Chengzhai ji*, 29:2a–2b. For an alternative translation, see Idema, *Insects in Chinese Literature*, 75. This rendition, however, appears to use a shorter version of the poem, taken from Jiang et al., *Qinchong dian*, 170:45a.

41. Kong Yingda, *Shangshu zhengyi*, 214 ("Taijia xia" 太甲下). See also Chen Li, *Baihu tong shuzheng*, 47 ("Hao" 號).

42. Shao, "Fengzhong tan," 1:406.

43. Yuan and Wu, *Yuejue shu*, 69 ("Waizhuan zhenzhong" 外傳枕中); for the same phrase with slightly different wording, see for example, Shanghai Shifan Daxue Guji Zhengli Zu, *Guoyu*, 658 ("Yueyu xia" 越語下); and Lu Jia, *Xinyu*, 20 ("Bianhuo" 辨惑).

44. Some scholars attribute references to general and prime minister bees to the *Youyang zazu* by Duan Chengshi (800–863); see, for example, Yang Shupei, "Zhongguo gudai dui mifeng de renshi," 244. The transmitted text does contain some references to bees; see Duan Chengshi, *Youyang zazu*, 17:168–69. However, there is nothing about drones in the present text, and hence the earliest account of drones is from the *Yinyang bianhua lu*.

45. Peng, *Shantang sikao*, 226:6a–6b. The importance of this description as the earliest known account in Chinese literature of drone bees is stressed in Yang Shupei, "Zhongguo yangfengshi zhi guanjian," 86.

46. For studies of the mating behavior of honeybees, see, for example, N. Koeniger and G. Koeniger, "An Evolutionary Approach"; and Winston, *The Biology of the Honey Bee*, 199–213.

47. This poem is quoted in Wu, *Songshi chao*, 36:741.

48. For studies of imperial-era literature about butterflies and bees that focus on their role as a metaphor for sexual activity, see for example Li Lu, "Tangshi de chunji kunchong yixiang yanjiu"; and Ji, "Kunchong shihua."

49. Thus the poem "Chunri" (Spring days) by Yang Shi (1053–1135) can be read as a landscape poem, or on another level as representing the longings of a secluded young woman for a passionate lover (Yang Shi, "Chunri," 68:21a–b). More obviously, in the poem "Hushang" (Out on the lake) by Fang Yue (1199–1262), the poet is describing the atmosphere once the partying men have departed: "The 'bees and butterflies' have gone home and the musical instruments fall silent" (*feng die yi gui xian guan jing*) (Fang Yue, *Qiuya ji*, 1:21a).

50. Early instances of the use of this metaphor can be found in the Song dynasty song lyrics Shao, "Pu hudie," 4:14a–14b, and Zhou Bangyan, "Liu chou," 81.

51. Oldroyd and Wongsiri, *Asian Honey Bees*, 5.

52. This aphorism is widely quoted; see for example Cai, *Mao Shi mingwu jie*, 11:4a. However, it does not appear in the transmitted text of the *Huashu*.

53. Bai, "Xianyuan dushang," 32:730.

54. Meng, *Meng Dongye shi ji*, 5:80.

55. Su, *Su Zhe ji*, 12:230.

56. For example, the "Yi feng xing" by Dai Biaoyuan (1244–1310) contains the line "Mountain bees guard their honey as they guard their homes" (*Shanfeng ying mi ru ying jia*), where the term used for "to guard" has strongly militaristic overtones (Dai Biaoyuan, "Yi feng xing," 8:22a).

57. Yuan Zhen, "Luofeng," 2266. There is also an interesting later reworking of this poem by Qian Qianyi (1582–1664) that eschews military metaphors in favor of familial and hierarchical images of bee society. This poem concludes, "They cull the flowers to entrance their ruler / They nibble wax to benefit their parent / They also observe the rituals of ruler and vassal / Lined up in their serried ranks they despise us hairless creatures"; see Qian Qianyi, *Muzhai chuxue ji*, 20b:425.

58. This alternative and much neglected tradition is outlined in Gao, "Luo Yin 'Feng' shi."

59. Shen Cai, "Da linmei," 6:5b.

THREE

Manchu Insect Names

GRASSHOPPERS, LOCUSTS, AND A FEW OTHER BUGS IN THE SEVENTEENTH AND EIGHTEENTH CENTURIES

Mårten Söderblom Saarela

Grasshoppers and locusts were part of Manchu everyday experience, and the Manchus accordingly had words for them. Yet in the Qing Empire that the Manchus established and centered on the capital of Beijing, the linguistic and conceptual world of rulers, administrators, and scholars was not limited to the Manchu words and notions that were carried along from "outside the pass" in Manchuria.

Within the conceptual world of Qing China, locusts and grasshoppers existed within a broader category of "bugs." They are remarkable within that category for occurring frequently in both literary and bureaucratic texts. Yet in order to situate locusts within the larger problematic of aligning Chinese and Manchu words for the natural world, I will make reference to other bugs, or *umiyaha* in Manchu. This word generally corresponded to Chinese *chong* 蟲, which, however, was varyingly used, at least in the canonical texts that were considered the foundation of morality and elite sociability. When not meaning simply "creature," *chong* could be "invertebrates and creeping creatures," which included, for example, turtles.[1] Chinese *chong* thus included more than simply insects, or arthropods, properly speaking.[2]

Umiyaha, by contrast, has cognates in other Tungusic languages that suggest that the etymon meant "maggot."[3] It thus appears that for the Manchus, the category of *umiyaha* was from the beginning more closely associated with insects in particular than Chinese *chong* might have been to some writers in antiquity, whose texts were still read in the Qing period. My focus, however, will be not on the category of *umiyaha* but on some of its members. The vocabulary used in reference to locusts and grasshoppers serves as an example of the development of nomenclature in three areas.

First, in the translation of canonical Chinese texts, the Manchu language was put into contact with a historically layered vocabulary for insects and other bugs (with the latter as the broader category, including a range of the phylum Arthropoda), locusts among them. Second, in bilingual dictionaries, often published commercially, Manchu words for bugs were juxtaposed with vernacular Chinese terms that were quite different from those used in the Chinese classics; they were drawn, rather, from the lifeworld of Qing China and came more easily to the dictionaries' compilers and readers. Third, Manchu administrators in the field reported on the presence and prevention of locusts as agricultural pests (a topic explored in much greater detail in David A. Bello's chapter in this volume). In this context too, the Manchu language was used alongside written Chinese. Bureaucratic and scholarly Chinese—simpler than the language of the classics but still distinct from the spoken language seen in commercial dictionaries—had its own way of talking about locusts and their lifecycle.

In these three contexts, Manchu writers and translators created equivalences between Manchu and Chinese. One way in which they reduced the differences that existed between the different languages and linguistic registers was through borrowing words from Chinese into Manchu. With time, they instead deliberately created new Manchu words that mimicked the Chinese semantically but not phonetically.[4] With bugs as with other things, the Manchu lexicon was to a great extent the product of a cross-linguistic encounter and the language reform that this encounter inspired.

LOCUSTS IN THE MANCHU *CLASSIC OF POETRY* OF 1655

The translation of *The Classic of Poetry* (Shijing)—the earliest collection of poetry in Chinese, with materials generally regarded to date between the eleventh and seventh centuries BCE—into Manchu showed what lexical resources early-Qing written Manchu possessed for talking about bugs. Yet it *ipso facto* also laid bare just how much Manchu terms differed from the famously rich vocabulary in the ancient canonical text. *The Classic of Poetry* contained numerous words for plants and animals: "From it we

become largely acquainted with the names of birds, beasts, and plants"
(*duo shi yu niao shou cao mu zhi ming*), Confucius is quoted as saying in *The Analects* (Lunyu).[5] Simply reading the poems of the classic was not enough for learning just what natural objects the names referenced, however. Indeed, *The Classic of Poetry* passages were often the *loci classici* for the words in question, which meant that to an average reader of literary Chinese, the names of birds, beasts, and plants were just so many floating signifiers.

A scholarly tradition developed to explain just what *The Classic of Poetry* meant. *Approaching Elegance* (Erya), an early lexicon that contained several chapters on flora and fauna (see chapter 1, this volume), had a close association with *The Classic of Poetry*.[6] *Approaching Elegance* is evidence that the classic's words for things like insects had to be explained even to readers already in Chinese antiquity. Over the centuries, philologists investigated the names, including those for bugs and insects, but, as expected, they did not agree on the creatures to which they referred. Translations of *The Classic of Poetry* into foreign languages, accordingly, varied in their treatment of the names for plants and animals.[7]

A Manchu translation of *The Classic of Poetry* was first published early in 1655 (SZ 11/12), about a decade after the conquest of Beijing.[8] It was printed in Manchu only and contained the main text of the *Classic* along with two layers of commentary. The philologist Chenyu Tu has recently shown that the Chinese edition used for the translation was *Compendium on the Classic of Poetry* (Shi zhuan daquan) from the early fifteenth century, an edition that remained popular and highly regarded in the early Qing period.[9] The main text of the Manchu translation was then used in a private or commercial edition probably dating from the late seventeenth century, as well as in at least one manuscript copy from the same period.[10]

Among the names for bugs in *The Classic of Poetry*, some were easily understood by learned readers of later times—or so they thought, as they assumed that the words in question meant the same thing in antiquity as in their day. Others words were less readily understandable. Some of the possibly hard-to-understand insect names were not translated at all, which meant they had to be glossed in the Manchu version for a reader to be able to make sense of them. For example, *fuyou*, rendered by two English-language translators as "ephemera" (in the sense of mayflies), was glossed but not translated in the Manchu *Classic of Poetry*.[11]

By contrast, in some cases, the Manchu translation made a rare Chinese word immediately intelligible by replacing it with a vernacular Manchu word rather than transcribing and glossing the original Chinese. For example, the *xiaoshao* in "Hills of the East" (Dong shan), which ancient authorities agreed was some kind of small spider, simply became a generic "spider" (*helmehen*) in Manchu.[12]

Furthermore, "Those Officers of the [Old] Capital" (Du renshi) mentions a *chai* (scorpion).[13] The Manchu translation has *hiyedz*, which is a loanword from the northern vernacular Chinese *xiezi*, a word still current in Mandarin today. The Manchu commentary followed the received Chinese version in describing the creature as a "bug that stings" (*šešere umiyaha*). However, the gloss that contrasted *chai* and *xie*, that was found in the Chinese base text *Compendium on the Classic of Poetry*, was not necessary in the Manchu version.[14]

The case of the locust is similar but more complicated because of the greater number of words used to refer to locusts and their relatives, the grasshoppers and crickets, and the more different cicadas. *The Classic of Poetry* contained quite a few of the words known from ancient Chinese sources to refer to these insects. The translators could transcribe the words, but if they wanted to gloss them successfully for a Manchu reader, the gloss required a detailed description (based on a Chinese commentary). If the translators chose to translate rather than transcribe, they would have to either coin new Manchu words to match the variety seen in the original *Classic of Poetry* or reduce that variety to the much smaller set of words that was available in Manchu at that time. The solutions opted for in the translation differed in the cases of cicadas on the one hand and locusts, grasshoppers, and crickets on the other.

At least four words in the main text of *The Classic of Poetry* were generally understood to refer to cicadas: *tiao*, which occurred several times; *tang*; and *qin*.[15] The common Chinese word, however, was *chan*, which occurred only in the commentary, not in the main text of the classic. Only this last word was translated by the Manchu court scholars. The word they used was *biyangsikû*, which was allegedly derived from the onomatopoeic *bing biyang*, which referred to the sound of the (northern Chinese) flute.[16] The other, literary Chinese words were transcribed rather than translated. Thus *tiao* became *tiyo* or *tiyoo*, *tang* became *tang* (transcribed the same but not homophonous), and *qin* became *cin*. In one instance, however, even the common Chinese word *chan* became *can umiyaha*, "the *chan* bug," rather than *biyangsikû*.[17] The difference in transcription (*tiyo* versus *tiyoo*) suggests that not all of these passages were translated by the same person.

Still, they evince a clear tendency not to translate rare names. Only the common name was translated (but at times even that was not the case).

For some reason, locusts and grasshoppers were treated somewhat differently than cicadas. Despite the plethora of names—greater, it seems to me, than in the case of the cicada—the Chinese commentators and textual authorities generally subsumed the different words under the umbrella term of "locust" (*huang*). This word was carried over into the Manchu translation.

In *The Classic of Poetry*, the word *zhong* in the title of the poem "Ye Locusts" (Zhong si) had always been treated as referring to a kind of locust.[18] The Manchu translators rendered it as *seksehe* and described it following the consensus in the Chinese commentaries as *huang* or *huangchong*, where *huangchong* is a vernacular Chinese binomen corresponding to the literary *huang*.[19] The Manchu commentary used this word and wrote that *seksehe* was "a kind of *huangchong*" (*hûwang cung ni hacin*). The Manchu version then described the color and features of the bug, which was also done in the standard Chinese commentary.[20]

In "Grass-Insects" (Cao chong), the eponymous insects are juxtaposed with *fuzhong*.[21] The latter has been identified as a kind of locust, if not simply a generic name for locust. Furthermore, ancient authorities identified the "grass-insects" themselves as a kind of locust as well.[22] In the Manchu translation, "grass-insects" becomes *sarpa*, "grasshopper," and *fuzhong* becomes *seksehe*, the locust from "Ye Locusts."[23] The Manchu commentary glossed *sarpa* as a "kind of locust" (*hûwang cung ni hacin*), repeating the gloss it used for *seksehe* in "Ye Locusts." (Here, the use of the vernacular binomen was not due to the commentary in *Compendium on the Classic of Poetry*, which did not use it in this case.) There is no gloss for *seksehe* in the Manchu "Grass-Insects."[24]

In "In the Seventh Month" (Qi yue), there is a locust, *zhong*, that "moves its legs" in the fifth month and another creature, *shaji*, that "sounds its wings" in the sixth. The Chinese tradition, known to the Manchu translators, identified *shaji* as similar to a locust.[25] Moreover, we read that in the seventh to tenth months, the cricket (*xishuai*) is active in various locations.[26] In the Manchu version of the text, *zhong* becomes *sengsehe*, which was probably a variant of *seksehe*, "locust." (*Sengsehe* and its variants might all have been onomatopoeic in origin.)[27] *Shaji* becomes *sarpa*, the grasshopper, and the cricket is referred to as *gurjen* in Manchu (elsewhere defined as "like the locust [*hûwang cong*] but smaller").[28] The Manchu translation followed the Chinese commentary on its source: "The locust, grasshopper, and cricket are one. They change according to the season and are called by different names." (*Sengsehe, sarpa, gurjen emu bime, erin be dahame, kûbulime ubaliyame ofi. Gebu be encu gebulehebi.*)[29]

In "Large Are the Fields" (*Da tian*), finally, four "noxious insects" (*ming, te, mao,* and *zei*) are transcribed (*ming, te, moo, dze*) and glossed as "four kinds of bugs," all of which are *hûwang tsung*.[30] The latter is Chinese *huangchong*, "locust" in a slightly different phonetic form (one that suggests the translator did not distinguish the Chinese initials *ch-* and *c-*).[31] The gloss followed a commentary quoted in *Compendium on the Classic of Poetry*.[32]

These examples mentioned in the preceding paragraphs show that archaic words that unambiguously referred to grasshoppers and locusts (*zhong, fuzhong, shaji*) were not retained as transcriptions in the Manchu version. Rather, they were translated using vernacular Manchu words for these common insects. The words that were arguably even rarer and more ambiguous (*ming, te, mao, zei*) were, however, transcribed. Naturally, a composite text like *The Classic of Poetry*, with its layers of commentary, did not present a coherent taxonomy of locust-like bugs. The Manchu version reflects this situation and incorporated the conflation of creatures like the locust and the grasshopper. The translation of this kind of canonical Confucian text, then, had little relationship with the study and combat of locusts among field officials, for whom the distinction of the two kinds of insects should have been important.

The Manchu version did, however, retain some order in the terminology by subsuming all words under the contemporary Chinese heading of *huangchong*, which in general was used where the Chinese authorities had *huang*. It is worth noting that the Manchu translators do not appear to have made conscious use of the variation in the native vocabulary for the creatures (*sengsehe* versus *seksehe*) in order to represent different ancient Chinese terms.

LOCUSTS IN MANCHU DICTIONARIES

A few decades after the publication of the Manchu *Classic of Poetry*, the development of Manchu-Chinese dictionaries led to further differentiation of the vocabulary used to talk about locusts and grasshoppers in written Manchu. In 1683, Shen Qiliang, a Chinese student of Manchu, published the first Manchu-Chinese dictionary, *Complete Book of the Great Qing* (Da

Qing quanshu/Daicing gurun-i yooni bithe) on the basis of his own work and manuscript material then in circulation in Beijing. As compilers of a dictionary that translated Manchu words and phrases into Chinese, Shen and his anonymous predecessors faced a problem opposite the one that the translators of *The Classic of Poetry* had to deal with. In *Complete Book*, the problem was often to find Chinese words that could translate a certain Manchu word, not the other way around.

The problem at times proved too much for Shen to handle. He "included in his dictionary roughly 300 Manchu words that lacked known Chinese translations," one authority writes, many of which referred to "flora and fauna common to the far north," whence the Manchus came.[33] However, Shen also quoted frequently from the Manchu translations of books like *The Classic of Poetry*, so that the vocabulary in *Complete Book* was partially a kind of translationese.[34]

Shen Qiliang's dictionary contained several entries that mentioned grasshoppers and locusts. The generic *sarpa* was listed, defined: as *zha*, probably short for the northern Chinese word *mazha* 虮蜡, which meant "locust" in the Beijing dialect and "grasshopper" in some other dialects; *diaolang*, likely "mantis"; and *mazha* 螞蚱, probably with the same meaning as the differently written *mazha* mentioned above.[35] *Sebsehe*, which was not seen in the Manchu *Classic of Poetry*, but which might be another dialect variant of the *seksehe/sengsehe* pair used there, was also glossed as *mazha* 螞蜡 (here written with a variant first character, which is not surprising given the word's vernacular character).[36] Finally, both *seksehe* and *sengsehe* were listed in Shen's dictionary as well. *Seksehe* was translated as *minghuang*, a word unknown to me that might perhaps have been taken from a gloss on *The Classic of Poetry*'s "Large Are the Fields," where *ming* was explained as a *huang* (see above).[37] *Sengsehe* appeared only in the compound word *hiya sengsehe*, translated literally in the dictionary as *hanhuang*.[38] Rather than referring to a kind of locust, the phrase should probably be translated as "drought and locusts," two agricultural problems that were commonly associated. The Chinese translations used in Shen's Manchu dictionary, then, represent a mix of vernacular expressions and phrases from classical literature, for which the Manchu lemmata that they translated probably originated as glosses.

If there was a problem with the words for grasshoppers and locusts in Shen's dictionary, it was not with finding a Manchu equivalent for literary Chinese words but matching a Manchu word to several vernacular

Chinese expressions that did not necessarily mean the same thing to all readers. As in the Manchu *Classic of Poetry*, the generic word for "locust" appeared there in several variants.

The decades around the turn of the eighteenth century witnessed the publication of several more Manchu-Chinese dictionaries. Some were arranged by topic, which placed them in the tradition of *Approaching Elegance*, whence much of Chinese insect classification originated. *Broadly Collected Complete Text in the Standard Script* (*Tongwen guanghui quanshu/ Tung wen guwang lei* [sic; < *lei* 類] *ciowan šu*), a 1702 edition of a topically arranged dictionary first published in 1693, and *Manchu and Chinese, Divided into Sections* (*Man-Han leishu*/Man han lei šu bithe) from 1700, both contained a section on "fish and bugs" (C. *yu chong*; M. *nimaha umiyaha*). As in ancient Chinese lexica of the *Approaching Elegance* type, these sections contained not only fish and bugs but also dragons and snakes. They also contained grasshoppers and locusts. *Broadly Collected Complete Text* had *sebsehe* as *mazha*, which was the translation of *sarpa* in *Complete Book*. In addition, *muhan sebsehe*, literally "male [perhaps in the sense of big] locust" was given as the translation of *guoguo*, which in other sources was used in reference to katydids or bush crickets. Finally, *sarpa* was *diaolang*, as in *Complete Book*.[39] *Manchu and Chinese, Divided into Sections* contained fewer relevant words: *seksehe* as *mazha* and, interestingly, *hûwang tsung umiyaha* as *huangchong*.[40] In sum, there was plenty of variation in which Manchu words were paired with which Chinese words in these books. However, both of them, like *Complete Book* (retranslations of quotes from classical Confucian literature aside), tended to match the Manchu words for locusts and grasshoppers with vernacular Chinese words.

Official standardization of Manchu vocabulary reached a milestone with the publication in 1708 of *Imperially Commissioned Mirror of the Manchu Language* (Han-i araha Manju gisun-i buleku bithe), which was a monolingual dictionary. This product of Kangxi court scholarship was, like *Approaching Elegance* and some of the private and commercial Manchu-Chinese dictionaries, arranged by subject matter. However, its categories were more narrowly defined than had been the case in its immediate predecessors. The *Mirror's* section on *umiyaha* contained only bugs. Quite a few words in this section probably referred to grasshoppers and locusts, but definitions were short and ambiguous.

The Kangxi dictionary contained only the form *sebsehe*, not *seksehe* nor *sengsehe*. Its definition was "long wings, two antennae, six legs" (*asha golmin, juwe salu, ninggun bethe bi*), which was hardly enough to identify it as a locust. However, the definition further quoted the passage in *The Classic of Poetry*'s "Grass-Insects" where this word occurs, which allowed an educated reader to identify it with the locust. As for *sarpa*, it was simply "a kind of *sebsehe*," followed, again, by a quote from "Grass-Insects."

Indeed, *sebsehe* is clearly used as a generic term (apparently covering our contemporary order Orthoptera and parts of the superorder Dictyoptera) in Kangxi's *Mirror*, under which individual species are subsumed. An alternative name for the praying mantis (*heliyen*) was "mantis *sebsehe*" (*heliyen sebsehe*). The *damjan sebsehe*, "carrying pole *sebsehe*," was something with a "wide body and long wings" (*beye halfiyan asha golmin*). The *hûwanta*, or "bald," *sebsehe* had a "deep yellow body, small wings, and cannot fly" (*beye sohon, asha ajige, deyerakû*).

Muhan sebsehe, familiar from earlier dictionaries, was listed in Kangxi's *Mirror* too, but it was no longer identified with the Chinese *guoguo*. Rather, this "gray and blackish, wingless, and big-bellied" bug, we read, "resembles other *sebsehe*." Yet it "does not lay eggs; larvae emerge like a string from the belly" (*fulenggi boco bime sahahûn asha akû, hefeli amba, gûwa sebsehe-i gese, cerhuwe waliyarakû, hefeli ci tonggo-i adali umiyaha tucimbi*). The dictionary added that "these are also called *tonggo midaha*, "string leech" (*erebe geli tonggo midaha sembi*).

The katydid, which "the Chinese call *guoguor*" (*nikan g'o g'o el seme hûlambi*—the Manchu here transcribed the Mandarin nominal suffix -*er*, which was not graphically represented in *Broadly Collected Complete Text*— was listed as *gergen* in Manchu: "Green body, short wings that are like those of the cricket, and a big belly. They make a call by grinding the two wings. . . . [The Chinese] raise them and listen to the sound of their call."[41]

Alongside these words, Kangxi's *Mirror* listed the words *jargima*, which referred to an animal with "a green body, long wings, incapable of flying long distances" that "make calls by rubbing its wings" (*beye niowanggiyan, asha golmin, goro deyeme muterakû, juwe asha karcame guwembi*; the word is derived from *jar*, referring to its sound),[42] and *cacarakû*, which meant a creature that was "ash-colored, red in the wings, and makes a call sounding like *ser ser* when it flies" (*fulenggi boco, asha-i dorgi fulgiyan deyere de ser ser seme guwembi*). This last word was borrowed from Mongolian and ultimately had onomatopoeic origins.[43] The dictionary noted that this bug was also called *usin bošokû*, literally a "field rusher," which to my ears has the ring of a vernacular term for a locust.[44] All of these words referred to grasshoppers or locusts, but ultimately the dictionary does not allow us to pin them down with any certainty.

In sum, written Manchu had quite a few words available for referring to grasshoppers and locusts after the publication of the *Mirror*. The dictionary established *sebsehe* as an umbrella term for these creatures, but the word might simultaneously have referred to a specific kind in common parlance; it is hard to tell.

LOCUSTS IN MANCHU MEMORIALS

At the same time that grasshoppers and locusts were variously translated in Manchu versions of classical Chinese texts and in Manchu-Chinese dictionaries, Qing government officials frequently discussed locusts in their memorials to the throne. Locusts, after all, were an agricultural pest of extreme importance and a frequent topic in reports on local affairs, be it in Manchu or Chinese.

Several kinds of Manchu government documents discussing locusts are extant. The routine memorials (*tiben*) now accessible in the archives of the Grand Secretariat (Neige), which routed them from the ministries to the throne, were at least in part translated into Manchu if submitted in Chinese. When submitted by bannermen like Ceke (fl. 1638–71) or Dung Tiyan Gi (fl. 1647–58), the Manchu version might have been composed already before the memorial was sent off from the field, although not necessarily before the Chinese.

In 1654, Ceke could refer to an outbreak of locusts—*huang* in the Chinese version—simply as a "bug calamity" (*umiyaha-i gashan*), as when "the bugs are eating all the grain in the high altitude areas" (*deken muhu ba-i jeku be geli umiyaha jekebi*).[45] A little more than two years later, in another of Ceke's memorials, "calamities of hail, locusts, and immature locusts" (*bingbao huangnan zai*) in the Chinese became "calamities such as hail, *hûwang cung,* and *seksehe* [grasshoppers?]" in the Manchu (*bono, hûwang cung seksehe-i jergi gashan*).[46] "Immature locusts"—*nan* or *nanzi* in Chinese—were not mentioned either in *The Classic of Poetry* or the early Manchu-Chinese dictionaries. They were, however, common in reports on crops. Around the same time as Ceke's last memorial, Dung Tiyan Gi used an almost identical phrase. Where the Chinese text had "calamities of locusts and immature locusts" (*huang nan zai*), the Manchu text read "calamities of *hûwang cung* bugs and grasshoppers" (*hûwang cung umiyaha, seksehei gashan*).⁴⁷

Curiously, the word *sarpa* for "grasshopper" was not used in these memorials. Furthermore, here *seksehe* was not, as its variant *sebsehe* would later become in the *Mirror of the Manchu Language*, the generic term for "locusts." The reporting officials instead used the Chinese word *hûwang cung* for this purpose. Judging by these memorials, it appears that in Manchu administrative prose of the 1650s, *seksehe* meant "grasshopper," and it was simply equated with the immature locust. Both grasshoppers and immature locusts might have been small, but they were not the same creature.

It is hard to believe that Qing field officials did not distinguish grasshoppers—which did not threaten crops—and immature locusts—which did. A possible explanation is that in the writing of this kind of report, the Manchu phrasing closely followed the Chinese. Thus when Chinese stylistic convention demanded a pair of noun phrases such as "locusts and immature locusts" (as in *bingbao huangnan*, quoted above), the Manchu translation followed it to the letter. The implication is that, first, these early Qing routine memorials primarily sought to communicate that there was a locust problem in the locality, without going into any details on the biological state of the locusts, and, second, that the Manchu version of the text, even though it might have been produced in the field before dispatch of the memorial, was a translation of the Chinese version, which thus constitutes the primary document.

It was, however, at times beneficial to farmers and to administrators of agriculturally important areas to draw a clear distinction between grasshoppers, locusts, and immature locusts. Accordingly, the different bugs were treated as different in at least some of the vernacular Chinese dialects, in Chinese learned discourse on insects, and by Qing administrators writing in Chinese. In fact, in the view of Qing officialdom, a clear grasp of the lifecycle of the locust with time appeared essential for successfully predicting, preventing, and managing outbreaks, as Bello's chapter makes clear. On June 27, 1752, a century after the routine memorials discussed above were written, the Qianlong emperor voiced a common opinion when he declared, "Generally speaking, locusts and immature locusts fundamentally belong to [the categories] of creatures born from moisture or born spontaneously (*shi sheng hua sheng*).⁴⁸ If fish and shrimp place small eggs by riverbanks and in low-lying damp areas, which then enter onto land, they will all change into locusts."[49]

In order to allocate resources to fight outbreaks, Qing officials in various parts of the empire submitted reports on the hatching and development of locusts. Not all of these were written in Chinese. Nor were they all bilingual in Manchu and Chinese, which the routine memorials from the 1650s had been, as discussed previously. Banner officials serving in Xinjiang after its conquest in the mid-eighteenth century, for example, generally submitted Manchu-only palace memorials to the throne.

But how to memorialize on locusts in Manchu if the terminology was imprecise or at the very least did not accord with the Chinese conceptual apparatus used to refer to these bugs? Unsurprisingly, simply calling the creature itself a "bug" and the immature locust a "grasshopper" was eventually unsatisfactory to Qing administrators. In 1752, the official Yenggišan (1694–1771) in a bilingual routine memorial referred to the immature locusts as "grasshopper *nandz*" (*sebsehe nandz*) using the vernacular Chinese term *nanzi* in Manchu while keeping the literary *huang nan* in the Chinese version of his memorial.[50]

LOCUSTS AND THE REFORM OF THE MANCHU LEXICON

The phrase in Yenggišan's memorial did not distinguish "grasshopper" and "locust," but it at least used an unambiguous term for the immature locust. Directly using the Chinese terminology in Manchu by transcribing Chinese words, as done in this memorial, was arguably a solution to the problem presented by the fluid Manchu terminology. After all, Manchu had for more than a century borrowed words from Chinese to discuss matters not previously treated at length in Manchu texts. Yet when the Qing court in the mid-eighteenth century decided to overhaul the Manchu lexicon, it very clearly rejected this option. Rather than standardizing existing Chinese loans and complementing them with new ones, the court and its officials weeded out Chinese words and coined neologisms with a Manchu-looking morphology.

The Qianlong reform of the Manchu lexicon is a topic that far exceeds the words for grasshoppers and locusts. Yet the history of matching Manchu and Chinese words for these bugs in the translation of *The Classic of Poetry* and the bilingual dictionaries goes a long way toward explaining a practical reason for divesting Manchu of its Chinese stock of words.

First, the potential supply of Chinese words was virtually endless, and if the court sanctioned it as a practice for enriching Manchu, writers of the language might feel encouraged to continue to import Chinese words whenever they felt the need for it. The Manchu vocabulary would thus remain in flux. Second, Chinese loans in written Manchu were simply transcribed according to their Mandarin pronunciation, without accounting for pitch tone, which differentiates words that would otherwise be homophonous. This process rendered monosyllabic literary Chinese words ambiguous. Perhaps in part for this reason, written Manchu predominantly borrowed from vernacular Chinese, which probably reflected how Chinese words were used in spoken Manchu by individuals proficient in both languages. But as the Manchu-Chinese pairings seen in the early bilingual dictionaries show, the vernacular Chinese vocabulary showed a great deal of dialectal variation (e.g., the meaning of *mazha* for either grasshopper or locust). Using vernacular Chinese words drawn from northern dialects could thus lead to ambiguity as well.

That said, an ideology of maintaining Manchu as an independent language, complete in itself, certainly also motivated the language reform. Such concerns are evident in the overhaul of the Manchu translations of Chinese works such as *The Classic of Poetry*. We also see it in the deliberations by the reformers that remain in the archival record.

In the archive of the Grand Council—the highest body of the Qing government from the second quarter of the eighteenth century onward—there are several Manchu memorials and brief lateral communications that discuss the coining of new Manchu words. Some of these are not very interesting, as they merely propose a word that semantically is a calque on the corresponding Chinese word but uses Manchu morphemes. A document concerning the coining of new Manchu words for "locust" and "immature locust" stands out among the ones that I have seen in that it proposes a new name on the basis of current ideas about locusts.

The document in question appears to be a lateral communication sent within the Grand Council, as it is not addressed to the emperor. The note is undated, but because of its placement in the archive, it was catalogued as dating from 1754, which is probably correct. I am tempted to conjecture that the note was written in response to questions raised by the translation of the imperial diary (*qiju zhu ce*) for the fifth lunar month of 1752, when Qianlong had spoken to his court about the spawning of locusts. It has been shown that in the Qianlong reign, the Chinese version of the diary was compiled with considerable delay, in one documented instance as late as the end of the ninth lunar month of the next year. It was subsequently translated into Manchu.[51] The translators might very well have hit upon the passage involving locusts from the fifth lunar month of 1752 sometime in 1754, which would explain the existence of the note. It reads, "Upon consideration: *huangchong*, 'locust.' A kind of grasshopper (*sebsehe*) with a body that is slightly bigger. Taking the ordinary pronunciation of *sebsehe*, I suggest we call the locust *sabsaha*. As for immature locust (*nanzi*), I suggest that we combine the two words [lit. characters] *use*, 'seed, insect egg,' and *honika*, 'fish fry,' to form *unika*. Please advise as to whether it is appropriate."[52]

The note thus proposed two new names. The first, *sabsaha*, was intended to once and for all differentiate locusts from grasshoppers by replacing the vowel *e*, which was sometimes identified as "feminine" (and occurred in words such as *hehe*, "woman," and *eme*, "mother") with *a*, which was "masculine" (and occurred in words such as *haha*, "man," and *ama*, "father").[53] Metaphorically, the two vowels could represent other distinctions, such as big versus small, or robust versus delicate. Thus the slightly larger body of the locust in comparison to the grasshopper probably inspired using the "male" vowel here. Whoever wrote this note did not seem to have considered using one of the several terms used for various locusts and grasshoppers (*jarqima*, *cacarakû*, *usin bošokû*) listed in Kangxi's *Mirror* and unambiguously redefining it as the generic name for "locust."

The other word, *unika*, was proposed as the word for immature locust. There was no existing Manchu word to work with here. Yet the anonymous Manchu scholar did not in this case create a calque on the corresponding Chinese expression (to late imperial users of Chinese, *nan* was a morpheme that could not be further semantically divided). Rather, the new word was formed in reference to current ideas about locusts. Above, I quoted Qianlong as voicing the common opinion that immature locusts were born from fish and shrimp eggs that ended up on land before hatching. Here, the new word *unika* is formed from two parts that reference fish and eggs.[54] The theory that fish and locusts had the same origin but differed because of their environment evidently motivated the new word.

Curiously, the neologism that was ultimately chosen for "locust" was not *sabsaha*, as proposed in the anonymous note. The new word was *sebseheri*, which was also clearly coined on the basis of *sebsehe*. We find it in the Manchu translation of the passage in the court diary dated 1752.[55]

The suggestions raised in the anonymous note were thus only partially accepted by the Grand Council.

According to precedent, newly coined Manchu words were circulated within parts of the bureaucracy once they had been fixed. Yet if a document announcing the new names for "locust" and "immature locust" still exists, none has thus far come to light. In 1749, however, the word *bingsiku* was circulated as the official translation of *chan*, the common Chinese word for "cicada." Clearly, the onomatopoeic *bing biyang*, which had already yielded *biyangsikû*, had been called upon to produce a new word.[56]

Other official documents show that new words for "locust" and "immature locust" were in use by the early 1760s. In 1761, one of the Grand Council's Manchu court letters and the palace memorial it cited still spoke only of the eradication of *sebsehe*, which was a word that, as we have seen, could refer to both locusts and grasshoppers.[57] The following year, however, Yunggui and Iletu reported on "flying grasshoppers (*dekdehe sebsehe*) and locusts (*sebseheri*) biting off the leaves of reeds and grasses."[58] "Locusts" (*sebseheri*) is seen in a court letter from the same year, and "immature locusts" (*unika*) in a memorial from 1763.[59]

One might think that *sebsehe* as used in Kangxi's *Mirror* could have sufficed as an equivalent of Chinese *huang*, with *sarpa* used for grasshopper (*mazha*). Yet by the mid-eighteenth century, *sarpa* might have fallen out of general use. In any case, in government documents, *sebsehe* was treated as the common word for grasshopper. Hence the new word *sebseheri*. The immature locusts were different, as Manchu does not seem to have had a word for them before the coining of *unika*.

Thus Qing administrators by the mid-1760s possessed Manchu terms for the dangerous insect pests that matched exactly with the established Chinese terminology. The equivalence between Manchu and Chinese usage was helpful to the Qing officials and clerks who wrote or handled these documents. Top-level administrative documents such as palace memorials, although usually monolingual, could be composed with reference to other documents of various kinds that were not necessarily written in the same language. Having an aligned conceptual apparatus facilitated composition of such documents. There was a need to distinguish grasshoppers and locusts, in Chinese as well as in Manchu.

Some of the aforementioned new words for bugs then made their way into books published by the court. The writing of these books, furthermore, in itself led to the coining of more new terms. Important in this regard are the revised Manchu translation of *The Classic of Poetry* and the bilingual and revised Manchu *Mirror*.

The revised version of *The Classic of Poetry* was finished in 1768.[60] The new edition, which was bilingual, omitted the commentary included in the original translation from 1655. It also revised the vocabulary. Words that had been transcribed and glossed in the first version, such the literary words *tiao* and *tang* for the cicada, were now translated using a common Manchu word, if one existed. The two words for cicadas, however, in one passage occurred in the same sentence, and thus could hardly be translated identically for reasons of poetical effect. The new word *bingsiku*, introduced almost two decades earlier, was now used to translate *tiao*, with the preexisting *biyangsikû* used to render *tang*.[61] In this case a word that had been coined to translate the common Chinese word for cicada (*chan*) was also used to translate its literary synonyms, with the effect of flattening the vocabulary in *The Classic of Poetry*. The lexical reduction notwithstanding, the word *bingsiku* might have been appreciated by a reader with a command of Manchu good enough to recognize the allusion to the onomatopoeic expression.

Other neologisms might similarly have been suggestive to fluent readers. "Ephemera" (*fuyou*) was now rendered as *dartaha*, which probably suggested a link to *dartai*, "temporary," in the mind of a fluent reader.[62] Yet *dartaha* was like the rest of the words in the text left without a gloss. The reader would have to already know the meaning of the Chinese word to fully grasp the meaning of the passage.[63]

The locusts and grasshoppers in the revised translation of *The Classic of Poetry* were handled with some finesse. All references to *hûwang cung/ tsung* were gone, because they occurred in the commentary that had been removed in the new version. *Fuzhong* and *zhong*, which had been *sengsehe/ seksehe* in the first translation, were now called *sebsehe*. The change is expected, as *sebsehe* was the term opted for in Kangxi's *Mirror* and subsequently became the standard form of this word. Similarly, *shaji* remained *sarpa*. The interesting case is that of the "grass-insects" (*cao chong*). This phrase too had been translated as *sarpa* in 1655. Now, the court translators sought to differentiate it from *shaji* by rendering it differently. With *sebsehe* being taken, they opted for another word. The choice was *jargima*, which to my knowledge did not occur in the 1655 translation of *The Classic of Poetry*. Yet the word was not a neologism either: *jargima* was one of the several words for grasshopper and locusts listed in Kangxi's *Mirror*.[64] No neologism for "locust" was used in the translation, even though the archival record shows that the neologism *sebseheri* was already in use at the time of its publication and ought to have been available to the translators.[65]

The different areas touched by the language reform—administrative documents and literary translations—were brought together in *Imperially Commissioned Mirror of the Manchu Language, Expanded and Emended* (Yuzhi zengding Qingwen jian/Han-i araha nonggime toktobuha Manju gisun-i buleku bithe), a dictionary and important milestone in the Qianlong overhaul of the Manchu lexicon that was finished in 1772–73. This book removed the quotations from classical texts seen in the entries of Kangxi's *Mirror* but added Chinese translations for all the lemmata. It also replaced the Chinese loans in the original with the neologisms coined in the intervening years.

The section for bugs (Ma. *umiyaha*; Ch. *chong*) listed the words for grasshoppers and locusts seen in Kangxi's original and added a few more. The definitions of the preexisting words stayed virtually the same, with the addition of Chinese equivalents: *sebsehe* was matched to *mazha* 螞蚱, the vernacular Beijing word for "locust" (and perhaps "grasshopper"); *sarpa* to *zhameng*, "grasshopper"; and *damjan sebsehe* to "carrying pole" (*biandan*), a literal translation. The "male" (*muhan*) or perhaps "big" *sebsehe* was called "ground locust [grasshopper?]" (*tu mazha*). *Tonggo midaha* was made into its own entry and glossed as the bug's offspring (*zi*). Other dictionaries—Kangxi's *Mirror* counting among them, if my reading is correct—listed it as a synonym for *muhan sebsehe*; perhaps the Qianlong court compilers made a mistake here.[66] Furthermore, the "bald" (*hûwanta*) *sebsehe* was a "block grasshopper" (*dunzi mazha*), *jargima* a "calling locust [grasshopper?]" (*jiao mazha*), and *cacarakû* a "gray grasshopper" (*huise zhameng*), which is how it was described in the Manchu definition.[67]

Several of the Chinese translations look like vernacular words and might have been words used in spoken Chinese at the time. Yet it is difficult to gauge the extent to which that was the case and, conversely, to what extent they on the contrary were *ad hoc* translations based on the Manchu definitions. It is even more difficult, if not outright impossible, to determine whether the Manchu and Chinese expressions—assuming both were actually used by people at the time—referred to the same bugs.

Among the Manchu neologisms listed alongside the preexisting words, several originate in the revised translation of *The Classic of Poetry* from 1768. The pest *ming*—which had been transcribed as *ming* in the 1655 translation and glossed there as a kind of *hûwang tsung*—had since been rendered as *mibsehe*, which was now lemmatized in the Qianlong *Mirror*. Its definition did not say it was a locust or *huang chong*, but was said to eat the center (*niyaman*) of grain, following the Chinese commentary to the relevant passage of *The Classic of Poetry*.

The new word for immature locust, *unika*, was lemmatized and paired with *nanzi*, as in the Grand Council note, and defined as the offspring of locusts. Predictably, the dictionary listed *sebseheri* as the Manchu equivalent of Chinese *huang chong*: "Similar to the *sebsehe*, it ruins crops. Both its head and body are yellow" (*Sebsehe de dursuki, jeku be gasihiyambi, uju beye gemu suwayan*).[68]

This entry shows what made the new word *sebseheri* differ from earlier terms used to refer to grasshoppers and locusts. The physical characteristics of *sebsehe* and *sebseheri* were similar, and both were yellow. Yet unlike any of the relevant words listed in Kangxi's *Mirror*, *sebseheri* was explicitly defined as an agricultural pest. What the Manchu administrators had wanted was a word that could unambiguously capture this aspect of the bug's interaction with humans. Through Qianlong's expanded and emended *Mirror*, the word received wide circulation.

CONCLUSION

By the 1770s, the vocabulary used in written Manchu to refer to locusts and other bugs had gone through substantial transformations. Since the time of the first translation of *The Classic of Poetry* and routine administrative reports on the agricultural situation in the newly acquired Chinese territories in the seventeenth century, Manchu dialect differences had been reduced in writing (*sengsehe* and *seksehe* both yielded to *sebsehe*). Chinese loans (*hûwang cung/tsung* and *nandz*) had come and gone. New words had been invented to reflect some of the variation in the literary Chinese vocabulary used for bugs (*mibsehe*), and others (*sebseheri* and *unika*) to align Manchu and Chinese bureaucratic language. In sum, the history of Manchu bug names is one of ad hoc adaptation and conscious planning within a government apparatus and an imperial scholarly world characterized above all by its plurilingualism.

This plurilingual bureaucracy and the knowledge that infused it, in turn, were facing a world of bugs of which some, like the locusts, appeared as serious agricultural pests. Manchu translators and administrators, while operating partially in a new language, stood in a tradition of bug classification going back to Chinese antiquity. At the same time as they faced a level of detail in the Chinese terminology—a distinction between "locusts" and "immature locusts"—that was initially not recognized in Manchu, their language presented an opportunity to avoid polysemy that the Chinese language had inherited from its ancient literary texts. The Manchu word for "bug" or "insect," *umiyaha*, was an everyday word. In topically arranged reference works that were influenced by the Chinese lexicographical tradition, "fish and bugs" included amphibious reptiles as per Chinese precedent. Yet the word *umiyaha* itself unambiguously meant "insect," and there was no ambiguity in the vocabulary comparable to that caused by the confluence of characters with different histories in the Chinese writing system.

NOTES

Masato Hasegawa, He Bian, Marc Winter, Federico Valenti, Wolfgang Behr, Martina Siebert, Daniel Burton-Rose, David A. Bello, Qiu Yuanyuan, José Andrés Alonso de la Fuente, and Nathan Vedal facilitated research, answered queries, provided references, offered corrections, or helped me read the sources used in this paper. I presented an earlier version of this chapter at the workshop "The Writing of Animals in the East Asian Cultural Imagery" (Dongya wenhua yixiang de dongwu shuxie), held at Academia Sinica (Taipei, Taiwan), December 8, 2020.

    1. See Valenti's chapter in this volume.

    2. For example, the graphic element 虫 in the standard script was used as a component of other characters as a shorthand for 蟲, even though the two characters had different histories. See Valenti's chapter in this volume and Wang Hui, "'Chong,' 'chong' zi chuyi."

    3. Tsintsius, *Sravnitel'nyĭ slovar'*, 280.

    4. Chinese proper names (e.g., names of the provinces) were retained as transcriptions.

    5. Legge, *The Chinese Classics*, 1:323.

    6. Needham and Lu, *Biology and Biological Technology*, 190.

    7. Nappi, *The Monkey and the Inkpot*, 24 (and 168–69, nt. 60).

    8. Pang and Volkova, *Descriptive Catalogue*, 77 (item 165).

    9. Tu, "On the Source Text of Ši Ging Ni Bithe (1654)." Cf. Ye, "Man-Han hebi *Qinding fanyi wujing sishu*," 10, including nt. 43; Yang Chin-Lung, "*Shi zhuan daquan*."

    10. Kim Chu-wŏn, Ko, and Chŏng, "Manmun *Sigyŏng*," 3–4. Cf. Beijing Shi Minzu Guji Zhengli Chuban Guihua Xiaozu, *Beijing diqu Manwen tushu zongmu*,

6–7 (item 0031), the date of which is suspect. Yang Fengmou and Zhang, *Dalian Tushuguan cang shaoshu minzu guji tushu zonglu*, 9.

11. Legge, *The Chinese Classics*, 1:220; Karlgren, *The Book of Odes*, 94. *Han-i araha Ši ging bithe*, vol. 7, n.p., in the poem "Feo io."

12. Ruan, *Mao shi zhengyi*, 128 (396 in the pagination of the series, ch. 8.2 in the original); *Shi zhuan daquan*, 8:26a (549). The translation of poems from *The Classic of Poetry* is based on Legge's translation of the phrases in question (Legge does not translate the titles themselves). On the etymology of *helmehen* in Manchu, see Tsintsius, *Sravnitel'nyĭ slovar'*, 481; Valenti, "Biological Classification," 117; *Han-i araha Ši ging bithe*, vol. 8, n.p., in the poem "Dung šan."

13. Ruan, *Mao shi zhengyi*, 226 (494 of the series, ch. 15.2 in the original); *Shi zhuan daquan*, 15:2b (688).

14. *Han-i araha Ši ging bithe*, vol. 15, n.p., in the poem "Du zin ši."

15. Chen Huan, *Shi Mao shi zhuan shu*, 1:706 (15:6b) states that *tiao* occurs three times: *Tiao* in "Xiao bian" 小弁 (Ruan, *Mao shi zhengyi*, 185, ch. 12.3); *Tiao* and *tang* in "Dang" 蕩 (Ruan, 285, ch. 18.1); and *Tiao* in "Qi yue" (where it is glossed as *tang*) (Ruan, 122, ch. 8.1). *Qin* is in "Shuo ren" 碩人 (Ruan, 54, ch. 3.2). See also Valenti, "Biological Classification," 75.

16. Tsintsius, *Sravnitel'nyĭ slovar'*, 83.

17. *Han-i araha Ši ging bithe*, vol. 8, the poem "Ci iowei" ("*tiyoo* is the name of a bug" [*tiyoo serengge umiyaha gebu*]); vol. 18, in the poem "Dang" ("*tiyo* and *tang* are both cicada bugs, [the scene described in the poem] sounds like the cicada" [*tiyo, tang serengge, gemu biyangsikû umiyaha be, biyangsikû-i guwere adali*]); vol. 3, in the poem "Šo zin" (C. *qin*/M. *cin* as "similar to the *can* [i.e., *chan*] bug but smaller" [*can umiyaha-i adali bime ajigan*]). This book is unpaginated. The Chinese source: *Shi zhuan daquan*, 12:12a (639), 18:6a (765), 3:32b (451).

18. Ruan, *Mao shi zhengyi*, 11 (279 in the pagination of the series, ch. 1.2 in the original); Valenti, "Biological Classification," 92.

19. Luo, *Mao shi cao mu niao shou chong yu shu xin jiao zheng*, 263: *huang lei ye*. The edition from which the translators were working included this canonical commentary plus a subcommentary, which used the binome instead: "*Zhong si* is simply a kind of locust (*huangchong*)" (Zhongsi huangchong zhi lei er). It is tempting to infer that the Manchu translators were translating this subcommentary. But the Manchu version then continues with the description of the bug, which is taken from the commentary, not the subcommentary. That is to say, the use of *hûwang cung* in the Manchu might not be the result of the translators working with the subcommentary in this instance.

20. *Han-i araha Ši ging bithe*, vol. 1, n.p., in the poem "Jung sy."

21. Ruan, *Mao shi zhengyi*, 18 (286 in the pagination of the series, ch. 1.4 in the original); *Shi zhuan daquan*, 1:38b (395).

22. Valenti, "Biological Classification," 92–93.

23. "Grasshopper" is apparently without cognates in other Tungusic languages: see Tsintsius, *Sravnitel'nyĭ slovar'*, 67.

24. *Han-i araha Ši ging bithe*, vol. 1, n.p., in the poem "Tsoo cung."

25. Luo, *Mao shi cao mu niao shou chong yu shu xin jiao zheng*, 264; Valenti, "Biological Classification," 103–4.

26. Legge, *The Chinese Classics*, 1:230.

27. I owe this information to José Andrés Alonso de la Fuente.

28. *Han-i araha Ši ging bithe*, vol. 6, n.p., in the poem "Si še" (i.e., "Xishuai"): *gurjen serengge umiyaha-i gebu, hûwang cung ni adali bime ajigan*.

29. *Han-i araha Ši ging bithe*, vol. 8, in the poem "Ci iowei"; *Shi zhuan daquan*, 8:10a (541, top panel). An association of these three creatures is not unique to ancient and Qing China: see Davies and Kathirithamby, *Greek Insects*, 134–35.

30. Karlgren, *The Book of Odes*, 166.

31. *Han-i araha Ši ging bithe*, vol. 13, in the poem "Da tiyan."

32. *Shi zhuan daquan*, 13:30a (671). See further Luo, *Mao shi cao mu niao shou chong yu shu* xin jiao zheng, 264. Other Chinese authorities, however, distinguished the four as very different species of pest. See Valenti, "Biological Classification," 126–28.

33. Schlesinger, *A World Trimmed with Fur*, 34.

34. For example, the separation of a *biyangsikû* as *qiuchan* (lit. "autumn cicada"), and *biangsikû umiyaha* as *hanchan* ("winter cicada") in Hayata and Teramura, *Daishin zensho*, 1:85. The dictionary includes the latter word in a phrase taken from the *Li ji*, which had not been published in Manchu translation at this time but which counted among the books that Manchu officials lectured on at court in the 1670s, from which unpublished material might have circulated. See Ye, "Man-Han hebi *Qinding fanyi wujing sishu*," 8–9.

35. "'Locust' in the Beijing dialect": Chen Gang, *Beijing fangyan cidian*, 188. "'Grasshopper' in some other dialects": this kind of variation is unsurprising; other communities, such as the ancient Greeks, might not have distinguished them either outside specialist circles. Davies and Kathirithamby, *Greek Insects*, 134. "Probably with the same meaning as the differently written *mazha* mentioned above": Hayata and Teramura, *Daishin zensho*, 1:100.

36. Hayata and Teramura, *Daishin zensho*, 1:105.

37. Hayata and Teramura, *Daishin zensho*, 1:105.

38. Hayata and Teramura, *Daishin zensho*, 1:223.

39. A-dun, *Tongwen guanghui quanshu*, 4:45a.

40. Sangge, ed., *Man-Han leishu*, 24:46a–b.

41. *Beye niowanggiyan, asha foholon, gurjen-i asha-i adali hefeli amba, juwe asha karcame guwembi. . . . ujifi guwere jilgan be donjimbi. Han-i araha Manju gisun-i buleku bithe*, 20:41b–42a.

42. Tsintsius, *Sravnitel'nyĭ slovar'*, 252.

43. Tsintsius, *Sravnitel'nyĭ slovar'*, 386; Rozycki, *Mongol Elements in Manchu*, 42.

44. *Han-i araha Manju gisun-i buleku bithe*, 20:42a-b.

45. Ceke, Routine memorial dated February 5, 1654 (SZ 10/12/19), Grand Secretariat database, call number 155801–001.

46. Ceke, Routine memorial dated October 25, 1656 (SZ 13/9/8), Grand Secretariat database, call number 152496–001.

47. Dung Tiyan Gi, Routine memorial dated September 28, 1656 (SZ 13/8/11), Grand Secretariat database, call number 152497–001.

48. The locus classicus for this terminology is Kumārajīva's translation of the *Diamond Sutra* (Jingang jing) in the early fifth century. See Muller, "The Diamond Sutra."

49. QSL, QL 17/5/16, 14:428b-29a.

50. Yenggišan, Routine memorial dated September 17, 1752 (QL 17/8/10), Grand Secretariat database, call number 015481–001. My translations here are intended to show what *words* were used in the Manchu: for example, "grasshopper" for *sebsehe*. I do not mean to say that Yenggišan was not in fact *referring to* grasshoppers through his use of this word. That is, I am translating what Yenggišan said, not what he meant.

51. Chuang, "Qingchao qijuzhu ce," 168 and 170.

52. *Baicaci*, 蝗蟲 [the Chinese characters are in the original document]. *Sebsehe-i duwali, beye majige ambakan, sebsehe-i an mudan be gaime,* 蝗蟲 *be sabsaha obuki,* 蟵子 *be, use honika juwe hergen be šošofi, unika obuki, acanara acanarakū babe dergici jorime tacibureo*. Manchu palace memorial or note file copy, 03-0172-0810-002, First Historical Archives, Beijing.

53. Söderblom Saarela, "Manchu and the Study of Language in China (1607–1911)," 336.

54. The means by which the word *unika* was formed (that is, through truncation of *honika*) was also used in the coining of many other plant and animal names. See von Zach, "Ueber Wortzusammensetzungen im Mandschu."

55. *Ilire tere be ejehe dangse* (Archival records of rise and repose), QL 17/5/part 2/*fulgiyan singgeri* [= *bingzi*], manuscript held at the National Palace Museum Library, Taipei, with the call number 故宮 009456, n.p. The new words are, as expected, also used in the Manchu translation of the *veritable records* for this event, which postdate the diary: *Daicing gurun-i g'aodzung yongkiyangga hûwangdi-i yargiyan kooli* (Veritable records for the Lofty Progenitor, the consummate emperor, of the Great Qing state), QL 17/5/part 2/*fulgiyan singgeri* [= *bingzi*], manuscript held at the National Palace Museum Library, Taipei, with the call number 故宮012976, 415:7a–8a.

56. Zhang, Cheng, and Tong, "Qianlong chao 'Qinding Xin Qingyu' (wu)," 39.

57. Zhongguo Diyi Lishi Dang'an Guan, *Qianlong chao Manwen jixin dang*, 2:368–69 (item 152, Chinese translation on 628–29).

58. Zhongguo Diyi Lishi Dang'an Guan, *Qingdai Xinjiang Manwen dang'an huibian*, 57:444–46 (relevant passage on 444).

59. *Sebseheri*: Zhongguo Diyi Lishi Dang'an Guan, *Qianlong chao Manwen jixin dang*, 3:283–84 (the word occurs on 84, item 337, Chinese translation on 524). *Unika*: Zhongguo Diyi Lishi Dang'an Guan, *Qingdai Xinjiang Manwen dang'an huibian*, 63:190–92.

60. Ye, "Man-Han hebi *Qinding fanyi wujing sishu*," 15.

61. *Yuzhi fanyi Shijing*, 7:3b (646). See also 3:100b.

62. *Yuzhi fanyi Shijing*, 3:92b (511).

63. The word *dartaha* was later entered into Ihing, *Qingwen buhui/Manju gisun be niyeceme isabuha bithe*, which is apparently a privately published copy held at Capital Library, Beijing, with the call number yi 乙·yi — 46, 1786, 5:10b with the translation *fuyou* and a reference to *The Classic of Poetry*, but without further information.

64. *Yuzhi fanyi Shijing*, 1:6b (417), 1:14b (421), and 3:101a (515).

65. Cf. Ye, "*Shijing* Manwen yiben bijiao yanjiu," 227.

66. For example, Li Yanji, *Qingwen huishu*, 7:4a (127).

67. *Yuzhi zengding Qingwen jian*, 2:32:61b–63a (338–39).

68. *Yuzhi zengding Qingwen jian*, 2:32:63a (339).

PART TWO

Insect Impacts on the Exercise of State Power

FOUR

Locusts Made Simple

HOLDING HUMANS RESPONSIBLE FOR INSECT BEHAVIOR IN EIGHTEENTH- AND NINETEENTH-CENTURY CHINA

David A. Bello

The greatest predator threatening preindustrial agrarian China was the locust, especially *Locusta migratoria manilensis* (the Oriental migratory locust) and *Locusta migratoria migratoria* (the Eurasian migratory locust). Prevailing Chinese official opinion associated the emergence of locust swarms with drought that would transform normally inundated spaces into damp ones. Since roughly the Song (960–1279) period, it was commonly believed that any fish or shrimp eggs deposited in these comparatively dry, but not too dry, spaces would eventually mutate into locusts. Furthermore, early detection was critical before immature locusts, with a capacity to infest only a limited locality, could sprout wings to ravage crops over much longer distances that complicated their eradication immensely.

This early modern (or, in Chinese dynastic terms, late imperial) conceptualization of locust reproduction fundamentally informed resulting human behavior, which was complicated by the need to consider the overlapping lifecycles of both locusts and cereals in the management of both. The consequent pressure exerted by locust behavior on imperial sociopolitical institutions designed to concentrate agricultural biomass as sustenance and revenue could bring out contradictions within those institutions as locusts blithely ignored administrative boundaries and agricultural peak seasons. Imperial Chinese administrators tended to respond to these contradictions by further regimentation of human behavior. In this way, they sought to simplify complex and substantially unpredictable locust behavior into a manageable problem—ideally one of personnel management, which their bureaucracy was best prepared to address. The Qing state, like any other, tended to oversimplify environmental complexity in an anthropocentric way for purposes of legibility. Anthropocentric legibility of one form or another has been an unavoidable orientation of human institutions past and present. The result has often been a praxis of determinism: environmental, economic, and even cultural.

Why and how were locusts made simple within environmental relations constituted from a dynamic intersection of human culture and ecological systems during the Qing dynasty (1644–1912)? The integration of entomological literature on locust biology is organic to this examination, but not in order to dismiss Chinese state and society as woefully ignorant of some scientific truth now possessed by (post)modernity. Instead, as in any other approach from economics to gender studies, an environmental analysis of cultures of the past is informed by the state of present knowledge, which critically applies new perspectives to understand both the successes and the shortcomings of a particular historical change more precisely.[1]

Here, an environmental analysis provides a more comprehensive multispecies context in which to understand attempts by Chinese state and society to reconcile the often-contradictory effects of intensive graniculture. Cereal cultivation produced not only more food for humans but also more habitat for locusts. In many respects, the state sought to reduce an environmental problem to a people problem. Even though the state was reasonably successful in making locusts simple along more accessible anthropocentric lines, nonhuman ecological dynamics pervaded human institutions to ensure locust behavior would continue to influence human behavior as long as grain cultivation persisted.

SOME PERSPECTIVES FROM ENVIRONMENTAL STUDIES

Despite its tendency to reduce environmental diversity to a more manageable monoculture, the state certainly recognized the complexity of locust development itself—a recognition clearly expressed in a 1759 recommendation to the throne titled "A Memorial That Respectfully Lays Out the Circumstances of Locust Catching" (Jing chen bu huang shi yi shu). Its author, Shi Mao (1697–?), as a member of the Qing censorate, was duty-bound to be respectful while being critical of anyone, up to and including his ruler, the Qianlong emperor (r. 1736–95), on behalf of the empire. In this instance, he was dissatisfied with the average Chinese farmer's lack of long-term perspective in the face of the persistent threat of locust infestation: "The capture of locusts cannot be done in a perfunctory or crude manner. If their source is not discovered and cut off—this being the prerequisite for their extermination—it will stoke their power intensively. There must be places for locusts to develop for a specific time when they can only creep. Then, people are required to expel them with necessary equipment and a methodical plan. Yet, most people are mired in the present that is before their eyes and neglect foreseeing distress from afar."[2]

The preoccupation with the present Censor Shi decried was with the agricultural supply of the Qing Empire, which left little leisure time to chase locusts between sowing and harvest seasons. Seasonal timing was critical for the cultivation of staple cereal plants, but it was also vital for the eradication of locusts—the primary animal threat to those plants. As with many who had concerned themselves with these matters, he recognized that there were developmental windows of opportunity that facilitated eradication: "Catching locusts is not as good as catching their nymphs, which is not as good as destroying their eggs."[3] The theme of his memorial was how to exploit such opportunities while efficiently handling the overlap between cereal and locust reproductive cycles.

In this instance and in terms of environmental studies concepts such as social ecological systems (SES) or niche construction theory (NCT), Shi was trying to keep the empire's agriculturally modified spaces (niches) resilient through dynamic adaptation of interdependent human social and nonhuman ecological relations, which formed a complex system. To put it even more technically, Shi was trying to deal with the conflict between an extended human phenotype—agricultural niches built to enhance food production—and locust phenotypic plasticity—the ability to sprout wings and swarm under the right conditions.

In simplest terms, the empire's people-constructed grain fields had room for only either cereals or locusts but no capacity for full double occupancy. As an anthropogenic construct, the unnaturally high concentration of cereals unintentionally provided living space for inordinately large masses of normally solitary insects. Chinese fields not only tried to maximize grain yield per unit of area but they also inadvertently increased the insect yield per unit of area. Fields, as manifestations of human "behavioral plasticity" or "extended phenotype" or "ecosystem engineering," actually created niche conflict between people and locusts. Range expansion for humans and locusts was enhanced but continuously contested.

Such dynamics, as informed by NCT and related concepts that concern the effects of complex or nonlinear systems, have been virtually ignored in the literature of Chinese environmental history, which is predicated— often implicitly—on dated equilibrium or linear assumptions. In this perspective, cereal fields are at equilibrium until disturbed by locusts, which humans must then control to restore the equilibrium of maximal yields. It is, however, this very tendency to maximize yields, by expanding locust food supply and habitat, that constructs the ideal niche for swarms to sustain themselves. From a less linear perspective, which includes considerations of NCT, disharmony dynamics, and SES, human efforts to enhance equilibrium simultaneously enhance the potential for disturbance.

Ecology (niche construction's capacity to expand habitat) is of more concern here than is evolution (niche construction's relation to natural selection).[4] Here, niche construction forms habitats that act as buffers to reduce environmental uncertainty. This "ecosystem engineering" entails an organism's modification of its surrounding environment. Although such a modification may be specially intended to shelter the initiating organism, it may also inadvertently establish or expand the habitat for other organisms as an "engineering web" that more favorably restructures ecosystem interconnections of energy and mass flows.[5]

LOCUST CONTROL: RECONCILING METAPHYSICAL AND MUNDANE MEASURES

Much of imperial Chinese culture was devoted to engineering cereal field ecosystems, not merely for subsistence or revenue, but also in order to cultivate a particular imperial subject identity, usually termed loyal subjects (liangmin) during the late imperial period.[6] Agriculture as "the root of the royal enterprise" (wangye zhi genben) had been recognized since antiquity as critical for the maintenance of the state in both material and social terms.[7] The Han dynasty text Comprehensive Discussions in the White Tiger Hall (Bai hu tong) provides an exemplary statement in its account of the Divine Husbandman (Shennong) or God of Agriculture: "Why is the Divine Husbandman so called? The people of antiquity all ate the flesh of beasts and birds, but when the Divine Husbandman arrived, the population was so great that the beasts and birds were insufficient. For this reason the Divine Husbandman, in accordance with the seasons and the gradations of soil quality, instituted plowing and weeding, [thereby] instructing the people in agriculture. [As stated in the 'Appended Phrases' of *The Classic of Changes*:] 'The people were thus mystically transformed to be made suited to it [agriculture].' Therefore, he is called the 'Divine Husbandman.'"[8]

This mystical transformation (*shen er hua zhi*) was understood to have worked upon a preexisting, unsustainable environmental relationship between people and animals—hunting—that changed it to a sustainable one between people and plants: farming. This transition was actually made historically. The conviction that "the means by which the state prospers are agriculture and warfare" (*guo zhi suoyi xing zhe, nong zhan ye*) had become a core concept of imperial centralization for warring states like Qin during the Eastern Zhou (771–256 BCE).[9]

The acceptance of agricultural relations as fundamental for empire locked Chinese states and subjects into particular regimens necessary to maximize cereal production, in turn committing human herbivores to protracted war with insect herbivores—especially locusts—for exclusive growing space. Locusts thus became a focus of human environmental management, in both ritual and applied terms. Ritual practice centered on regulation of the metaphysical responses to human environmental competition with locusts. Locust control manuals, like Chen Chongdi's (1826–1875) *Manual on Locust Control* (Zhihuang shu, 1874), included ritual provisions among their applied eradication measures. Onsite "works" (*chang*) would be set up in infested areas not only to coordinate mundane eradication operations but also to provide infrastructures for the metaphysical operations of making burnt offerings of incense and yellow paper inscribed in large character format to the Divine Husbandman and other tutelary deities of agriculture. Authorities considered official ritual a critical process in the ongoing construction of a loyal subject identity, which was traditionally conflicted about locust eradication.[10]

The mysterious or uncertain nature of outbreaks precluded a full social consensus on locust metaphysics by affording too much space for an excessively wide range of interpretation. This overextensive scope long predated 1874, but, paradoxically, was an enduring legacy of a likewise long-lived cultural consensus on locust outbreaks visible from some of the earliest records of Chinese civilization onwards. Prior to the Tang dynasty

(618–907), what Andrea Janku has termed a "moral reading of disasters" prevailed; it was firmly established no later than the Western Han dynasty (202 BCE–8 CE).[11] Environmental catastrophes like floods, droughts, and locusts were consistently interpreted as expressions of divine displeasure with rulers' failure to govern benevolently. Under these circumstances, eradication was not an option. Moral reform was the only acceptable response to what was considered a potentially fatal rejection of dynastic legitimacy by nature spirits. Agents of divine judgement, like locusts, were strictly left alone to fulfill their destructive mandate.[12]

An unprecedented shift in official thought and practice toward active eradication of locusts emerged in a 715–16 court debate over an official response to a serious outbreak in Shandong. Chief Minister Yao Chong (651–721) staunchly and successfully took up this activist position against a formidable range of court opposition and resistance by local provincial officials. His act inspired elite admiration and commemoration through-out the remainder of the dynastic period. Yao decried popular attitudes toward locust outbreaks broadly similar to those alluded to in Chen's manual, which was published over a thousand years later: "Alas, at this time the common folk of Shandong all burn incense, ritually prostrate themselves and set up altars to pray for heaven's mercy. They watch the locusts devour their crops, not daring to touch them. . . . If only people wholeheartedly put forth an unrelenting effort, the locusts could definitely be exterminated!"[13]

Yao's effective handling of the Shandong outbreak inaugurated state planning to institutionalize mundane locust eradication across the en-suing dynasties, Song through Qing. By 1075, one of the earliest official promulgations of mundane locust control regulations had appeared. Its statutes included many subsequently standard policies, such as the award of grain in exchange for captured locusts and official supervision of stan-dard eradication methods of digging up eggs and capturing, burning, and burying insects. By 1182, there were provisions to punish official failures to report outbreaks and to personally supervise the implementation of control measures. During the Yuan dynasty (1271–1368), a centralized system of locust control reaching into subprovincial localities was de-veloped. Its main provisions centered on the implementation of regular regional inspections by central government officials to ensure the proper management of eradication—including a system of reportage to evaluate the extent of the disaster and the appropriate tax relief in response. There was also an increasing focus on preemptive measures against locust eggs. Further refinements to the Song–Yuan periods' foundational structure of institutionalized mundane eradication were added in the late imperial (or Ming–Qing) period.[14] Generally speaking, trends in locust eradication moved toward more pragmatic eradication, less inhibited by metaphysical concerns and greatly encouraged by material incentives.

Nevertheless, the late imperial period did not implement wholly mundane locust eradication. Another Shandong account, from the brush of the celebrated Ming official and agricultural encyclopedist Xu Guangqi (1562–1633), affirms the persistence of a divisive late imperial tradition of peasant reverence for locust outbreaks. He first invoked the Shandong outbreak of 715–16 as a canonical example of the harmful effects of peasant moral inaction. He then used this example to castigate contemporary subjects in "Shandong and Shaanxi [who] all can be observed superstitiously sacrificing to" locusts "in worship and consider it a taboo to harm or touch them." Xu's solution, likewise based on more material motives, was to persuade peasants to eat locusts like they would eat shrimp, which he conventionally believed were transformed into locusts when wetlands dried out.[15] During the succeeding Qing dynasty, the Kangxi emperor (r. 1661–1722) in 1694 could still fume that "some rustic fools generally hold that locusts cannot be caught and should be allowed to leave on their own. This sort of ignorant talk should be in particular prohibited. The capture of locusts to avoid disaster lies entirely within human affairs."[16]

The mundane eradication procedures of applied agriculture the Kangxi emperor so expressly preferred, however, did not operate so rationalistically in practice. Considerable complications arose from an intersection between human institutions and ecological processes. These processes are complex and still not fully understood, but it is possible to identify some of the main ecological factors that contribute to locust outbreaks—factors that were reasonably well understood during the Qing.

THE CLIMATE FOR LOCUST REPRODUCTIVE HABITAT

The most significant ecological system least accessible to human intervention in the context of locust control was climate, especially the cycle of flood and drought and corresponding temperature variations. Generally speaking, ground that is kept just wet enough without excessive moisture or dryness is prime locust reproductive habitat. Consequently, marginal zones along China proper's two longest rivers, the Yangzi and the Yellow, are ideal grounds for the spawning of locusts as they cycle from dry lands during periods of low precipitation to inundated areas in floodplains, shorelines, and wetlands in times of high precipitation. However, interaction of a number of complex ecological factors creates great regional differentiation in terms of locust reproduction and swarming outbreaks in these river basins.

One climate factor generally considered critical is how warm a winter will be, which will affect the formation and development of locust eggs, accordingly. The minimum temperature for mating in L. m. manilensis, for example, appears to be around 18°C/64°F. Ovum development and hatching in this subspecies require a minimum temperature of 15°C/59°F–16°C/61°F), and once laid, the egg itself can only survive a day or so at temperatures under -25°C/-13°F and only about five days at -20°C/-4°F. Since locust eggs must overwinter, the maintenance of seasonal temperatures within these ranges determines the size of the locust population, and the potential scale of the outbreak, in the following late spring and summer. Developmental stages of the immature locust nymphs, or "instars," at this time then require temperatures of at least 20°C/68°F and no more than 42°C/107.5°F. Locusts may bask in the sun to offset lower temperatures, an ability that likely allows them to mature, mate, and lay eggs in more northerly places like Hebei Province by early October, when the average air temperature stays below 21°C/70°F.[17] In sum, for a locust to get from ovum to maturity, ideal seasonal temperatures need to stay relatively warm at all stages of its development. Locusts will not be able to get off the ground without considerable stretches of minimal temperatures in the high teens and low twenties Celsius (mid- to high sixties in Fahrenheit).

Soil water content is another vital condition for locusts at the egg-laying stage. Optimum content is 10 percent to 20 percent, allowing egg clusters to reach two hundred thousand to four hundred thousand per square meter. Under conditions of total submergence, eggs can last only about fifteen days. These requirements render shorelines that are normally above regular water levels prime reproductive habitat. Little Ice Age (ca. 1400–ca. 1900) conditions that probably kept China proper somewhat drier than normal may also have expanded locust habitat.[18]

According to incomplete statistics compiled for a wide variety of disasters from 1644 to 1839, there appears to be a rough correspondence between frequency of locust outbreaks and droughts and floods. This correspondence is most evident in the provinces of Shandong and Zhili. Among the eighteen provinces and the northeastern region (i.e., Manchuria), Shandong had the most outbreaks (121) during this period, had the second-largest number of droughts (1,358), and came in third for floods (2,385). Zhili had the second-largest number of outbreaks (104), experienced the most droughts (1,725), and came in second for floods (2,994). Overall, Shandong and Zhili account for 31 percent of total outbreaks during this 196-year period, 34 percent of the droughts and 33 percent of the floods.[19] Although far from definitive, these figures suggest a connection within the Shandong-Zhili region between what appears as the empire's center of locust outbreaks and one of its major centers for drought and flood.

Despite a general consensus on parameters of locust reproduction and development, it has been difficult to find a similar consensus on whether there are more locust outbreaks in a generally cold year or in a generally warm one. It has been the standard view that locust reproduction and growth require relatively warm temperatures, which would ideally include warmer winters.[20] More recently, some evidence has emerged to explain how locusts might be able to flourish in eastern China even under the rather forbidding conditions of the Little Ice Age.[21] One 2011 study found that the flood-drought cycle may increase with climate cooling—commensurate with that of the Little Ice Age in drier, colder China proper—to expand locust habitat by leaving behind more ground just damp enough for reproduction. It remains unclear, however, how locusts adapt to much lower average temperatures.[22]

It is actually a flood-drought cycle that is advantageous to locusts. "Heavy droughts usually cause" locust outbreaks "in the same year" while "heavy flooding usually causes outbreaks . . . the year after the flooding." Serious drought "dries up rivers or lakes" to provide "more suitable habitats like wet banks" for locust egg-laying. In cases of heavy flooding, this drying-out process is delayed until the following year "as water dries up in the flooded areas" to, again, produce appropriate reproductive habitat.[23]

Serious flood-drought frequency seems to have increased in the Yangzi Delta, from the sixteenth into the eighteenth centuries, and with a similar pattern for serious drought in the lower Yellow River during much of the Little Ice Age.[24] While the precise relations between locust outbreaks and climate are still in dispute, there does seem to be a basic consensus that "drought," which here includes the drying up of flooded areas, is a critical mechanism for the outbreaks. Late imperial records confirm this association, anecdotally, as evident in the following quotes selected from just over a century between 1686 and 1792.[25]

1. "Nowadays, when the heavens are in drought, there will be locusts, and it is to be feared that there may be great neglect of administrative affairs."

2. "It is yet unknown whether there will be continuous rains this year with a short drought, come spring, from which the locusts will be born again."

3. "Last year it rained continuously, and it is yet uncertain that, if this spring there is a slight drought, the eggs left behind by locusts will hatch anew to then become a disaster to the distress of our people."

4. "Last winter there was little snow in the north, and this spring there has been scant rainfall, so there is still insufficient moisture—[causing] a genuine fear that locusts will easily spawn to the harm of agricultural affairs."

5. "During last winter there was little rain and snow in the north, so that We [the Yongzheng emperor] fear immature locusts will spawn this summer."

6. "We [the Qianlong emperor] have heard that last winter on Jiangnan's Zhaoyang Lake water dried up, turning roe into locust offspring."

7. "Locusts are essentially the sort of insect that is born from moisture and direct metamorphosis.[26] They spawn most easily on shorelines and in damp lowlands."

8. "Last year in Henan, the Yellow River flooded. Departments and districts near the river all remain deluged, and there is deep concern that the eggs left by aquatic creatures were transformed into locusts."

9. "The salt supervisor at Changlu, Da-se, memorializes that 'water is pooling in Tianjin, so a free-flow will be released from thirteen ditches and flood gates. The total land that will be dried out is 17–18 *li* long and 8–9 *li* wide.' . . . An imperial decree responded: 'Good . . . but there is the further matter of locusts. Areas that have dried out should also receive attention because they are especially prone to producing these creatures.'"

10. "Locust offspring mostly arise from places where dampness from pooled water dries out to produce locust eggs after a year's interval. After the heat and rain in the following year, there is again steaming

and sun-drying, then spawning commences. Now, last year, in the Miyun area, which is a highland, there was not much rain water and absolutely no flooding, so how can immature locusts suddenly be born there? Furthermore, locusts are mostly fish eggs that have been transformed, which is something everyone knows."

These examples convey the prevailing late imperial conviction that there were direct connections between locusts and fluctuating water levels. This relationship often suggested to observers that locusts were some sort of aquatic spawn that had undergone a morphological transformation into insects due to climate cycling between inundation and aridity over several successive years. This concept is perhaps most succinctly stated in Xu Guangqi's magisterial compendium, *Comprehensive Manual of Agricultural Administration* (Nongzheng quanshu): "Lands that produce locusts . . . must be places that suddenly overflow and suddenly dry out."[27] In most instances, the climate conditions were beyond state controls, although in example number nine it is obvious that people could take measures to avoid active contributions to enhancing locust reproductive habitat in the course of water control measures. Indeed, there is some evidence to suggest that certain forms of water control that resulted in the preservation of wetlands also unintentionally preserved locust reproductive habitat.[28]

In other cases, great care was taken to avoid creating more locust habitat during agricultural clearance, which could greatly complicate the process. One 1773 report on such an operation in Zhili was particularly concerned with the potentially detrimental effects of establishing pools for water storage, which "over time," would become spawning ground "for fish and shrimp." Should the artificially accumulated "water dry out," however, these creatures "would leave eggs clinging to the grass and mud that would everywhere turn into locust offspring that would spread to agricultural fields to their detriment." It was proposed that channels be dug to keep the water level under control to avoid both flooding and drying out.[29] Such precautions could inhibit locust habitat expansion, if not in precisely the same way officials believed.

Throughout the history of locust interaction with the imperial Chinese state, human constructs of locusts were not purely anthropogenic but formed from a selective intersection of locust behavior and human response. The coincidence of the two might not only produce more effective control measures but also could forge some practical translingual links between different human cultures. As noted in Mårten Söderblom Saarela's contribution to this volume, by the 1760s, Qing administrators were working with equivalent terms for locusts bilingually in Chinese and Manchu. This cross-cultural collaboration "was helpful to the Qing officials and clerks" working to cross-reference official reports on infestations covered by the empire's two most important administrative languages. A linguistic equivalency was thus made possible in large measure by the behavioral consistency of locusts across Chinese and Inner Asian cultures.

THE GROUNDS OF LOCUSTS' SWARMING HABITAT

The existence of premodern misconceptions about locust transformation is unsurprising, in light of how much remains to be discovered even with the powers of contemporary technology. For example, it was only in in 2015 that scientists isolated the workings of the initial chemical trigger for swarming behavior, or "density-determined phase polyphenism." Surges of the neurotransmitter serotonin change select species of normally solitary and comparatively ground-bound grasshoppers into winged masses of ferociously gregarious locusts. Such potent chemical jolts are the results of "increasing population density" and are "directly induced by stimuli from other locusts in close proximity" through receptor mechanisms of touch, sight, and smell of other insects in the same condition. The "continual exposure to stimuli from other locusts . . . drives the process of transformation onwards through positive feedback."[30]

Grain fields, as niches produced by environmental relations between people and cereals, seem almost deliberately constructed to promote such locust-swarm-generating-and-sustaining gregariousness among normally solitary grasshoppers. The clumping of food that is a deliberate structure built into grain fields may, in turn, clump grasshoppers together in an increasingly coordinated swarming fashion, or, in more technical terms:

> Because the probability of having an active neighbour is greater when
> foods are clumped rather than scattered, the strength of entrainment
> and phase-coupling of individual activity cycles is also greater, which
> results in emergence of synchronized movement and feeding within groups.
> Synchronization of activity will increase the intensity of mutual stimula-
> tion during periods of activity and hence accelerate population gregariza-
> tion. In contrast, when resources are scattered, activity in one locust stim-

ulates activity of any solitarious near neighbours, but usually the response is to move away, eliciting a wave of dispersal among scattered solitarious locusts and inhibiting gregarization.[31]

High concentrations of food initially bring solitary insects together, then establish more uniform behavior patterns as they all begin to feed at the same time in the same fashion and place, which continues to stimulate group action via serotonin-driven receptor mechanisms in individual bodies. In contrast, dispersed food sources scatter individuals with accompanying behavioral and chemical effects that stop swarming.

Food is an important stimulant in terms of quality as well as quantity, although locusts are not normally thought of as discriminating eaters. Many species of grain are unnaturally rich concentrations of proteins and carbohydrates for both insects and humans and provide a desirable food source for both because of the absence of repellent chemicals in them. Generally, "grasses and a few other plants are readily acceptable" to locusts "because they do not contain deterrent chemicals in sufficient quantity to limit feeding." Tannins, for example, are chemical compounds organic to plants that naturally concentrate and refine proteins. Humans often pleasantly experience tannins as the astringent taste of wine. Insects like locusts, in contrast, have an intensely unpleasant experience when ingesting tannins; so intense in fact that tannins in sufficient concentration will deter locusts from eating away a plant. The whole botanical family of grasses (Poaceae or Gramineae), which includes cereals, generally lacks these natural deterrents. Furthermore, some research has shown that temperate grasses containing high concentrations of carbohydrates exerted some of the most powerful stimulus to locust appetites.[32] In effect, as a consequence of human-intensive cultivation of high-carbohydrate cereals lacking in natural insect repellents, graniculture can simultaneously, and inadvertently, raise locusts.

In sum, grain fields not only attract locust swarms, they may even generate and prolong them. Unlike climatological factors, locust behavioral factors that contributed to swarming went unremarked by dynastic authorities. Even if the relevant biological knowledge was possessed by dynastic authorities, it is difficult to imagine that it would have resulted in a reduction of grain acreage. The stimulating effects of monocropped cereals on locust swarming were all too apparent, even if their triggers were not fully comprehended. The empire, however, had long acclimated itself to outbreaks.

LOCUSTS MADE SIMPLE

Given the complexities of climate and locust biology, which are even now far from perfectly understood, it is not surprising that the Qing state's strategy for locust control was mainly reactive and heavily dependent on popular implementation. In the sense that insect outbreaks "could only be solved through communal action and communal solidarity," Qing environmental governance was not so very different from the approach of the postwar Japanese government's eradication operations against flies and mosquitoes in the 1950s and 1960s, as discussed by Kerry Smith in this volume.

Qing environmental governance was also effective in support of community eradication especially because of its relatively firm foundation of environmental governance, which included ever-normal granary reserves that could be used to make good food shortfalls in outbreak districts. Such an infrastructure of robustness is a keystone of what I have elsewhere termed a system of "imperial arablism" that ordered China proper's primary environmental relations between people and cereal cultivars.[33] Prompt actions by people to eradicate locusts as quickly as possible were critical because people were the main component over which the dynasty had the most control. In this respect alone, dynastic administration was anthropocentric. Indeed, this is why ritual practices—which enhanced the more mundane mobilization of human resources—mattered at all throughout the imperial period.

Thus, it was critical that locusts be made simple to facilitate state eradication. This did not mean ignoring the effects of climate or biology, but it did mean an excessive reliance on human intermediaries and institutions that were, at best, indirect and somewhat unwieldy methods to deal with outbreaks. Although dynastic authorities were aware that crows and ducks would eat locusts—and there were some attempts to rely on them to do so—the main dynastic strategy was to rely on people, through the activation of provincial, prefectural, and district administrations to coordinate peasant resistance to locusts.[34]

This strategy entailed a number of challenges that, to a significant degree, rendered locust control procedures mainly dependent on control over humans to carry them out. The first of these challenges was simply to persuade a critical number of people that locusts could and should be controlled. Yao Chong had successfully begun to overcome official reluctance, but late imperial authors like Xu Guangqi and Chen Chongdi reveal that the peasantry—the most important human resources for effective locust eradication—remained difficult to enlist. This conviction existed even in highly developed and urbanized regions such as Suzhou, where a 1627 incursion "was considered by some to be divine, so they did not dare catch them." The author of this account, Shen Shouhong (1645–1722), felt bound to cite the canonical Confucian works *The Classic of Poetry (Shijing)* and *Spring and Autumn Annals (Chunqiu)*—along with a detailed account of Yao Chong—in condemnation. Yet, it is difficult to understand how Shen thought these exemplars would move peasants. Perhaps this is why he also made more pragmatic arguments in his "On Catching Locusts," when he asserted that "flood, drought, and locusts are all disasters from the heavens. . . . If one encounters a flood or drought, does one not act to drain it off or conduct irrigation?"[35] Nevertheless, appeals like Shen's are difficult to explain in the light of peasant beliefs like those noted by Zhili governor-general Fang Guancheng (1698–1768), who recorded in 1752 that peasants there were convinced catching locusts would bring more of them.[36]

Another seventeenth-century essayist, Chen Fangsheng (fl. 1684), advocated having peasants eat locusts. Apparently, this was a common practice in the Jinan region of Shandong. Chen had also seen peasants dishing them out while serving as an official in Tianjin. They were commonly served up in markets and also stored dried in winter, "tasting the same as dried shrimp." In contrast, he had seen that Shaanxi peasants considered harming, or even touching, locusts a taboo. When he told them they were edible, these people were "shocked" and "very suspicious" because they thought that eating them would make the consumer's temperament violent. Chen explained the different regional responses to the idea of edible locusts as the effect of ecology upon culture. Shandong people, "knowing shrimp perfectly well," simply saw locusts as the terrestrial version of this aquatic staple.[37]

Rural convictions about locusts appear here as regionally specific, which doubtlessly hindered central organization and implementation of locust eradication. Indeed, conditions were not even uniform in a single province, if the Shandong accounts of Chen Chongdi and of Chen Fangsheng are both correct. Regional ecological diversity certainly had a significant influence on rural culture, as Chen Fangsheng implied. This particular difference, however, did not just arise between watery and drier regions. Because conditions were generally too wet for locusts to thrive provincially, Guangxi outbreaks came exclusively from more congenial habitats in the less water-saturated north. This gave outbreaks a much more mysterious and unpredictable character that encouraged supernatural explanations from the perspective of the peasants—who were not even trained in preemptive eradication. The ability of swarms to travel far from their places of origin was a critical factor in the formation and persistence of this regional cultural conviction.[38]

There were additional, more pragmatic dynamics operating in rural areas beyond religious taboos, ones that were directly related to peasants' material interests. Some basic motives for farmers to avoid reporting were laid out in a 1760 memorial by the distinguished official Chen Hongmou (1696–1771). Chen explained that eradication in his jurisdiction was generally carried out by poor landless people who dug up locust egg-masses for a state bounty. Financial incentives, however, appeared insufficient in the face of difficult climate conditions, and the poor remained "not very enthusiastic" about digging in soil that was often still frozen. Chen also thought that landlords and tenants might not police even their own fields because once immature locusts emerged, they may "hop elsewhere, not necessarily eating up all one's crops. There is, moreover, the concern that in mobilizing farmers to catch them, fields of sprouts will be trampled. This is the reason they neither catch them, nor report them to officials." Human mobilization for preemptive egg eradication was particularly challenging because of climate and individual cost-benefit assessments. Chen was also forced rely on the willingness of village authorities to inspect isolated locust reproductive areas "in the hard stones of the mountain peaks or the reeds at the edges of marshes where people seldom tread and where there are neither landlords nor assigned officials."[39]

Zhou Tao (fl. 1739) submitted a 1752 memorial on the preemptive eradication of immature locusts and eggs that elucidated further human resource problems. Zhou observed that residents of villages where no outbreaks had occurred would be reluctant "to be scattered about elsewhere to assail and catch locusts. They will only fear to abandon agricultural tasks." Their "attachment to their native places" would prompt individuals and possibly whole villages—in collusion with local officials—to buy their way out of obligations to mobilize to assist neighboring locales. Zhou even thought that these corrupt officials could actually encourage such defections on a mass scale as they moved about the countryside extorting bribes.[40]

Peasants were reluctant to assist nearby locales, which might still lie a considerable distance away on foot. Despite the ability of locusts to cover large distances quickly, peasant localism was quite reasonable in light of the environmental circumstances under which they lived. Stopping locusts at any stage of their development did not precisely coincide with the agricultural calendar. Searches for eggs and immature locusts could often interfere with spring planting. Winged locusts matured in tandem with the ripening of crops in summer and fall.

In addition, not all locust swarms attacked every farm in every direction. The extreme cultural constructs that could be cobbled from this unpredictable behavior are exemplified in an essay on locust eradication by the noted Confucian philosopher Lu Shiyi (1611–1672). Lu held a concept of infestation only slightly different from the prevailing wisdom challenged by Yao Chong. Lu's essay sought to clarify the metaphysical conditions under which locusts would selectively attack grain fields. When they descended on a group of plots, Lu observed that "some are eaten and some are not; although the fields are in the same locale, it is as if they are cut off by a boundary." Lu held that some "spiritual" (*shen*) power was at work in every circumstance, but the locust themselves were neither spirits nor led by spirits. Instead, locust behavior was determined by a kind of moral patchiness: variations in local peoples' adherence to the Confucian values of filial piety, fraternity, parental compassion toward their children, simplicity, and frugality. If people in one place practiced these values, then they "should not undergo a calamity from the [obstructed] circulation of cosmic *qi*, and the spirits must therefore protect them so that the locusts will not cause a disaster." Other places that did not would, in contrast, be visited by such a disaster because "the spirits would certainly not protect them." For this reason, because "customs are not uniform, good and evil dissimilar, and the circulation of cosmic *qi* variable, then the spirits must make distinctions in exhortations and warnings. Locusts in consequence will arrive at some places to feed and not at others."[41]

Recent research on locust feeding behavior suggests that selective swarms are driven by nutritional requirements that work to maintain a consistent ratio between protein and carbohydrate intake as the insects feed on the wide variety of grass species, including grains, that generally attract them.[42] This dietary factor helps explain why locusts "arrive at some places to feed and not at others." But such complex behavior—which remains incompletely understood—could easily demonstrate to Confucian farmers that their plots were under no threat from the locusts in the next village. Lu's essay exemplifies a Confucian attempt to simplify locust behavior to facilitate the control of humans under confusing ecological circumstances.

Zhou Tao provided further reasonable justifications for peasant reluctance to participate in state-orchestrated eradication operations. He acknowledged that people with no property to protect would be enthusiastic about locust eradication because it would provide them numerous opportunities to pillage the crops of their distressed neighbors, trampling their fields in the process. The result, in Zhou's view, would cause "more harm than the locusts." He went so far as to accuse these people of actively concealing sites where eggs or immature locusts existed to allow them to spread and develop into a disastrous opportunity for plunder. Moreover, local officials' efforts were often useless. Zhou had heard that in some places, when an outbreak was at its height, unprepared officials "frequently with hands tied, had no more policy than to koutou at the shrine of General Liu Meng to pray for his spiritual power to drive them off."[43]

Another 1752 memorial, from Shuntian—the Zhili prefecture that contained the capital—stated that peasants were reluctant to fulfill their primary locust eradication duty to report a local outbreak because they feared their crops would be trampled during the eradication operations. This fear was a major reason, he implied, for their devotion to the spiritual powers of General Liu Meng.[44] Here, it is possible to see peasant attempts to simplify locust outbreaks as resistance to the unintended social dynamics of state eradication operations. Of course, these chaotic social circumstances were driven by the ecology of locust behavior interacting with human culture to produce an environmental relationship that was too complex for either state's or society's preferred degrees of control.

A little over a decade later, Governor-General Fang Guancheng would face a major outbreak in his Zhili jurisdiction that spilled over into neighboring Shandong. A fairly well-preserved record of the ensuing eradication operations reveals in detail the complex interplay of human and ecological elements that the state sought to simplify in order to effect timely control of locusts. One of the primary challenges was coping with the fact that locust swarms ignored provincial jurisdictional boundaries, which central officials worried would allow their local counterparts to deny responsibility for locust control in administratively ambiguous areas.

In July of 1763, the throne began receiving reports of hopping and flying locusts from districts and departments along the Zhili-Shandong border, centered in the Zhili prefectures of Jiaohe and Tianjin. An initial imperial edict in response immediately expressed concern over local officials' "bad habit of constantly keeping boundaries firmly in mind for mutual use as a pretext to avoid responsibility."[45] One of the most important tasks of eradication was to determine the origin of the outbreak for both locust habitat control and disciplinary measures against any lax officials. Prevention was intended to eliminate locusts at the egg or hopper stages before they could sprout wings and do more extensive damage by easily crossing potentially conflicted administrative boundaries both within and between provinces.

The first regulation duly listed in the "disciplinary actions" section in the Qing manual of precedents was a 1709 prescription for impeachment of officials who had failed to personally inspect known outbreak areas and supervise prompt eradication in their jurisdictions on the pretext that locusts "had flown in from a neighboring jurisdictional boundary."[46] In 1770, regulations concerning this issue had become even more detailed and impassioned. After an extended tirade against local bureaucratic prevarications concerning control of a Zhili outbreak in the summer of that year, the Qianlong emperor declared:

Locusts when first born hop around, so all leave traces that can be tracked. Even though they grow wings and take flight, they, after all, are never far from the ground. How are they able to surpass distances of over one hundred *li*, form swarms, and stop to congregate? Even if they fly at random into adjoining boundary zones, local officials ought to gather men with the utmost urgency to eliminate them and protect agricultural fields. If they are too mindful of boundaries and use neighboring jurisdictions as a pretext, a long delay will be the result. How will this be any different than their spawning within one's own jurisdiction? Furthermore, it will be absolutely impossible to eradicate completely the evil offspring of flying locusts from whence they arose. . . . There is no need to ask from whence they arose. . . . Henceforth, local officials who are lax in the capture of locusts will be punished, as will those areas where flying locusts currently exist. There is no need to inquire into tracing whence they came, which will result in shifting the blame. Let this be an order![47]

The emperor's views about the anthropogenic origins of locust disasters are characteristic of an imperial administration committed to converting every environmental problem into one of human management. This is, indeed, a major reason for his exasperated revision of the regulations that insist on holding some local official somewhere responsible for an outbreak of winged locusts. While he appears to acknowledge officials cannot be held responsible for such outbreaks, Qianlong was actually seeking to make them more responsible for controlling locusts by removing an obstacle to jurisdictional cooperation. He made his conviction on this matter quite clear elsewhere in his declaration when he praised imperial commissioners dispatched to handle the 1770 outbreak. In addition to punishing local officials who were shifting blame among themselves, Qianlong dispatched central government imperial commissioners free of such local entanglements, who "went forth to exert themselves in collaboratively handling matters. The result was a timely and complete extermination that caused no harm to crops. It can thus be seen that arresting locusts is not a matter beyond human strength to carry out."[48]

It is possible that some of the Qianlong emperor's convictions were formed from his experience of the 1763 outbreak, when he also successfully sent imperial commissioners to prevent a major disaster. In an early report on the situation, Manchu grand councillor Agūi (1717–1797) and Fang Guancheng stated that "every department and district sees them [locusts] come from a certain direction, then at once makes the accusation they have arisen from a neighboring jurisdiction in that very direction. This is actually not true, but is the malpractice of shifting the blame as [the locusts] actually change direction and multiply."[49] Initial reports had indeed put the blame on Dacheng in southern Shuntian Prefecture, but at the insistence of the emperor, an official, Qian Rucheng (?–1779), was dispatched to the area and revealed no outbreak had occurred there. It was ultimately decided that the source of the outbreak, which included both hopping and flying locusts, lay in Jiaohe District in central Jianhe Prefecture. Jiaohe's magistrate, Gan Yi (n.d.), was duly accused of failure to report an outbreak.[50] Subsequent reports indicated the main areas of locust reproductive habitat were not readily accessible. In their report to the throne, Agūi and Fang Guancheng claimed locusts had spawned in reed-filled wetlands "difficult for human effort to overcome." Even the emperor himself acknowledged that locusts could easily hide in such terrain.[51]

It is hard to reconcile this admission of the emperor's with his 1770 statutory declaration. His own extensive administrative experience surely could not have informed such hasty generalizations, so easily challenged by his own statements elsewhere in the record. Admittedly, the Qianlong emperor was a busy man, and the system of court letters, which the emperor dictated rather than wrote out himself, was deliberately intended by his father, the Yongzheng emperor, to reduce the throne's enormous daily load of paperwork.[52] Yet further consideration of the administrative system in which he labored occasionally reveals a more collective tendency to reduce environmental problems—which may certainly *involve* humans—to *exclusively* people problems. This was a regime in which Manchurian banner foragers were reprimanded for fulfilling their pheasant quota with underweight birds and Mongolian banner pastoralists were fined for wolf mortalities inflicted on their herds. It is, thus, not surprising that their Enduringge Ejen—"Divine Lord," the standard Manchu term for the Qing emperor in memorials—adopted a bureaucratic mentality that oversimplified the management of the human-ecological relationships on which his regime ultimately depended.[53]

In the instance of the 1763 locust outbreak, the emperor had been informed that in the southernmost areas of Tianjin prefecture, an extermination operation was conducted with four thousand to five thousand people, who spent four days clearing out locusts (not counting the extra time spent digging up eggs). Nine locales in Yanshan had been cleared when seven new areas of "newly born locusts" were discovered.[54] Such operations were, moreover, conducted under the pressure of spring and fall sowing and harvesting schedules. Agricultural circumstances in the district of Jiaohe in Hejian Prefecture were especially pressing. In the infested space:

> There is no early-ripening rice or sorghum; all are late planted grains and beans only 3–4 inches tall and there is much thick undergrowth among those that had just emerged from the ground. When questioned, peasants of every village stated "at the time when the spring wheat was about to ripen, there was a locust outbreak, entirely consuming all the early-ripening rice and sorghum. The spring wheat was also harmed in places. The late-ripening rice, grains and beans were, consequently, all turned over and replanted but there was no strength left for hoeing.[55]

This primary farming situation was difficult enough under existing ecological conditions in the district, which had flooded the year before.

Under these already disastrous conditions, there is little wonder that that district magistrate Gan Yi "did not pursue [locust] capture with urgency and, furthermore, engaged in intentional concealment and made no detailed report, which resulted in the spread of the disaster."[56] Indeed, according to one report by Agūi and Fang Guancheng, areas drying out from flooding were converting fish eggs previously laid underwater into terrestrial locust eggs.[57] Even if such radical phenotypic plasticity was biologically impossible, the hydrodynamics of flooding and drying out could easily have helped to create outbreak conditions.

Human relations with plants also inadvertently contributed to outbreak conditions that could synergistically combine with comparatively less anthropogenic ecological factors like flooding. Aside from feeding the locusts with their early plantations of sorghum and other crops, which probably stimulated crowding and swarming, human use of nearby wetland reed stands likely also helped to maintain locust breeding habitat. As officials deliberated on reaching a long-term solution to the area's suddenly serious locust problems, a consensus grew that something had to be done about its widespread reed marshes.

Agūi, Fang Guancheng, and another senior official, Qiu Yuexiu (1712–1773), submitted a long memorial to the throne on September 24, 1763. A few days earlier, Guan Yinbao had declared major extermination operations successfully concluded with minimal damage to crops.[58] One of the critical events that had helped to finish off the swarms was well beyond human control: the onset of a colder, wetter autumn than usual, which was termed the White Dew season (*bailu jie*). Their memorial quoted a previous communication that "there is, at the present time, a white dew amidst the watery lowlands, reed marshes and small lakes that has . . . entirely eliminated the flying locusts." Before the swarms died off, however, "they were seen hanging upside down from reeds depositing their eggs, which are feared numerous." Consequently, an edict, quoted in their memorial, decided that

> it is essential to formulate an appropriately timely eradication method. Qiu Yuexiu was previously concerned about the water surface taken up by reed marshes in a swamp and, consequently, deliberated uprooting them. Moreover, Giking once looked into the management of immature locusts, and it also happened that reeds were burned off.

Yet, these sorts of reed marshes spread to fill the horizon, and people who dwell near lakes avail themselves of these natural advantages. So, it would be impractical to throw the reeds away all at once just to catch the immature locusts. Those left behind will germinate in this lowland marshy area, which will only make it a swamp for sprouting a locust plague. These seeds thus sown are an even greater disaster for the people's livelihood— naturally proper weight should be given to deliberations and control. Let it be decreed that Agūi et al., in conjunction with the said supervisors, will decide whether the use of fire is urgent at this time, or to wait until after mowing, then burn all root and branch to ensure this legacy of disaster is cut off so that people are not harmed.[59]

The memorial then quoted another decree regarding flying locusts in Jinghai. It said the swarms originated "amidst swamps and from the grasses and reeds of beaches and rivers," not from more settled zones around Dacheng. The decree concluded from this information that

> it seems the lakes and reed thickets of the marshlands truly nurture the growth of locusts. If the reeds and grasses are entirely burnt up suddenly, it is further to be feared that this will unavoidably impede the livelihood of the poor who live near the lakes and mow for a living. Locust eggs generally cleave to the earth for growth. The colder the weather, the deeper they are buried. Nothing is more effective than waiting to mow, then firing root and branch. Since this will clear out the eggs, next year's reeds will increase in size, from which people's livelihoods will continue to benefit.

The memorialists responded with a proposal that the current reed lands of locust reproductive habitat should be inundated by canals cleared of reeds and dug out to transform their eggs back to fish and shrimp. This procedure would have actually drowned the locust eggs. One section of the lake where eggs were unearthed was to be mowed and burned, or "deeply plowed." The remainder would be left intact to provide reeds for local consumption with the hope that the canals would flood any remaining low-lying areas hosting locust eggs. This large-scale transformation of wetlands would probably have disrupted locust reproductive habitat but certainly would not have eradicated it. Instead, new wetland boundaries would gradually form at the edges of waterways and in the new reed stands, which as the memorial stated, would probably expand.[60] In effect, a new habitat would be created for locusts because

humans still depended on reeds, to say nothing of waterways and crop-
lands that locusts also shared.

CONCLUSION

The state could not make locusts sufficiently simple without simultaneously simplifying the management of its mainstay cultivators in ways that
were impractical and likely unsustainable. Indeed, the state could not
even finally simplify its regulations to eliminate the divisive bureaucratic
hunt for which jurisdiction bred a given locust swarm. An 1803 case pitted
Anhui officials against Jiangsu ones accusing each other regarding which
province had neglectfully nurtured an outbreak that year. Jiangsu was
ultimately blamed, but the Jiaqing emperor (r. 1796–1820) issued an edict
whose lament would have surprised his royal father, who had considered
the problem resolved in 1770:

> From Shandong ['s administrative perspective, the locusts] originated
> within the boundaries of Jiang[su]; in contrast, from Jiangsu's [administra-
> tive perspective]; they originated in Shandong. Provincial officials are al-
> ways punished rather severely where locust swarms have arisen. So, there is
> frequent mutual recrimination in hopes of avoiding responsibility—a truly
> evil practice. A locale may, beyond expectation, meet with locusts. Regard-
> less of whether they sprout from within one's own boundaries or swarm in
> from another district, they should always be caught and wiped out imme-
> diately; why search out where they came from? If each side shifts the blame
> to the other, locust eradication will be neglected, and this situation will
> steadily expand until it critically impedes agriculture.[61]

As in so many instances in the Qing record, people appear here as the
main state problem. From an environmental perspective, however, there
were other contributing factors beyond imperial reach—physical transformations of locusts, hydrological cycles, crop seasons. The problem of
locust outbreaks could never be that simple.

NOTES

1. For a more general discussion of these issues, see the introduction. There are
certainly studies that "seek to place [locusts] at the center of historical analysis" in
a revisionist attempt to reduce anthropocentrism by shifting attention to "histo-

ries of human relationships with the insects themselves" (Few, "Killing Locusts in Colonial Guatemala," 62–63, 83–84). However, these studies still tend to present locusts exclusively in terms of their historical human cultural constructs. This approach provides minimal consideration of how locusts have always behaved outside these constructs, and so elides the insects' deep influence on human culture. This is precisely why entomological literature is a prerequisite for decentering humans in historical analysis of their mutual relations. The present volume directly addresses the "humanities" problem raised by Few that "insects do not fit into historically and culturally constructed binaries that historians of human-animal relationships wish to critique" (64).

2. Shi, "Jing chen bu huang shi yi shu," 2:1076a–b.

3. Shi, "Jing chen bu huang shi yi shu," 2:1076a–b.

4. For detailed discussion of NCT and evolution, see Scott-Phillips et al., "The Niche Construction Perspective," 1231, 1234–35.

5. Kendal, Tehrani, and Odling-Smee, "Introduction," 787; Odling-Smee et al., "Niche Construction Theory," 5–6, 8.

6. For further discussion of this process of what I have called "imperial arablism," see my *Across Forest, Steppe and Mountain*, 22–23, 40–43.

7. Xu, *Nongzheng quanshu jiaozhu*, 3:1805.

8. *Bai hu tong* 1.4; translation adapted from Tjan, *Po Hu T'ung*, 1:233. For further context for the *Classic of Changes* quotation, see Kong Yingda, *Zhouyi Zhengyi*, 1:86c.

9. Pines, *The Book of Lord Shang*, 133.

10. Chen Chongdi, *Zhihuang shu*, 7a–8a.

11. Janku, "'Heaven-Sent Disasters,'" 233–34.

12. Rothschild, "Sovereignty, Virtue, and Disaster Management," 784.

13. This passage is translated in Rothschild, "Sovereignty, Virtue, and Disaster Management," 793.

14. For transdynastic overviews of state locust control policies, see Zhang Yihe, *Zhongguo huangzai shi*, 160–78, 192–213, and Ni, "Zhongguo lishi shang de huangzai ji zhihuang," 48–51.

15. Xu, *Nongzheng quanshu jiaozhu*, 3:1301–3.

16. QSL, KX 33/4/13, 5:780b.

17. Yu, Shen, and Liu, "Impacts of Climate Change," 2; Tu et al., "Growth, Development and Daily Change," 134, 137, 138.

18. Yu, Shen, and Liu, "Impacts of Climate Change," 2; Chen et al., "Hydroclimatic Changes in China," 104.

19. Adapted from Li Xiangjun, *Qingdai huangzheng yanjiu*, 214. The remaining provinces analyzed by Li rank far behind Shandong-Zhili for outbreaks. They are, in order: Henan (66), Shanxi (63), Jiangsu (52), Shaanxi (38), Zhejiang (21), and Anhui (19).

20. Yu, Shen, and Liu, "Impacts of Climate Change," 8–9.

21. Conditions during the Little Ice Age are subject to many qualifications,

including its likely different precipitation effects in North and South China, respectively. Yu, Shen, and Liu, "Impacts of Climate Change"; Chen et al., "Hydroclimatic Changes in China."

22. Tian et al., "Reconstruction of a 1,910-Y-Long Locust Series," 14521–26. A study by many of the same authors also found preexisting locust abundance from the previous year or decade an important factor in promoting outbreaks. Stige et al., "Thousand-Year-Long Chinese Time Series," 16188–93. Both studies, however, were limited to the Yangzi Delta.

23. Z. Zhang and Li, "A Possible Relationship," 68.

24. Q. Zhang, Gemmer, and Chen, "Climate Changes and Flood/Drought Risk," 65; J. Zhang et al., "Decadal Variability of Droughts and Floods," 3218.

25. The ten quotes are from, respectively, QSL, KX 25/6/4, 5:345b; KX 32/10/9, 5:758b–59a; KX 34/1/16, 5:805b; KX 41/3/10, 6:109b; YZ 10/intercalary 5/12, 8:578a; QL 9/6/3, 11:807b; QL 17/5/16, 14:428a–b; QL 17/5/20, 14:428b–29a; QL 28/3/24, 17:646a–b; QL 57/7/12, 26:932a–b.

26. On the terms *shisheng* and *huasheng*, see Söderblom Saarela's contribution in this volume.

27. Xu, *Nongzheng quanshu jiaozhu*, 3:1300.

28. Bello, "Consider the Qing Locust," 63.

29. Ge, *Qingdai zouzhe huibian*, 254–55.

30. Rogers and Ott, "Differential Activation," 1–2. "Density-determined phase polymorphism," used in much of the older literature cited here, is currently being replaced by the newer term, "density-determined phase polyphenism," which emphasizes that the insects' physical transformation is environmentally induced rather than wholly determined by genetic factors internal to locust physiology. See Meir and Simpson, *Advances in Insect Physiology*, 5–6.

31. Meir and Simpson, *Advances in Insect Physiology*, 217–18.

32. Bernays and Chapman, "Deterrent Chemicals," 1, 14, 16. As in any examination of environmental processes, much has been oversimplified in this account. Locusts appear to eat selectively, including intake of less nutritious food, under certain conditions. Chambers, Simpson, and Raubenheimer, "Behavioural Mechanisms," 1513–23.

33. Bello, *Across Forest, Steppe and Mountain*, 13, 40–48.

34. Lu Shiyi, in his "Chu huang ji," noted that Zhenjiang Prefecture successfully employed "hundreds of ducks" to waddle through the rice paddies to "get rid of all the immature locusts in a jiffy" (2:1073b–74a). For an implausible suggestion regarding crows, see QSL, YZ 2/7/1, 7:350b.

35. Shen Shouhong, "Bu huang shuo," 2:1068b–69a.

36. Hu, "Zou fu buhuang jingguo qingxing zhe," QL 17/5/21, 3:138a–39b.

37. Chen Fangsheng, "Bu huang fa," 2:1070b–73a.

38. Lu and Liu, "Guangxi de huangshenmiao yu huangzai," 145–52.

39. Chen Hongmou, "Chutu nanzi zecheng dianhu souchu xi," 2:1080a–b.

40. Zhou Tao, "Jing chou chunan miezi shu," 2:1079a–b.

41. Lu Shiyi, "Chu huang ji," 2:1073b–75a.

42. Chambers, Simpson, and Raubenheimer, "Behavioural Mechanisms," 1513. When possible, locusts appear to eat selectively in order to maintain a particular balance of protein to carbohydrates that may change in ratio depending on the developmental stage of the feeding individual, its species, and surrounding ecological conditions. To the extent external conditions have "exerted selective forces on the neural and physiological processes of behavior," locusts can be considered "to contain a 'model' of their external environment, partly acquired genetically and augmented through direct assessment and feedback" (1520–22). In this perspective, the insects literally and dynamically embody their environmental relationships.

43. Zhou Tao, "Jing chou chunan miezi shu," 2:1079a–b. Shrines of General Liu Meng had been established in the Song to repel locusts, but they received full official support only in the first decades of the eighteenth century. They were centered in Jiangsu and Zhejiang Provinces. North China also had shrines to other locust-fighting spirits (Zhang Yihe, *Zhongguo huangzai shi*, 185–90). Selective official patronage could be read, in part, as a state attempt to reduce the problematic diversity of local beliefs regarding the spiritual status of swarms.

44. Hu, "Zou fu buhuang jingguo qingxing zhe," QL 17/5/21, 3:138a–39b.

45. QSL, QL 28/6/14, 17:703a–b.

46. *Da Qing huidian shili*, 2:418b.

47. *Da Qing huidian shili*, 2:420a–b.

48. *Da Qing huidian shili*, 2:420a–b.

49. Agūi, "Zou bao gongtong dongban pubu huangnan fangfan deng yuanyou zhe," QL 28/7/11, 18:441b–43a.

50. Qian Rucheng, "Zou fu qinwang chakan Dacheng nannie shi xi jinjing zhe," QL 28/7/21, 18:524b–26a; Guan, "Zou xie ming congkuan mian qi ge qi ren reng zhuce zhe," QL 28/7/18, 18:505a–b; QSL, QL 28/6/24, 17:720b–21a. Gan's superior, Zhili's provincial administration commissioner, Guan Yinbao, requested he not be impeached. Guan, "Zou xie ming congkuan mian qi ge qi ren reng zhuce zhe," QL 28/7/18, 18:505a–b.

51. QSL, QL 28/7/22, 17:746a–47a; Qian Rucheng, "Zou fu qinwang chakan Dacheng nannie shi xi jinjing zhe," QL 28/7/21, 18:524b–26a.

52. Bartlett, *Monarchs and Ministers*, 103–12.

53. Bello, *Across Forest, Steppe and Mountain*, 4–5, 103–6, 134–36.

54. Agūi, "Zou bao du bu huangnan qingxing zhe," QL 28/6/29, 18:343a–44b.

55. Fang Guancheng, "Zou wei yanxing canzou Jiaohexian xianzhi Gan Yi huini nanzai zhe," QL 28/6/20, 18:229a–30a.

56. Fang Guancheng, "Zou wei yanxing canzou Jiaohexian xianzhi Gan Yi huini nanzai zhe," QL 28/6/20, 18:229a–30a.

57. Agūi, "Zou bao gongtong dongban pubu huangnan fangfan deng yuanyou zhe," QL 28/7/11, 18:441b–43a.

58. Guan, "Zou bao chakan nannie pubu jinjing zhe," QL 28/7/24, 18:554b–55a.

59. Agūi, "Zou fu soubu huangnan ji jieyu zizhong qingxing zhe," QL 28/7/27, 18:564b–66a.

60. Agūi, "Zou fu soubu huangnan ji jieyu zizhong qingxing zhe," QL 28/7/27, 18:564b–66a.

61. Bello, "An Intermittent Order," 27.

FIVE

A Silkworm Massacre

AGRICULTURAL DEVELOPMENT AND LOSS OF INDIGENOUS DIVERSITY IN EARLY TWENTIETH-CENTURY KOREA

Sang-ho Ro

Various silkworms have lived under human custody for millennia in East Asia. Among the diverse species of Bombycidae, *Bombyx mori* (K. Wŏnjam; C. *Yuancan*) is one that is especially well protected and tended to thanks to its high-quality protein fiber: silk. Utilization of the insect for making silk of better quality and greater quantity was carefully researched and transmitted from one generation to another, and human knowledge on its nature built rich entomological discourses on the present-day taxonomical class Insecta. As neighbors of China, where silk production originated, Koreans were familiar with the presence and utility of varieties of the family Bombycidae and used silk in their daily lives. When the modern Korean state promoted sericulture as a form of agricultural development, sericulture and the silk industry underwent rapid transformation geared by the Japanese colonial state and its Agricultural Experiment Station (J. Kangyō Mohanjō; hereafter AES). An ecological niche for the insects was developed in the process of Japanese colonization of Korea, which integrated Korea into the larger territory of imperial Japan between 1910 and 1945.

The readjustment of the ecological niche could not help but be complicated because the Chosŏn dynasty (1392–1897) had treated *Bombyx mori* as an essential player of Confucian statecraft, public ceremonies, and international trade. The modification of tradition became inevitable, encountering modern industrial needs, which demanded new methods and varieties. After the Japanese empire annexed Korea in 1910, *B. mori* variants, such as *Matamukashi, Koishimaru,* and *Aojuku,* which Japanese breeders had engineered, began to migrate to the Korean peninsula.[1] The Korean Silk Production Act (J. Chōsen Sangyōrei) in 1919 made illegal the private breeding of silkworms and placed the insects' population under state control. Subsequently, various *Bombyx* strains and wild silk moths (most likely *Antheraea yamamai*) quickly disappeared from Korean farms as well as public discourse. At present, only small numbers of old "Korean" *B. mori* strains survive in laboratories in South Korea and Japan.[2] Japanese agricultural development realigned human-and-insect relations and re-formed the ecological environment of Korea into an imperial monoculture for silk production.

In the historical shift, however, many factors, which seemingly contra-dict one another—such as Confucian tradition and modern science, colo-nizer and colonized—showed a surprising level of functional correlation. In Chosŏn Korea, *B. mori* embodied a long tradition in which humans, biological information, and public organizations defined their appropri-ate roles with their engagement with the insects.[3] From an early period, *B. mori* became a fictive and actual agent of Confucian moral economy in which "men till and women weave" (K. *namgyŏng yŏjik*). As evident in this oft-quoted phrase, sericulture symbolized two crucial economic ac-tivities that sustained individual livelihood and communal ethical norms in tandem with agriculture.[4] Nonetheless, the heavy weight of tradition did not suffocate a new idea and method of utilizing *B. mori* differently. While the Confucian state employed *B. mori* as an ethical agent, the mod-ern Japanese state protected the insects in state-authorized farms and genetically engineered them for industrial development. So, the modern state rewrote the symbiotic terms between the Confucian state and the worms. As the public research institute of agricultural science, the AES took charge of reconfiguring sericulture in these new terms. These sci-entific experts supported new silkworm classifications and duly divided them into "good" and "bad" variants. Korean reformers and farmers agreed to and executed the plan of replacing the native silkworms with new *B. mori* in a short time and on a massive scale. The history of this silkworm massacre reveals the dynamic amalgamation of human collaboration with and betrayal of insects in the agricultural development of colonial Korea.[5]

KOREAN THREADS AS SUBSTITUTE FOR CHINESE SILK

Grain and silk textiles were two quintessential products of a proper Confucian state. Confucian rulers had a duty to feed their subjects and clothe them. In this regard, agriculture and sericulture farms had enjoyed a special status and value in East Asia, where Confucian rulership constituted a political ideal. The Chosŏn dynasty, which implemented Confucian ideals to an extent unprecedented in Korean history, shared the same concept that a virtuous ruler should manage an economy for food and attire. At the same time, the adoption of idealized Confucian norms posed a particular problem to Korean rulers due to ecological differences between the peninsula and China, where early Confucian texts were produced. Variations in Korean climate and habitat meant that producing silk textiles in the peninsula was not easy. There existed economic burdens and environmental differences between the real and the ideal. Most of all, the Chinese aesthetic standard and high quality of silk production, including dyeing and embroidery, dominated the taste of the Korean *yangban* aristocracy. Sumptuary regulations (*kŭmmun*) prohibited low-ranking officials from wearing Chinese silk textiles (*saranŭngdan*), yet the popularity of Chinese silk was intense enough to cause severe trouble in trade relations with Ming China (1368–1644).[6] Chinese silk entered Chosŏn Korea legally and illegally through various channels, with the mismatch between supply and demand driving up prices for consumers on the peninsula.[7]

The Sino-Korean silk trade was under the careful supervision of the Korean throne. The court-chartered merchants based in the capital (present-day Seoul) monopolized the trade. As one of Six Guilds of Chartered Merchants (Yugŭijŏn), Sŏnjŏn (silk traders; also called Ipchŏn) imported the foreign textiles and supplied them to the royal palaces and other wealthy consumers. Since the silk merchants paid silver to Chinese partners, they maintained close financial transactions with the state. Moreover, their business was sensitive to international silver prices and the Korean reserve of silver. For instance, the Border Defense Council (Pibyŏnsa) found that the silk merchants failed to supply Chinese silk because of the shortage of silver in the country in 1781. The issue drew the attention of the highest level of the state, the king and his councillors. King Chŏngjo (1752–1800) discussed the matter with Prime Minister Sŏ Myŏng-sŏn (1728–1791), hinting that special financial aid would be given to them. The minister, however, argued that such assistance would not be proper.[8] This episode illustrates that the king and close advisers officially monitored the supply of Chinese silk.

When a royal order of emphasizing thrift and banning luxury (*sogŏm kŏch'i*) was issued in 1787, Chinese silk symbolized extravagance that needed to be put under control. A year before, Yi Tong-hyŏng, fourth royal secretary (*chwabusŭngji*), initiated the action against luxury and urged prohibiting the import of Chinese silk.[9] It was five years later that the king and his councillors first noticed the shortage of silver and silk. The king deliberated Yi's views with the Border Defense Council. Yi demanded the complete shutdown of importation, writing, "People in our country do not appreciate what is made in our country, but they admire Chinese goods and demand Chinese silk." As a result, "the price skyrockets and [we] lose silver." For this reason, the council also agreed on imposing limitations on the use of imported Chinese silk, whereas it opposed banning importation. After about three hundred officials presented their own opinions on the issue, the king finally banned trade in embroidered Chinese silk (*yumun*).[10] However, state-mandated thrift was a temporary measure in a time of economic hardship, a futile effort to suppress demand. The Border Defense Council hesitated to prohibit importation because the country could not help but require Chinese silk as long as the expensive taste of Korean nobility persisted. According to the council, the embargo would cause severe trouble in public affairs and private ceremonies since nothing could replace Chinese silk, which was needed for garments.[11]

We can find evidence that the outflow of silver to pay for Chinese goods triggered new thinking and actions in Korean agriculture in the late eighteenth century. In 1787, the king ordered that female attire in noble families should be made from domestic textiles (*hyangjik*).[12] The shortage of silver and silk was no longer a passing phase. The country was experiencing a severe financial setback in the late eighteenth century. The Korea-Japan trade in Tongnae (in present-day Pusan) was shrinking in the mid-eighteenth century, drying up the vital Korean source of silver. This consequently damaged the silver reserve for trading with the Chinese.[13] The order to use domestic textiles coincided with a growing call for a new industrial policy among eighteenth-century Confucian reformists. For example, Pak Che-ga (1750–1815) proposed a plan for fostering international and domestic trade by opening Korean ports. Moreover, he argued that Korean agriculture should adopt advanced technology from abroad and increase productivity.[14] Kang P'il-ri (1713–1767), governor of Tongnae (Tongnae *pusa*), in the same vein imported the vines of sweet potato from Edo Japan (1600–1868) and successfully transplanted them in the country for the first time. Farmers in the south welcomed such experiments and continued cultivation themselves.[15]

In the early nineteenth century, academic interest in domestic agricultural products steadily grew outside of officialdom. Korean silkworms received the first academic attention from Yi Kyu-kyŏng (1788–?). He wrote about Korean sericulture and its techniques in his encyclopedia, *Yi Kyukyŏng's Collection of Individual Essays in Myriad Topics* (Oju yŏnmun changjŏn san'go). According to his survey, Korean silkworm breeders avoided *B. mori*. Only in Hamgyŏng Province, the northeastern borderland, did farmers use it. But, in the other regions, people shared a belief that *B. mori* would bring about a natural disaster.[16] Instead, Korean silk farmers raised their own favorite strains. Yi recorded that people in Hwanghae Province produced silk textiles from giant cocoons after catching wild silk moths, *Antheraea yamamai*. Called *yajam*, *Antheraea yamamai* cost less and was more sustainable for farmers of moderate means because they could feed the insects with many different kinds of leaves. If Yi was referring to *Antheraea yamamai*, the farmers must have woven comparatively rugged textiles from Tussar silk of lesser quality. Varieties of wild silk moths must have existed in Chosŏn Korea, as they did in Qing China (1644–1912) and Edo Japan.[17] Tussar silk, essentially a product of less discriminating foraging rather than of exclusive mulberry cultivation, would have been a cheaper alternative to Chinese silk for many who could not afford to enjoy the luxury item.[18]

In 1876, Japan compelled the Chosŏn dynasty to trade outside of the Sinocentric tribute system. The opening stimulated domestic interest in developing Korean agricultural goods. Koreans saw that Qing China and Meiji Japan (1868–1912) achieved remarkable success by selling silk to the West in the new multilateral trading system. Soon after the opening, King Kojong (1852–1919) struggled to maintain his political leadership when his policies to open Korea encountered severe opposition. However, despite the political unrest, the earliest effort to learn new sericultural technology appeared in 1884, when Qing troops were stationed in the country after suppressing the Imo Mutiny, which occurred two years earlier. The publisher Ch'ŏnghakkwan expressed a hope that Koreans could enrich people and country by learning the Chinese silk techniques. The Korean press published *Essence of Sericulture* (Chamsang ch'waryo) in 1884. Its Korean editor, Yi U-kyu, compiled this work by reprinting a Chinese book of the same title (*Can sang jiyao*), written by Shen Bingcheng (1823–1895) in 1871, and adding some supplementary chapters.[19]

Simultaneously, Meiji Japan also caught Korean attention concerning agricultural renovation. In 1881, a Korean mission to Japan (*Sinsa yuramdan*) gave young Koreans Yu Kil-chun (1856–1914), Yun Ch'i-ho (1865–1945), and An Chong-su (1859–1896) a rare opportunity to explore the outside world. Among them, An visited Tsuda Sen (1837–1908) and learned of his efforts to acquire agricultural science from the West.[20] Returning from Japan, An hurried to write *Agrarian Administration, Newly Compiled* (Nongjŏng sinp'yŏn). It was first published in woodblock in 1881 and later in modern type in 1885.[21]

In the 1890s, the circulation of new information in sericulture triggered real investment beyond the small circle of government officials. We can find a case of private investment in a short memoir of Chi Sŏk-yŏng (1855–1935). Known for his pioneering efforts to introduce the cowpox vaccination technique, he was appointed governor of Tongnae during the Kabo Reform of 1894–96. In this capacity, he met a Japanese sericulture expert completing a tour in Korea. In their meeting, the Japanese expert related that he had met a Korean farmer named Kim Hŭi-myŏng in Hado-myŏn, Kyŏnggi Province, where the capital was located. Kim owned a large orchard of Chinese white mulberry trees (*Morus alba*). Around 1885, he had started farming B. *mori* after retiring from a public post in Seoul. However, soon after he started the new business, he found that all of his neighbors opposed his plan, claiming that the cost of producing silk textiles was normally nine times greater than the profit. In response to this skepticism, Kim considered quitting the silk business. But then he heard that "many countries are getting prosperous and strong (*hŭngwang*) with sericulture." In response, he sought out "those who visited many countries" and made his own inquiries. His first investment was to purchase different varieties of Chinese mulberry trees from abroad and transplant them in his farm.[22]

By 1895, Kim's mulberry orchards had grown large enough to impress the Japanese sericulture expert. The "beautiful mulberry trees" lined up in thousands of *Morus alba* that France, the United States, and Hangzhou in China used for silk production. After his country-wide tour, the expert strongly agreed that Kim had developed the farm in the right direction.

That is, the increase of Chinese mulberry trees would not only boost the productivity of Korean sericulture but also lower the cost. According to the Japanese observer, Korean farmers typically fed their silkworms, which were likely Bombyx variants, with the leaves of mountain mulberry (Morus bombycis Koids/K. San sang) and mulberry thorn (Cudrania tricuspidate/K. Hyŏng sang). Since they used these indigenous wild mulberry trees, it cost less to feed mulberry silkworms than planting Chinese mulberry trees.

However, the popular choice had several setbacks. First, the local farmers competed to collect the leaves before others took them. As a consequence, the time of feeding cocoons tended to be rushed. In addition, malnutrition of the worms was common.[23] Finally, the Japanese advised that Chinese mulberry trees should be propagated on the peninsula to raise productivity. From this, it is evident that beginning in the 1890s both Koreans and Japanese were in accord concerning the future direction of developing Korean sericulture: transforming ecology for a better economy.

The Japanese female Buddhist missionary Okumura Ioko (1845–1907) testified that Morus alba was rare in the peninsula. In 1898, Okumura founded the Kwangju Vocational School in Kwangju, in the southwestern province of Chŏlla. A sister of Okumura Enshin, a Buddhist monk of Shinshū Ōtani-ha, from 1877 on Okumura Ioko engaged herself in Korean affairs to propagate the Buddhist commitments she shared with her brother. In 1897, they chose Kwangju as their mission field. The city had recently suffered severe damage from flooding, and they expected that promoting the local economy and developing agriculture would appeal to Kwangju residents.[24] As part of this strategy, Okumura Ioko attempted to import new B. mori strains from Japan. Ioko's daughter Okumura Mitsuko accompanied her in this mission. Mitsuko had worked at the Tomioka Silk Mill in Gunma Prefecture, where she learned silk reeling.[25] In April 1898, they succeeded in hatching B. mori eggs of the Japanese strain Koishimaru. It did not take long for their plan to stall. The Koishimaru died of starvation because the Okumuras could not find enough food. In response, they decided to test Korean mulberry silkworms, reasoning that they would have more dietary options. In their experiment, it was known that the Korean Bombyx variants entered the pupal phase after only three moltings while the Koishimaru did so after four moltings. Additionally, these moltings consumed only thirty-one days, whereas the Japanese silkworm took thirty-four days. Okumura Ioko determined that the silk threads from the Korean Bombyx strains were satisfactory in strength and flexibility, but she did not give up her plan of importing the Japanese variety to the peninsula. She planned to transplant one thousand *Morus alba* (known by the names Ichihara, Yōkaichi, and Nezumigaeshi in Japan) to Korea.[26]

Korean efforts to develop sericulture also intensified in the first decade of the twentieth century. In December 1900, the minister of agriculture, commerce, and industry, Kwŏn Chae-hyŏng (1854–1934), submitted a plan to open a new Bureau of Sericulture (Chamŏpkwa).[27] He vehemently claimed that silk production would benefit "a national mission" and "private business" altogether. In particular, the ministry wanted to monitor silkworms' varieties and conduct new testing and education for farmers.[28] The opening of the Bureau of Sericulture in 1900 marked the beginning of a new industrial policy by which the dynasty attempted to end the old dependence on Chinese silk. The so-called "artificial sericulture" (*in'gong yangjam*) became a new subject of recruiting government officials, and many textbooks on sericulture were published in the first decade of the twentieth century.[29] Coinciding with the new policy, a group of aristocrats and sericulturists established a private corporation, Korean Silk Corporation (Tae-Han Cheguk In'gong Yangjam Hapcha Hoesa), in early 1900.[30] The company established a new orchard of Chinese mulberry trees at Yŏngdŭngp'o after purchasing about ten thousand trees from Kim Hŭi-myŏng at Hado-myŏn. The construction of mulberry orchards shows that Koreans wanted to enhance the habitat of *B. mori* for better productivity. As the new public and private ventures got launched, the Korean monarch again posed himself as the sponsor of silk production and *B. mori*, supporting the foundation of a new school of sericulture in Seoul in 1900.[31]

In this manner, Korean sericulture was gradually changing its status from a minor supplement of the Sinophile state to a major industry of the modern nation-state. The efforts to develop Korean silk appeared from the mid-eighteenth century, when the heavy dependence on Chinese goods grew burdensome financially. Korean *Bombyx* variants and *Antheraea yamamai* played a significant role in the domestic production of a substitute, *hyangjik*, for Chinese silk. However, the opening of Korea ended the short boom of raising Korean *Bombyx* strains and wild silk moths for domestic use. Korean reformist elites and investors attempted to learn Chinese and Japanese sericulture and to transform their ecology to accommodate *B. mori*. Still, Korean local strains maintained their population in Korean farms, as they adapted better to the local environment, especially Korean forestry, than foreign *B. mori* strains. The natural scarcity of Chinese mulberry trees made it difficult and risky to raise B. mori. For this reason, the primary agenda of developing Korean sericulture was to expand the silviculture of Morus alba in Korea. That is, Korean habitat was converted to Chinese or Japanese habitat to accommodate silkworm biology. In contrast, the foraging behavior that distinguished Korean Bombyx variants from other East Asian B. mori types had become a relatively a minor issue. The primary goal of new sericulture, which was concerned not with subsistence but with profit, was to feed all available Bombyx variants by providing them with the ideal habitat, modeled on places like Hangzhou.

SELECTIVE BREEDING OF BOMBYX MORI
IN COLONIAL KOREA

The outbreak of the Russo-Japanese War in 1904–5 suddenly changed the course of development. In 1905, Meiji Japan forced Korea to accept the Japan-Korea Treaty of 1905, by which it became a protectorate of the Japanese empire. Korean sericulture and agriculture became the first place where the imperial leadership intervened immediately. Koreans had pursued the same goal and showed little disagreement on the Japanese-style development itself. Kwŏn Chae-hyŏng, who then changed his name to Kwŏn Chung-hyŏn, was a vocal supporter of promoting Korean sericulture at the top level of the government. He warmly welcomed Itō Hirobumi (1841–1909), the architect of the protectorate and the first resident-general of Korea, and continued to collaborate with the new imperial hegemon. In September 1905, he again became the minister of agriculture, commerce, and industry and approved the signing of the Japan-Korea Treaty as a member of the cabinet.[32]

So, the Japanese empire, to some extent, hijacked Korean agricultural development and reframed it as a colonial mission. The imperial use of science made a remarkable difference between before and after 1910. In particular, modern biology became an ideological and practical tool for building a colonial hierarchy: colonizers and the colonized. Also, both Koreans and the peninsula ecosystem were not much distinguished in the colonizer's perspective, for both were the objects of scientific colonization.[33] In agriculture, the central apparatus of imperial science was the AES. From the beginning, AES researchers were investigating Korean sericulture as their major research field. The AES was founded in 1906 as a joint venture of Korea and Japan, and the Japanese government granted funds by which it employed twenty full-time Japanese staff. Because the Korean government was planning to open its own AES, Itō Hirobumi claimed that building the two separate facilities of the same mission would be a waste. For this reason, the Korean government decided to donate the vast land of Suwŏn to the future AES on the condition that Japan would later transfer the facility to the Korean government.

Suwŏn, a castle town designed in the late eighteenth century, was surrounded by extensive arable lands. Many grounds belonged to the Yi royal family and its close relatives. The AES started with the fifty-nine hectares of rice paddies (about 67 percent of the AES lands) that it received from the Yi royal family.[34] In 1907, the School of Agriculture (Nongnim Hakkyo) also moved near the AES in Suwŏn. And in 1918, it developed into the College of Agriculture (Nongnim Chŏnmun Hakkyo).[35] As a new hub of agricultural science research and education, the AES continued to hire Japanese staff until the Japanese annexation of Korea, at which time the facility returned to Japan's possession.[36]

The AES empowered Japanese experts to establish themselves as the authority on *Bombyx* strains in Korea. While Koreans rapidly lost their previous role as a mediator of connecting the country to new knowledge, the Japanese at the AES determined the direction of Korean sericulture. Miyahara Tadamasa (b. 1867), for instance, first came to Korea in 1906 after working as a sericulture expert in Yamanashi Prefecture. He graduated from the College of Agriculture at Tokyo Imperial University and built his career as an expert in modern sericulture.[37] In 1903 and 1904, Miyahara published two books on sericulture and accepted the position of the head of the Yongsan branch of the AES.[38] In 1913, he moved to the main campus of the AES in Suwŏn when the *B. mori* Breeding Lab (J. Gensanshu Seizōsho) was relocated to Suwŏn.[39] Then, he was promoted to the head of the lab in that year and received another appointment to the chair of the Sericulture Experiment Lab (J. Sangyō Shikensho) in 1917.[40]

The establishment of the AES caused a dramatic change in the ecology of Korean silkworms. Japanese *B. mori* strains constructed by artificial breeding began to migrate from the archipelago to the peninsula under the thorough care of the AES. Why did the AES decide to replace the local *Bombyx* strains with modern *B. mori*? The AES researched *B. mori* varieties and their characteristics in order to determine the best strain for industrial use. In the late 1900s and 1910s, the AES conducted various experiments to compare the Korean *Bombyx* strains with the Japanese strains. In 1907, the Yongsan branch imported *Matamukashi* from a Japanese breeder, Iwata Tarō, in Ibaraki Prefecture. It tested the Japanese *B. mori* variants' adaptability to Korean ecosystems and worked to discover any difference between the Korean and the Japanese varieties. In the same year, the AES in Suwŏn also brought another variety of *Koishimaru* from the Tokyo Sericulture School. In 1911, the AES again purchased *Matamukashi* from Aichi Prefecture.[41] The Yongsan branch continued the same project in 1912 and 1913, when it imported *Hakuryū* from three breeders in Nagasaki Prefecture and *Aojuku* from the Tokyo Sericulture School.[42]

The consistent efforts of settling Japanese *B. mori* in Korea were based on new classification systems of silkworms. As seen above, Korean and Japanese developers before 1900 did not seriously consider the biological differences between Korean and Japanese *Bombyx* strains. The reconceptualization of *B. mori* as one genetic lineage took place in Meiji Japan, especially by scientists led by Toyama Kametaro (1867–1918).[43] After the Russo-Japanese War, Toyama began to explain the law of inheritance to the public. He claimed that breeders could select and promote positive characteristics of the worm artificially. Mendelian genetics profoundly transformed the Japanese biology of "the silkworm."[44] The essence of Toyama's plan was to redefine the industrial silkworm by selective breeding. And his idea of standardizing Japanese silkworms became the backbone of the new sericulture policy in 1910s Japan. Silkworm Breeding Farms opened in 1911, and these state-authorized facilities obtained an exclusive right to choose which *B. mori* strains could mate and spread their genetic characteristics in the next generation.[45]

Thus, the Japanese colonization of Korea happened at the exact moment when the modern state artificially reconstructed *B. mori*. In colonial Korea, the state pushed the same policy unilaterally and ignored preexisting folk practices, know-how, and local silkworms as the sign of colonial "backwardness." In a public speech in 1912, Terauchi Masatake (1852–1919), the first governor-general, presented science as a self-evident tool of the new colonial regime. He described the condition of Korean sericulture in a condescending tone, saying, "In Korea, sericulture still remains premature." He seemed not to know about Korean efforts to follow the Japanese model during the previous decades, imagining colonial Korea as a tabula rasa, where the empire should develop it *ab ovo*. He claimed that Korean soil and climate were suitable for silk production, but Korean sericulture needed "proper improvement methods" (J. *kairyō*). He argued that the

improvement was an exclusive right and duty of the Japanese colonial
state. It does not at all surprise us that he included Korean *Bombyx* strains
and *Antheraea yamamai* in the colonial evaluation of the "bad" (J. *furyō*).
It seemed to him that the Japanese civilizing mission should standardize
the silkworm population in Korea by replacing "bad" worms with "good,"
productive, imported worms. In the announcement, Terauchi directly
ordered importation of *Matamukashi, Koishimaru, Aojuku, Araya,* and
Hakuryū from Japan.[46]

In 1912, there already appeared a sign that the population of the native
worms was decreasing. When the colonial authority identified them as the
"bad," Korean farmers responded to the order positively. According to a
report in *Maeil Sinbo*, the number of "native" (*chaerae*) silkworms dropped
quickly. Korean farmers accepted the claim of the "badness" and partook
in replacing the "bad" worms with the "good." Also, the overall production
of silkworm eggs did not go smoothly in the year, so the paper expected
Koreans to purchase more eggs from Japan in the next year.[47] This means
that Korean farmers had a new option and considered buying more productive strains from Japan rather than simply depending on Korean breeders. The AES also conducted various scientific experiments to support the
claim. It tested the industrial efficacy of Korean *Bombyx* strains from 1912
under Miyahara Tadamasa. Two staff members—Nagaoka Tetsuzō and
Im Han-ryong—joined the research project. The test result of verifying
the claim was released in the sixth Annual Report of the AES in 1912.[48] It
concluded that Korean local strains could not be industrialized as effectively as Japanese *B. mori* were. As Korean silk was no longer a substitute
for Chinese silk in the domestic market, the farmers and researchers both
prioritized developing a quality that would be suitable for industrial use.

It is an open question for now whether there existed distinctive *B. mori*
variants in the peninsula. I have no evidence to determine if Koreans in
the Chosŏn period had constructed their own artificial strains, which we
may call "Korean" *B. mori*. At least, it seems that some AES experts in the
1910s were confident that the "Korean" *B. mori* was a valid member of the
genus *Bombyx*. In a series of experiments, Nagaoka discovered that Korean
strains had a unique feature of three moltings (J. *sanmin*).[49] According to
his report published in 1914, he collected the Korean worms from seven
different locations: Sangju-ŭp, Pian-ŭp in North Kyŏngsang Province,
Kŏch'ang-ŭp, An'ŭi-ŭp in South Kyŏngsang Province, Imsil-ŭp in North
Chŏlla Province, Ch'ŏlwŏn-ŭp in Kangwŏn Province, and Sŏngch'ŏn-ŭp

in South P'yŏngan Province. As a result, 11,342 eggs of *Bombyx* strains were gathered at his lab from these places.[50]

First, he measured the percent of successful hatching. Eighty percent of the eggs were hatched in the seven groups except for Sangju and An'ŭi (38.1 percent and 36.8 percent respectively). Given the result, he jumped to the conclusion that "we should admit that Korean silkworms generally show a low chance of hatching." Second, he noted that Korean *Bombyx* strains spent more days than Japanese *B. mori* before entering the larva stage in the same condition. The Sangju samples took twenty-one days, and the Pian only ten days. The An'ŭi group required the most days, with twenty-three. If his sampling adequately represented the condition of Korean *Bombyx* strains, those from North Kyŏngsang and North Chŏlla Provinces ironically proved the excellent quality of their health and growth (Pian: 95.8 percent of hatching and seven days; Imsil: 98.4 percent and ten days). Curiously, however, Nagaoka concluded that "it becomes clear that Korean silkworms have no commercial value."[51] Nagaoka decided that the appearance of Korean *Bombyx* mutants was a result of careless breeding practices and that the colonial authority should stop them. Korean breeders, he argued, did not know how to classify the worms and instead allowed their inbreeding repeatedly. In such a condition of state noninterference, there was no chance of improvement.[52]

Indeed, the autonomy that independent breeders and their local *Bombyx* strains had enjoyed came to an end soon. State-monitored standardization and quality control started, and the environmental accommodation for the critical biota (Chinese mulberry trees and modern *B. mori*) was established. In 1919, the colonial state announced new legislation banning private breeding. On April 24, 1919, the Korean Silk Production Act introduced a licensing system in sericulture. Korean farmers must receive an official license from a provincial governor to raise *B. mori*.

More importantly, the farmers were required to use only the eggs of standard *B. mori* distributed by public agents. In other words, no one could produce silkworm eggs for private sale. The colonial authorities monopolized the power to verify which varieties of *B. mori* could live as the proper insect partner of the state and its industry.[53] The eggs of *B. mori* were kept solely in the AES, provincial breeding centers, and sericulture schools. If anyone wanted to import silkworm eggs from abroad, they required the approval of the governor-general. Even if the governor-general approved the import, the eggs and larvae had to pass a medical inspection. Article no. 14 of the Korean Silk Production Act clearly stated, "If necessary, the governor-general of Korea can limit the kinds of B. mori for silk production, egg production, or trade."[54] The preexisting Korean strains systematically got screened out from industrial reproduction. Korean farmers thus had little reason to preserve the "bad" Bombyx strains and their eggs.

Korean sericulture developed dramatically in the first and second decades of colonial rule, along with the state's heavy policing and quality control. On the one hand, the colonial state harshly punished any violators who raised "bad" silkworms.[55] On the other hand, the state built a country-wide supply channel of standard B. mori eggs, making sericulture more accessible to Korean farmers. As historian Holly Stephens notes, Korean farmers actively answered the industrial policy and started sericulture with more information and eggs in the 1910s. The cooperation between Korean silkworm farmers and the colonial authority appeared at various social levels because they agreed to boost silk production.[56] Between 1910 and 1923, Korean silk production multiplied by fifteen times. Later in 1932, it reached six hundred thousand koku (about 108 million liters). It was a surprising increase in comparison to thirteen thousand koku (about 2.34 million liters) in 1910. In the meantime, the old methods of sericulture disappeared. For instance, only 161 households produced Tussar silk in 1929, and three years later, none raised Antheraea yamamai anymore.[57]

Where did Korean Bombyx strains and Antheraea yamamai go? The wild moth can survive without human care, but B. mori has little chance to sustain itself alone. From what we can see in the 1910s AES documents, Korean Bombyx strains were once dominant varieties at major production sites. At present, however, only a few of them have been preserved at laboratories. In 2000, two Korean researchers, Si-Kab Nho and Jae Man Lee, confirmed ten kinds of B. mori that have distinctive genetic identities in South Korea and Japan. They are called k30, k18, k301, k303, k304, k120, and ki20 in South Korea. In Japan, j300, j301, and j304 are categorized by Korean origin. "There are meager numbers of them conserved, and conservation efforts are found at merely a few places," the two researchers say.[58] They also claim that what they call Korean "native" B. mori has distinctive genetic characteristics. Furthermore, it is interesting that these two scientists cannot find any other scientific reports on the worms other than the papers published by the AES in the 1900s and '10s. For almost one hundred years, the presence of the Korean *Bombyx* strains has remained in oblivion not only among ordinary people but also among researchers.

Given many other examples of animal extinction in modern Korea, the worms are possibly fortunate to find shelters at labs. Although South Korea attaches a high cultural and symbolic value to the tiger, Koreans warmly welcomed the campaigns for hunting tigers in the colonial period.[59] In a similar vein, Korean farmers were willing to improve agricultural productivity instead of preserving tradition if new crops and modern varieties became available. As a result, many of the so-called native strains were marginalized and forgotten in fields. In the case of rice varieties, the Korean natural landscape dramatically changed with the systematic introduction of modern *Japonica* rice in the 1930s. Korean native rice strains reached about 200 varieties (including *Indica* rice), and modern *Japonica* rice has 117 varieties. Although modern rice has high yields, scientists are rediscovering the value of indigenous rice varieties for genetic diversity.[60] Seen in this light, the breakup of Koreans and "Korean" *Bombyx* strains may not be an extraordinary story. However, it is tragic that the humans unilaterally broke the trust with their old insect partner. The story of the Korean silkworms also echoes similar cases of human enthusiasm for economic growth and selection of monocrop farming, which ultimately threatens the ecological niches of other species.

To sum up, Japanese *B. mori* strains such as *Matamukashi*, *Koishimaru*, *Aojuku*, and their hybrids began to colonize Korea in the 1910s. They arrived at the peninsula as what Alfred Crosby, writing on European introductions to the Americas, termed "portmanteau biota."[61] Their migration from Japan to Korea would not have been possible without the Japanese empire and its industrial-strength intervention in the lifecycle of insects. Japanese *B. mori* was an essential agent for constructing imperial dominance and was handsomely rewarded with new habitat and offspring. Equally important is that Korean farmers themselves had no objection to the migration of Japanese silkworms. When the colonial state ordered them to abandon their old partner, they quickly accepted the new partner for industrial productivity and wealth. As *B. mori* and other silk-producing organisms no longer had a symbolic value in the Confucian regime, farmers made a rational choice in modern economic terms when they switched silkworms. They also had incentive to do so because the colonial state had already validated modern *B. mori* as its partner.

CONCLUSION

The ecological niche of silkworms began to transform when the modern state policed their reproduction and required specific genetic characteristics. It was an artificial selection of the industrially fittest that the state enforced. B. mori had enjoyed human custody in its long history of interaction and dependence on humankind. The Confucian state in East Asia had established a prototype of functional correlation between humans and B. mori. This symbiosis remained intact even in the modern age. Still, it is striking that the new definition of "virtuous" insects forcefully narrowed the genetic diversity of B. mori into only a few strains that satisfied industrial needs. As a result, the most industrially productive varieties chosen by the state became dominant and expanded their habitats to new foreign lands at the hands of empire builders. This territorial expansion of imperial B. mori occurred from Meiji Japan to Chosŏn Korea between the 1880s and the 1920s, causing a precipitous decline of traditional Bombyx strains. This "silkworm massacre"—an intentional disposal of indigenous varieties—unveils a dark shadow of modern agricultural development in East Asia and an intriguing alliance between the modern empire and modern insects.

Local varieties of silkworms in the peninsula flourished in the eighteenth and nineteenth centuries. Although the king and queen of Chosŏn publicly positioned themselves as guardians of Korean sericulture, the Confucian state did not actively develop domestic silk production. The Yi royal house had intransigently maintained a cultural preference for high-quality silk imported from Ming-Qing China. When the Korean regime found it increasingly difficult and expensive to buy Chinese silk, the court urged thrift and less dependence on foreign textiles. "Local fabrics" gradually increased in value and became a substitute for imported goods. A broad spectrum of biological varieties existed in the silk-producing organisms as the habitats of B. mori were scarce in the peninsula. B. mori never became dominant in Chosŏn because Korean farmers were reluctant to raise them for various reasons: high cost and low return, the lack of Chinese mulberry trees, and folk taboos. So, the premodern correlation between indigenous humans and insects enjoyed comparative autonomy from the Confucian state. It safely preserved a free space for local silkworm variants to survive, depending on the independent choices of breeders.

The silk-producing organisms were for preindustrial subsistence and cultural values.

The opening of Korean ports and the news of Japanese commercial success in the silk business evoked criticism and suspicion of old practices. Initially, Chinese books and techniques drew the attention of Korean reformers in the 1880s, and in the following decades, Japanese knowledge and skills were translated and circulated. Developing Korean sericulture became a primary interest of reformers such as An Chong-su and Chi Sŏk-yŏng. Japanese Buddhist missionaries, including Okumura Ioko, also attempted to introduce Japanese *B. mori* and new techniques in Kwangju. In the early stage of agricultural development by both Koreans and Japanese migrants, the lower-maintenance endemic varieties remained integral to their plans. They agreed that *B. mori* from Japan would starve to death in Korea because there were insufficient mulberry trees to feed the hungry caterpillars. The Korean *Bombyx* strains, which had become less standardized without artificial breeding, had a decisive advantage in the survival race, for they had adjusted to the Korean agroforestry ecosystem. At the same time, a development-oriented mentality drove modernizers of private and public sectors to abandon the preexisting equilibrium; modern humans had a right to change the ecosystem to better the national economy.

The Japanese colonial empire thus was congenial to Korean sericulturists who wished to utilize insects for building a modern economy. Although this development plan was not something new to Korean elites, it made the colonial state distinct in its mobilization of science and scientists outside Korea. The colonial regime imposed on the Korean ecosystem a dichotomy of "good" and "bad" insects. Following the opinions of the AES, the empire selected certain varieties and permitted only those strains to propagate in Japan and its colony. All of a sudden, the others lost their right to live. In colonial Korea, imperial control over insects' mating and population commenced with the Korean Silk Production Act. The migration of Japanese *B. mori* varieties to Korea proceeded quickly and systematically without facing any Korean resistance. Soon, the local *Bombyx* strains completely disappeared in farms and scientific discourses after a few research papers identified them as "bad" ones. Tussar silk made from *Antheraea yamamai* followed the same fate, as Japanese *B. mori* became a dominant variety in Korea. How could the old alliance between Koreans and their local varieties break apart so quickly and without hesitation? A possible answer is that agricultural development forged an apolitical alliance between Koreans and the Japanese empire. It was apolitical because none would oppose utilizing the insects for humans' common economic interests. From the perspective of the Korean *Bombyx* strains, nonetheless, it was bitter betrayal and cruel massacre after all their mutual dependencies.

Insect-focused history illustrates the need for understanding Korean agricultural development beyond human affairs. It is striking that the age-old union between the silk-producing worms and Koreans was never entirely secure or stable, even under the Confucian regime. The emergence of the modern state forcefully rewrote it in different terms. Conserving local varieties never received support or attention in colonial Korea, even though Korean farmers became increasingly dependent on the colonial empire and empire-authorized egg suppliers. Thus, colonial reliance on the imperial metropole proceeded with the functional alliance between Korean farmers and the empire. The new functional correlation does not imply political consent to Japanese colonial rule. Instead, the modes of engaging insects were based on state prerogatives in the premodern and modern eras. In this regard, the empire of Japanese *B. mori* successfully and relentlessly altered the old ecosystem in Korea. Who, except Shakespeare, would shed a tear for poor insects?

> The poor beetle, that we tread upon,
> In corporal sufferance finds a pang as great
> As when a giant dies. (*Measure for Measure*, 1604)

NOTES

1. It is difficult to identify "Korean silkworms" with one species, *Bombyx mori* (domesticated mulberry-eating silkworm), because there are great genetic variations of silkworms in the families Bombycidae and Saturniidae (non-mulberry eating). Before the colonial regime standardized *B. mori* in sericulture, it is possible that the Korean peninsula had many different kinds of the silk-producing worms, such as *B. mandarina*, *Antheraea yamamai*, and *B. mori*. See Arunkumar, Metta, and Nagaraju, "Molecular Phylogeny of Silkmoths."

2. Nho and Lee, "Hyŏnjon hanŭn Han'guk chaeraejong," 10–11; Nho and Lee, "Tongwi hyoso mit RAPD."

3. In many countries and cultures, silk has generated special meanings especially from the unusual sense of touching soft and smooth fabrics. See LeCain, *The Matter of History*, chap. 5.

4. In Confucian gender ideology, women were expected to produce textiles, the use and exchange of which forged and secured proper social relations. During the Chosŏn period, the court initiated a top-down implementation of the idealized gender relations described in the Confucian canon. Although the Confucian ethics spread in the society slowly and steadily over centuries, the Yi royal family and *yangban* aristocrats accepted the gender ethics and division of labor as their own ideal faster than any others; see Bray, *Technology and Gender*, 186–87. Regarding changes in notions of silkworms in the late Chosŏn period, see Ro, "Shifting Perceptions of Insects." On the emergence of new scientific discourses on Korean fauna and flora, see Ro, *Neo-Confucianism*. For Chosŏn policies on sericulture in the seventeenth and eighteenth centuries, see Nam, "18-segi Yŏngjodae yangjam" and "17-segi yangjam chŏngch'aek."

5. Regarding the Japanese colonial development of Korean agriculture, see Stephens, "Agriculture and Development in an Age of Empire"; T. Kim, *Kŭnhyŏndae Han'guk ssal ŭi sahoesa*; Yi Yŏng-hak, "1920-nyŏndae Chosŏn chongdokbu"; Oh, "Tae-Han chegukki in'gong yangjam."

6. Regulations on clothing can be found as early as the late fifteenth century. In 1472, the court ordered punishment for commoners and merchants who wore embroidered Chinese silk dresses. In 1493, it announced that smuggling Chinese silk would meet severe punishment; see Pak and Ko, "Chosŏn wangjo sillok e kiroktoen," 749.

7. Ku To-yŏng, "16-segi Chosŏn tae-Myŏng sahaeng muyŏk," 744, 748–49.

8. *Pibyŏnsa tŭngnok*, entry for Chŏngjo 5/3/21. The silk merchants also sold Chinese silk to other service branches (Kungbang) of palaces and ministers. However, some powerful *yangban* clans purchased silk from them at a low price or on account. For example, in 1781, it was reported to the king that a man named Song Nak-kyu had an unpaid bill of 820 *nyang*. *Pipyŏnsa tŭngnok*, entry for Chŏngjo 5/11/12. On the Six Guilds and their relations with the government, see Miller, "The Myŏnjujŏn," 188, 192–197.

9. *Chŏngjo sillok*, entry for Chŏngjo 10/1/22.

10. *Pibyŏnsa tŭngnok*, entry for Chŏngjo 10/2/06. In *Chŏngjo sillok*, we can see only the opinion of the Border Defense Council. Yi's argument is recorded in more detail in *Pibyŏnsa tŭngnok*.

11. *Pibyŏnsa tŭngnok*, entry for Chŏngjo 10/2/06.

12. *Pibyŏnsa tŭngnok*, entry Chŏngjo 11/10/5.

13. C. Kim, "Chosŏn hugi tae-Ch'ŏng muyŏk," 5.

14. Sin, "Pak Che-ga," 318.

15. Ro, *Neo-Confucianism*, 59–60.

16. Ro, "Shifting Perceptions of Insects," 60–61.

17. Ro, "Shifting Perceptions of Insects," 59–60. There was another variant of the Saturniidae, *Antheraea pernyi* (common name Chinese oak silk moth).

18. Additional research is necessary before concluding that *hyangjik* meant Tussar silk. The counterpart of *hyangjik* was Tangjik (Chinese textiles). So, the term *hyangjik* could include many local textiles including Tussar silk. For instance, King Yŏngjo mentioned that *hyangjik* was coarse and less sophisticated than Tangjik. *Sŭngjŏngwŏn ilgi*, Yŏngjo 7/4/19.

19. The Korean book, *Chamsang ch'waryo*, has thirty-one chapters in total, twenty-one of which were copied from Shen's *Can sang jiyao*, with minor editing. The illustrations are identical with those in Shen's work. It seems that the Korean editor, Yi U-kyu, added ten extra chapters for the purpose of helping Korean readers understand Shen's book.

20. As a member of the Japanese diplomatic mission, young Tsuda Sen traveled to the United States in 1867 and developed his interest in modern agriculture. After the Meiji Restoration, he tested planting new crop and vegetable species in Tokyo. In 1873, he visited Europe and learned from a Dutch agriculturist, Daniel Hooibrenk, then published a book, *Nōgyō sanji* (Three topics in agriculture, 1874). Uchida, "Kaikaki ni okeru Nippon," 99.

21. Yi Sŏn-a, "19-segi kaehwap'a ŭi nongsŏ," 62–64. In the book, An introduced plant anatomy and explained the six basic parts of plants: the root, the stem, the bark, the leaf, flowers, and seeds. An, *Nongjŏng sinp'yŏn 3-kwŏn*.

22. Chi, "Sangjam mundap," 6.

23. Chi, "Sangjam mundap," 6.

24. They confidentially received financial support from the Ministry of Foreign Affairs in Japan. Okumura Enshin believed that Koreans would be more interested in practical affairs than "the current international situation of the Orient." Yamamo'to, "Tae-Han chegukki Kwangju," 224–26, 232.

25. Yamamo'to, "Tae-Han chegukki Kwangju," 234.

26. "Sanshi hōkokusho." Ichihara was used in the Jōbu area (present-day Saitama and Gunma Prefecture). It sprouted early, and the large leaves were a rich source of nutrients to silkworms. Yōkaichi sprouted late, and its leaves were thick and oily. This mulberry strain was also preferred in the Jōbu area. See Shimamura, *Tsūzoku yōsan hihō*, 11–12. In the Edo period, Japanese sericulturists had paid the most attention to temperature control and the living conditions of the worm, including their food. Empirical information on how to care for and harvest mulberry leaves was a major part in the Japanese sericulture texts of the Edo period. The accumulation of empirical knowledge was shared among silkworm farmers in wood-block publications. The circulation of empirical know-how continued in the Meiji period, while a new generation of experts in Tokyo gradually achieved hegemony in the scientific discourse. Tuchikane, "Meiji ki no Nihon yōsangyō," 42, 44–45.

27. Kwŏn changed his personal name to Chung-hyŏn later in 1903. In the late nineteenth century, he was one of the reformist officials who supported the opening of the country. After visiting Japan in 1888, he had worked in Tokyo as the Korean ambassador from 1891 to 1893. When the Russo-Japanese War broke out, he became a vocal supporter of the Japanese military and its presence in Korea. In 1910, when the Japanese empire annexed Korea, he received a title of viscount from the empire. See "Kwŏn Chung-hyŏn."

28. Kwŏn, "Nongsanggongbu chamŏpkwa sŏlch'i rŭl ch'ŏngham."

29. For example, Yokota Katsuzō's *Jinkō yōsan kagami: Ichimei Yokota yōsanki no Shiori* (1898) was translated into Korean in 1900 and 1901. For further discussion, see Oh, "Tae-Han chegukki in'gong yangjam," 153–54.

30. In 1899, seven Koreans completed a program at the Japanese School of Artificial Sericulture. They became leading experts of developing Korean sericulture in the first decade. Oh, "Tae-Han chegukki in'gong yangjam," 126–31.

31. Oh, "Tae-Han chegukki in'gong yangjam," 131–32.

32. Sŏ, "Kwŏn Chung-hyŏn, Yi Chi-yong," 57–58. Andre Schmid also found the self-deprecating nature of the civilizing mission, which accorded with Japanese colonial ideology. Schmid, *Korea between Empires*, 102.

33. The Meiji government consistently propagated its scientific advancement as a proof of Japanese superiority in Korea. As early as in 1877, the Japanese navy dispatched the physician Yano Yoshitetsu to open a modern clinic, Saisei Giin, in Tongnae. In 1883, the Japanese army took the facility over from the navy. When Japanese diplomats demanded the opening of the Japanese medical clinic in Tongnae, they claimed that Western medicine would impress Koreans and make them be more dependent on and respectful toward Japan. See Hasegawa, "Chosŏn hugi Han-Il ŭi hakkyo ryusa," 103–4, 115–16.

34. King Chŏngjo gave fertile fields in the west of Suwŏn to the house of Lady Yi, his paternal grandmother. Hasegawa, "Chosŏn hugi Han-Il ŭi hakkyo ryusa," 17.

35. One of the alumni from the school was Chang Myŏn (1899–1966), who became the prime minister of the short-lived Second Republic of Korea. In 1947, the former colonial College of Agriculture joined new Seoul National University when the US Army Military Government in Korea established the university. See Ku Cha-ok, "Sŏdunbŏl ŭi kŭndae nonghak kyoyuk," 99, 108.

36. Kim Yŏng-jin and Kim Sang-kyŏng, "Han'guk nongsa sihŏm yŏn'gu," 25.

37. "Miyahara Tadamasa," 508.

38. Chōsen Sōtokufu Kangyō Mohanjō Sangyō Shikenjō, *Sangyō shikenjō jyūnenbo*, 13.

39. Chōsen Sōtokufu Kangyō Mohanjō Sangyō Shikenjō, *Sangyō shikenjō jyūnenbo*, 1.

40. Chōsen Sōtokufu Kangyō Mohanjō Sangyō Shikenjō, *Sangyō shikenjō jyūnenbo*, 13.

41. In 1912, Kigami Tsunezō wrote a short report on the history of the AES proj-

ects to import the Japanese silkworm varieties. Chōsen Sōtokufu Kangyō Mohanjō Sangyō Shikenjō, *Sangyō shikenjō jyūnenbo*, 55.

42. Nagaoka Tetsuzō in Suwŏn and Kigami Tsunezō at Yongsan wrote an annual report together. Chōsen Sōtokufu Kangyō Mohanjō Sangyō Shikenjō, *Sangyō shikenjō jyūnenbo*, 58–60.

43. Onaga, "Silkworms, Science, and Nation," 174–75. In Meiji Japan, the public monitoring of silkworms started in 1898 with the promulgation of the Act of Inspecting Silkworms (J. Sansho Kensahō). In the following decade, the state inspection focused on the prevention of an epidemic among the worms. However, the state did not interfere with the genetic inheritance of the worms, at least according to the Act of Preventing Silkworm Diseases (J. Sanbyō Yōbōhō) of 1905. Tomizawa and Esaki, "Sanshu kensahō shikōki," 54.

44. Onaga, "Silkworms, Science, and Nation," 180–82.

45. Onaga, "Silkworms, Science, and Nation," 208.

46. Terauchi, "Chōsen sōtokufu kunrei dai-11-go," 106.

47. "Chaerae chamjong tun'gam," *Maeil Sinbo*, September 16, 1912.

48. Miyahara, Nagaoka, and Im, "Chōsen zairai sanshu shīku seiseki," 212.

49. Nagaoka, "Chōsen zairai sansho," 2.

50. Nagaoka, "Chōsen zairai sansho," 3. The breakdown by county is 1,489 (Sangju), 480 (Pian), 1,937 (Kŏch'ang), 1,462 (An'ŭi), 631 (Imsil), 2,698 (Ch'ŏlwŏn), and 2,645 (Sŏngch'ŏn). For these figures, we can assume that these places in Kyŏngsang, P'yŏngan, Kangwŏn, and Chŏlla Provinces were the major centers of sericulture until the 1910s.

51. Nagaoka, "Chōsen zairai sansho," 6.

52. Nagaoka, "Chōsen zairai sansho," 2.

53. Farmers could raise "other kinds," but they were not allowed to sell the eggs. The production of Tussar silk legally from wild silkworms continued in the 1920s.

54. "Seirei no. 10 Chōsen sangyōrei," *Chōsen Sōtokufu Kanpo*, no. 2010 (April 24, 1919), 345.

55. "Seirei no. 10 Chōsen sangyōrei," *Chōsen Sōtokufu Kanpo* no. 2010 (April 24, 1919), 346.

56. Stephens, "Agriculture and Development," 223–26.

57. Yi Yŏng-hak, "1920-nyŏndae Chosŏn chongdokbu," 21.

58. Nho and Lee, "Hyŏnjon hanŭn Han'guk chaeraejong," 10–11; Nho and Lee, "Tongwi hyoso mit RAPD."

59. Seeley and Skabelund, "Tigers—Real and Imagined."

60. Kwon et al., "Urinara chaeraebyŏ," 189–91.

61. Crosby, *Ecological Imperialism*, 270–71.

SIX

"Lives without Mosquitoes and Flies"

ERADICATION CAMPAIGNS

IN POSTWAR JAPAN

Kerry Smith

Movie audiences never actually get to see the stinking, mosquito-infested sewage pond that sets the plot of Akira Kurosawa's classic 1952 film *Ikiru* (To live) in motion. As the film begins, a group of women have arrived at the Public Affairs Department to ask for the city's help dealing with the pond. "My child has sensitive skin, and that water has given him an awful rash," says one. "Plus it breeds mosquitoes like crazy. And it stinks, besides," says another. "Can't you do something? It would make a great playground if you filled it in."[1] The women's bureaucratic odyssey is just beginning, and Kurosawa's portrayal of officialdom's near absolute indifference to their plight is as brilliant as it is concise. In the end it is only long after Watanabe, the mortally ill department chief and the film's protagonist, has taken on the women's cause as his own that we see where the odiferous pond once was and the new playground that has replaced it.

Kurosawa's film is a good place to open an investigation into Japanese efforts in the 1950s to eradicate mosquitoes and flies, in part because it helps suggest how commonplace and serious worries about disease-carrying insects and the conditions that produced them were in the 1950s.[2] Outbreaks of typhoid fever, dysentery, and Japanese encephalitis were ongoing public health problems in Japan for many years after the end of World War II and persisted even as the date for the opening ceremonies of the 1964 Tokyo Summer Olympics grew near. *Ikiru* also captures a moment of considerable uncertainty about the nation's values in the aftermath of the war and as the American Occupation came to a close. How Japanese communities chose to deal with flies and mosquitoes in the 1950s has a great deal to tell us about how those uncertainties were being addressed.

Over the course of the 1950s and early 1960s, many of Japan's urban neighborhoods, towns, and farm and fishing villages were part of multi-year projects working toward the eradication of flies and mosquitoes from their midst. Most of that work was done under the aegis of programs—some of them ad hoc and local, others more persistent and regional or national in scope—that one way or another made the achievement of a better life for average citizens and their communities contingent on the extermination of both insect foes. If the Ministry of Health and Welfare's reports are to be believed, in 1964 roughly six out of ten Japanese, or around sixty-three million people, resided within the boundaries of one of the "model districts" involved in mosquito and fly eradication.[3] Even if only some small fraction of that number was actually aware that the campaigns were underway, it seems worthwhile to reflect on the meanings associated with the eradication of flies and mosquitoes in Japan at that moment.

Japan in the 1950s was no stranger to campaigns designed to encourage citizens to think and act in ways that furthered the pursuit of democracy and economic growth or highlighted the appeal of a "Bright, New Life" to rural and urban households alike. For example, in August 1955, the cabinet of Prime Minister Ichirō Hatoyama announced that it was launching a national "New Life Movement." This was an endorsement of projects that had been underway for some time rather than a brand-new initiative in its own right. Historians interested in questions about how the practices of daily life changed after the war and the American occupation that followed, and in the implications of those changes, have explored some of these campaigns at length.[4] These studies have shown how public and corporate campaigns that offered to improve women's lives by providing them with more appliances and better kitchens, or teaching them to make more rational use of their time, also functioned to define the purpose of those lives as best spent playing the roles of good wife and wise mother. Along similar lines, Laura Neitzel's recent study of the advent of *danchi* housing in the '50s and early 1960s shows how those new configurations of domestic space reproduced a division of labor that ideally suited the needs of a growing Japanese economy.[5]

Despite their ubiquity, the national "Campaign for Lives without Mosquitoes and Flies" (Ka to hae no inai seikatsu undō), which the Hatoyama cabinet endorsed months before it offered its support to the New Life

Movement, and projects like Tokyo's "Campaign to Get Rid of Mosquitoes and Flies" (Ka to hae o nakusu undō), on the other hand, have largely gone unremarked by historians interested in this era.[6] One reason that initiatives like these have fallen below scholars' radar is that in the end none of the eradication efforts worked, at least not to the extent that their advocates had once claimed was possible. While residents of many of the communities that participated in the insect control efforts had positive things to say about the campaigns' effects, the goal of outright eradication remained out of reach. Mosquitoes and flies continued to be a part of the lives of most Japanese, however much people might have wished otherwise. Compared with the "successes" of China's "Four Pest" campaigns of the late 1950s and early 1960s, for example, an argument can certainly be made that Japan's insect control efforts were of limited significance in the end. One might conclude that for most people, the campaigns changed little in the registers that interest historians most.

Another reason that the intellectual and physical labor that went into these campaigns has been overlooked is that much of it was either directed at or performed by women, at a time when the New Life Movement and other lifestyle reform efforts were focused on them as well. Critics of the New Life Movement liked to joke "that the movement was just a bunch of women swatting flies," a perspective as dismissive of the efforts to get rid of the insects as it is of the women doing that work.[7] The interventions of the lifestyle reformers were in many ways also more legible and more concrete—literally—than the results of efforts underway at the same time to rid communities of mosquitoes and flies. Lifestyle reform often left improved kitchens and bathrooms in its wake and attracted the attention of corporations anxious to leverage newly rationalized and distinctly gendered divisions of labor to their own benefit. The fly and mosquito eradication programs attracted relatively little interest from the private sector, and since the lifestyle reform campaigns themselves also endorsed improvements in the handling and disposal of garbage and insect control, the differences between the sets of projects are easily elided.[8]

One reason to look more closely at the "Campaign for Lives without Mosquitoes and Flies" and its counterparts is to get a better sense of the scope of the changes in daily life that average Japanese aspired to in the 1950s. We seem to have underestimated the importance opinion-makers and the people doing the work of eradicating these two pests attached to the prospect of a "bug-free" Japan. In addition, and in keeping with the themes of this volume, a close study of that era's discourses about mosquitoes and flies speaks to changes underway not only in how much experts and laypeople knew about these insects and their behaviors but also in their faith in their own capacities to instrumentalize that knowledge for the greater good.[9] Public health officials and other experts shared their advice and ideas when they instructed citizens in how and why to combat the flies and mosquitoes in their midst, as is also reflected in a series of didactic, educational films produced in support of the anti-insect campaigns. They also wrote detailed assessments of the campaigns' progress for their peers; these appeared in a variety of professional journals.[10] Reporters from Japan's major daily newspapers covered local and national iterations of the attempts at eradication at length. The *Mainichi* and *Yomiuri* newspapers in particular were enthusiastic promoters of the different campaigns, offering awards and public recognition to individuals and communities that seemed to be making the most progress toward their goals. Finally, as noted above, the scale of popular participation in at least some element of the different eradication campaigns means that they were features of everyday life for a great many Japanese.

Tensions existed between what the presence of flies and mosquitoes implied about Japan's place in the world in the 1950s and what their hoped-for absence said about the nation's future. The work that went into eradicating these insects is a good place to look to understand how new ideas about the proper application of science and technology, the boundaries between public and private spaces, and even gender roles (about which the ideas were perhaps not so new) were put into practice as Japan transitioned from defeat to recovery to something approaching affluence.

FLIES, MOSQUITOES, AND PUBLIC PERCEPTION BEFORE THE SECOND WORLD WAR

In late August 1927, police in Tokyo arrested two men for sneaking into a Kameidō Ward government office and making off with containers filled with the bodies of some seventy thousand dead houseflies. The flies had been collected by ward residents as part of a city-wide fly-catching contest, which promised to pay a bounty of 1/1,000 of a yen per "head." The two enterprising thieves simply helped themselves to the fruits of their neighbors' labor. The burglars collected the 70 yen reward for themselves and set about spending the money at a series of local drinking establishments. The police reportedly caught up with them after one was overheard remarking to the other, in none too quiet a voice, "Flies are worth a lot!"[11]

They hadn't always been.[12] As Setoguchi Akihisa has shown, it wasn't until the early twentieth century that people began to refer to "harmful insects" (gaichū) as a category distinct from both agricultural pests and insects in general.[13] The new label reflected the growing body of scientific work linking certain insects to the spread of diseases like filariasis, malaria, and a variety of enteric illnesses. Japanese public health experts were well aware of discoveries by Ronald Ross, Walter Reed, and others of the role of flies and mosquitoes as disease vectors.[14] So too were the officers responsible for health and hygiene in the Japanese military; they encouraged their soldiers to view flies and other potential disease vectors as threats well before civilians in Japan proper were advised to do the same.[15] The 1897 Law for the Prevention of Infectious Diseases (Densenbyō Yobōhō), for example, didn't mention insects at all. It wasn't until 1922 that the law was amended to make insect control a mandatory element of public health policies in the nation's villages, towns, and cities.[16]

In the absence of community-wide efforts to deal with mosquitoes and flies, families and individuals focused on practices that would keep insects out of homes and other lived-in spaces. Families turned to netting, flypaper, and traps to keep pests away as best they could, and in the late 1800s to domestically produced pyrethrum-based insecticides as well.[17] Pyrethrum-derived powders were found to be relatively safe for use around people and other mammals and had an almost immediate effect on insects that came into contact with them. Japanese consumers would have encountered pyrethrin first in flea-powders, but by the turn of the century, manufacturers were also offering pyrethrin-infused incense sticks that, when burned in sufficient numbers and in relatively confined spaces, kept mosquitoes at bay. Longer lasting, more convenient "mosquito coils" were on sale by 1902. Pyrethrin powders and liquids (dispensed in aerosol form via handheld sprayers) for use against flies, mosquitoes, and other insects found around the home were widely available on the eve of the Second World War.[18]

Large-scale efforts to mobilize the public against insects harmful to public health began in Japan around the time of the First World War. Officials called on citizens to help eradicate flies after a cholera outbreak in Yokohama in 1916, for example, in an effort to prevent the spread of the disease. Other cities took a more proactive approach and began urging residents to collectively take up arms against local fly populations during the summer months. Osaka celebrated its first "Fly Catching Day" on July 1, 1920, an event the city marked with a parade and other fanfare. Handbills distributed along the parade route read, in part:

> Flies are born in filthy places and grow up in filthy places. Each little body carries as many as five hundred thousand germs.
>
> When a fly lands on food or a drink, those and other germs are left behind. Those germs are ones brought from toilets and other filthy places. Isn't it to be expected that you'd get sick if you consumed it?[19]

Tokyo's first fly-collecting/killing contests followed just a few years later, after the Great Kantō Earthquake of September 1923 left much of the city in ruins. Tens of thousands of people displaced by the disaster had ended up in makeshift housing, and by the next summer, city officials had grown concerned that the crowded conditions and poor sanitation common in the temporary barracks would trigger outbreaks of dysentery, typhoid fever, or other illnesses. The call to Tokyoites to do everything they could to rid the city of flies was one of the plans they came up with to try to curtail the spread of contagion.[20]

The competitions soon became a regular summertime event in the city, to which residents responded with enthusiasm (the two thieves mentioned earlier among them). Even in less successful years, officials reported tallies of as many as 50 million dead flies; in years when conditions were more conducive to the fly population, Tokyoites might collect as many as 140 million.[21] In the summer of 1938, the *Asahi* reported that so many flies had been collected for the city's most recent "Catch a Fly Day" that were they to be laid head-to-tail on the Tokaido rail line, the little fly corpses would stretch from Tokyo Station all the way to Kyoto.[22]

Campaigns like this served multiple goals. The prevention of contagion was certainly one of them, but the public was also encouraged to view the elimination of flies as evidence of improvements of a different sort as well. Officials announced a national antifly campaign in the weeks leading up to the Taishō emperor's 1915 enthronement ceremony, for example, as part of a suite of preparations to help mark the occasion.[23] Along similar lines, municipal governments in Tokyo and elsewhere made getting rid of flies a part of their plans in the 1920s and early 1930s to push back against characterizations of their cities as crowded, dirty, and dark.[24] In these contexts, there seems to have been no expectation that these attempts to make flies less numerous and less visible would be anything but short-term measures, with short-lived effects, but with value nonetheless.

OCCUPATION, THE AMERICANS, AND DDT

The end of the war brought some six million Japanese back from a former empire and battlefields that stretched from Manchuria to New Guinea. They returned to a country devastated by the war and under the authority of the forces that had brought Japan to its knees in August 1945. The vast apparatus of occupation wielded by General Douglas MacArthur, supreme commander for the allied powers (SCAP), and the Americans under his command quickly set about remaking just about every aspect of how the Japanese state and its citizens interacted and toward what ends. Those interventions included changes in the policies and institutions responsible for public health, and thus also practices for the prevention of contagion. Initially the Americans' concern for the health of the Japanese was a function of SCAP's desire to protect its own soldiers and staff from such worrisome diseases as Japanese encephalitis and typhoid fever. (Sexually transmitted diseases were also a serious problem, but one that required interventions of a different sort.) It did not take long, however, for SCAP to expand the scope of its efforts to include the parts of Japan where Americans were not.

Both at the time and retrospectively, it was not at all uncommon for American occupation officials to overstate the degree to which their reforms represented a sharp break with presurrender Japanese policies. Where public health is concerned, the Americans seem to have concluded that the rather dismal state of affairs that greeted them when they arrived in Japan reflected historically lax attitudes toward sanitation and an ongoing failure to understand the roles of flies, mosquitoes, and other insects as disease vectors.[25] That assessment was inaccurate; although it is true that medical entomology as a field lagged behind its American counterpart at the time, on balance much of what US observers saw as an absence of modern attitudes toward hygiene and insect control was instead the inevitable by-product of the widespread privations of wartime. Japanese practices around sanitation and the control of infectious diseases had been reasonably effective until the closing months of the war.

That said, the Americans did affect Japan's postwar approach to "harmful insects" in at least three ways of interest to us. First, the occupiers highlighted the threats these insects posed to public health at the same time that they introduced practices and tools designed to mitigate those hazards. A number of the films the Americans made sure were shown to Japanese viewers as part of SCAP's campaign to use movies as a conduit for the dissemination of American ideals and norms, for example, focused on public health and infectious disease.[26] Among those were several from a series of animated short films that Disney had developed for distribution in Latin America in collaboration with the Office of the Coordinator of Inter-American Affairs. Disney's "The Winged Scourge," originally released in 1943 and the first of the "Health for the Americas" shorts to be screened in Japan, told the story of how Disney's Seven Dwarfs came to learn about malaria and the role mosquitoes played in its transmission. The cartoon then followed the dwarfs' efforts to contain the spread of the disease by killing as many mosquitoes as they could and taking precautions to protect themselves against any that survived those efforts. Dopey, Grumpy, Doc, and the others are shown using insecticide on a local pond to kill mosquito larvae, filling in swampy areas near their home, and taking care to always sleep under mosquito netting at night, among other measures.[27]

How persuasive these films were for a Japanese audience is hard to gauge, given that the stories they told were all set in impoverished rural communities in Central America or Mexico as imagined by Disney's animators. That the films were also clearly condescending toward their intended audiences couldn't have made it a given that Japanese viewers would respond positively to their recommendations. At the same time, the cartoons did convey information about how flies and mosquitoes helped spread diseases, and about the steps that people could take to protect themselves and their families. Even for those viewers for whom these were familiar concepts, it would not have been lost on them that the Americans were suggesting that they themselves take the initiative to protect themselves and their families.

At the same time that the Americans were flagging these hazards to public health in Japan, people all over the country were being subjected to close encounters with one of the unmistakable symbols of America's scientific might: dichloro-diphenyl-trichloroethane, or DDT. The US military had turned to DDT late in the war as a defense against the malaria-transmitting anopheles mosquito, and SCAP was quick to put it to similar use in and around American bases and other facilities in occupied Japan.[28] And while one could argue that the purpose and efficacy of those practices would have been hidden from most Japanese, at least initially, the same could not be said about the other ways the chemical was deployed by occupation forces. Many, many Japanese were forced to undergo invasive and often humiliating delousing procedures in the early years of the Occupation, during which American troops or their surrogates used handheld dispensers to spray DDT powder into the hair, under the clothing, and onto the bodies of adults and children alike.[29] It was not lost on Japanese public health professionals that if the means of DDT's application was one sign of American power, the new chemical's impressive efficacy was another. One doctor recalled what happened after a visiting American medical officer ordered that the hospital at which he worked be deloused: "With DDT, the lice were exterminated right away. With this illustration [of American scientific power], we thought it was only natural that Japan lost the war. A problem about which we could do nothing was instantaneously solved by the occupation forces."[30]

By the time the Americans began using DDT in Japan, its reputation as a particularly lethal and long-lasting insecticide was well established. Unlike pyrethrins, which tended to lose their efficacy when exposed to sunlight, DDT remained toxic to insects long after it was introduced into the environment. That it seemed to pose no direct threat to mammals was another factor in its widespread adoption; there appeared to be few downsides to using it whenever and wherever harmful insects were found. After an initial period in which the United States simply imported large quantities of DDT in concentrate form for distribution to public health officials, Japanese chemical companies began producing it themselves under license.[31]

Less dramatic than DDT's introduction into Japan but still significant for how the anti-insect campaigns of the 1950s developed was Japanese access to several other new and highly effective synthetic pesticides. Benzene hexachloride (BHC), for example, became available not long after DDT first went into general use.[32] Like DDT, it was quickly adopted by farmers, but it was soon available to consumers for use at home or at the workplace as well. Chūgai Pharmaceuticals Varsan (Barusan) brand of BHC-based insecticides first went on sale in 1954. Consumers could choose from among a variety of Varsan products: it was sold in incense form, as a sprayable liquid, and (ingeniously) as the heat-activated "Varsan Ring," which, when installed on the neck of any properly oriented electric light bulb, slowly released its BHC-laden vapors into the room. The Varsan product line was marketed as deadly to flies, mosquitoes, cockroaches, and other household pests.[33]

In the United States, DDT and its kin played important roles in moving antipest campaigns beyond tactics like "swat-the-fly" and toward the pursuit of outright eradication. Paul Müller, who first developed DDT for use as an insecticide (and would win the 1948 Nobel Prize in Physiology and Medicine for his efforts), suggested in 1945 that this new product could "send malaria mosquitoes, typhus lice and other disease carrying insects to join the dodo and the dinosaur in the limbo of extinct species, thereby ending these particular plagues for all time."[34] "Echoing his predecessor as president of the American Association of Economic Entomologists," writes Edmund Russell in War and Nature, "Clay Lyle called in 1947 for the 'complete extermination' of gypsy moths, houseflies, horn flies, cattle grubs, cattle lice, screwworms, and Argentine Ants."[35] Officials in Oklahoma and Idaho were among those nationwide who launched large-scale fly eradication projects in their respective states. The US Junior Chamber of Commerce, writes Russell, "inspired by the 'anti-fly wars' in Idaho and elsewhere . . . launched a national campaign for 'total annihilation' of flies. Because flies were suspected of carrying polio and other diseases," Russell notes, "1,500 branches of the Jaycees joined 2000 communities in a 'DDT blitz' to improve public health by creating a 'fly-free America.'"[36] While there is no reason to think that these American campaigns directly inspired the ones that emerged in Japan a few years later, I mention them here to point out that the Japanese faith in the efficacy of new technologies like DDT was hardly unique.

A third American intervention into public health and insect control began with the Occupation's efforts to do away with the hygiene associations (eisei kumiai), the long-standing local bodies that served as the primary channel between communities and the Japanese state's public health apparatus. SCAP officials argued that the hygiene associations embodied undemocratic, top-down practices that the Americans were in Japan to dismantle; some also suggested that the groups had never been that effective to begin with.[37] In 1948, SCAP's Public Health and Welfare Section ordered existing hygiene associations dissolved and installed new "sanitary teams" in their place. These teams were charged with more or less the same responsibilities as the associations they replaced, namely the monitoring and control of infectious disease, the maintenance of proper standards of hygiene and waste handling, and insect control. While the hygiene associations and the sanitation teams did differ in that the latter were supposed to better reflect the democratic, locally empowered spirit of Occupation-era reforms, in practice it was not uncommon for communities to simply adapt the associations they already had to whatever the new American nomenclature happened to be.[38]

As was the case with many of SCAP's other initiatives, the Public Health and Welfare Section's intervention was less revolutionary than its advocates at the time claimed. Like the hygiene associations, the sanitary teams targeted flies, mosquitoes, and other potential disease vectors at the village or neighborhood level; like the hygiene associations, they seem to have been reasonably effective in general, with some variation across communities.[39] In 1950, however, as part of an across-the-board (American-mandated) reduction in spending, the national government abruptly eliminated all funding for the sanitary teams.[40] Simultaneously, it shifted responsibilities for infectious disease prevention and other public-health-related activities to local governments and began requiring that each assign personnel to pest control duty. There is no evidence to suggest that Japan's villages, towns, and cities were ever eager to take on these new burdens, but the Ministry of Health and Welfare chose to cast the move in positive terms. Ministry officials suggested that the Japanese people were finally free to set their own priorities and to make decisions for themselves about how best to keep their communities healthy and clean. Instead of dictating to communities how they should go about dealing with public health issues, as it had in the past, the government's new role would be to assist grassroots, local initiatives.

TOWNS WITHOUT MOSQUITOES AND FLIES

The Hatoyama cabinet's 1955 announcement that it would launch a national "Campaign for Lives without Mosquitoes and Flies" didn't so much reveal a new initiative as it allowed the administration to associate itself with work that had already been underway for several years. Villages and towns all over Japan had started systematic efforts to eradicate mosquitoes and flies within just a few years after the end of the war. At the time, neither SCAP nor the Japanese government in Tokyo was actively encouraging communities to do this on their own—there was no pest eradication bandwagon for anyone to jump onto—so the precise number of towns and villages doing the work is not clear. What we do know is that by 1949 there were enough communities trying to eradicate mosquitoes and flies for the Ministry of Health and Welfare to begin designating some of them as "Environmental Hygiene Model Districts" (Kankyō eisei moderu chiku). Designation brought limited support from the ministry in the form of small grants and technical assistance, and public recognition of work well done. One of the ministry's goals in using the "model site" nomenclature, as the label implies, was to encourage other communities nearby to adopt the strategies of their successful neighbors, with relatively little investment of effort on the central government's part. It named fifty such sites by the end of 1949, added another hundred the following year, and by late 1954 was reporting that it had awarded the label to more than 3,500 towns and villages.[41] The ministry also worked closely with newspapers and other media to build public interest and support for eradication projects.

Much as the Hatoyama cabinet came late to the anti-fly and -mosquito campaign, the ministry too was capitalizing on initiatives that it could not take credit for having helped launch. Public health officials in Nagasaki, for example, started their own five-year "Project to Establish Hygienic Cities, Towns, and Villages" in the summer of 1951.[42] Hiroshima's "Movement to Create Hometowns (kyōdo) without Mosquitoes or Flies" got underway in 1952, and in 1954 Chiba, Hyogo, and Tochigi Prefectures each announced that they too would begin supporting local anti-mosquito and -fly efforts.[43]

Antipest campaigns in cities like Tokyo, Yokohama, and Osaka also predate the Hatoyama government's decision to provide a national framework for them. Tokyo's administration was helping distribute insecticide and sprayers by 1953 and had started designating neighborhoods already active in eradication efforts as "Model Hygiene Districts" around the same time. The city named a sector of Kita Ward as a model district in June 1954, for example, in recognition of the work that the women of the Yanagita Fujinkai had been doing to rid their corner of Tokyo of mosquitoes and flies. As one of the Fujinkai's members pointed out to a reporter sent to cover the announcement, she and her neighbors had actually been doing that work since 1947.[44] A few months later, when the Mainichi newspaper announced that the Mitanichō neighborhood in Meguro Ward had been chosen to receive one of its Environmental Hygiene Awards, it was in recognition of the work the women's association there had been doing since 1951, work that its members said had made it possible for them to now live in "a town without either mosquitoes or flies."[45]

Each of these communities launched its eradication campaign independently of the others, for reasons specific to its circumstances. At the same time, it seems safe to assume that concerns over public health and an understanding of the roles that mosquitoes and flies played as disease vectors were important factors for those towns, villages, and neighborhoods that decided to move ahead with eradication efforts. In 1950, the short educational film "The Town with No Flies" (Hae no inai machi) told the story of how one community came to define the presence of flies as a problem and of what it did next. Its themes certainly resonate with what we know about the emerging public discourse around flies and mosquitoes in the late 1940s and early 1950s.

Local anti-mosquito and -fly campaigns were getting underway at more or less the same time that Japanese documentary filmmakers were reestablishing themselves in the new postwar environment. The timing was serendipitous for both. SCAP's insistence on sweeping reforms in the Japanese educational system and its fondness for movies as a reliable means for reaching the masses led to an early 1950s boom in the production of documentary and educational films. Iwanami Productions (Iwanami Eiga Seisakusho), for example, one of the most influential of the postwar Japanese documentary film studios, got its start in 1950 with the release of the first installment in its Compendium of Social Science Teaching Materials series.[46] Iwanami Productions would eventually release a great many more movies before it went out of business in the 1990s, but the very first film in its extensive catalog was "The Town with No Flies."

Production work on "The Town with No Flies" began in 1949, and filming on location in Mitsukaidō in southwestern Ibaraki Prefecture finished the following June.[47] The entirety of the twelve-minute film takes place in and around an anonymous and unremarkable town, home to a large school, a busy main street lined with shops, and well-kept residences set amid farm fields. There is nothing in the way the film portrays the community to suggest that it is special in any way. The schoolchildren who are the story's protagonists are engaging and comfortable in front of the camera, but their curiosity and actions are presented to viewers as nothing out of the ordinary.

The film opens with a close-up of a nearly empty metal bento box, in which several houseflies are shown walking across or resting on a few scattered grains of rice clinging to the bottom of the container. The camera then zooms in even closer, so that a single grain of rice and the single fly feeding on it fill the screen, before the scene shifts again and we see that the lunch box belongs to one of a dozen or so middle school students eating at their classroom desks. Several of the students try to shoo flies away from their meals as one of the boys remarks that there are suddenly a great many of them, now that the warmer weather has arrived.

Together he and others in the school's Health Unit decide to address the problem by organizing a school-wide fly-catching activity. We see the students patrolling the classroom and the school grounds armed with flyswatters and watch as they dispatch one fly after another. "We caught a lot!" the narrator reports, over a scene depicting a dead fly being carefully picked up with chopsticks and dropped into a can already filled to the brim with the remains of other flies. "When we counted them all up," the boy continued, "we had killed almost ten thousand of them!" The classroom is declared fly free. All of this transpires in the film's first minute and a half.

The respite from the annoying flies is short-lived, however, and the insects are soon back in force. "Where can they be coming from?" our narrator wonders, posing the question that propels the story forward. One of the points the film makes early on is that the conditions that allow flies to breed in such large numbers and in such proximity to people are almost always the result of changes that humans made to the environment. As the students begin exploring their surroundings more carefully, for example, they discover a garbage-strewn, fly-infested corner of the schoolyard that they identify as the source of their problems. This is where the flies are laying their eggs, the students conclude, and they resolve together to watch carefully over each stage in the fly's life cycle. Thanks to some skilled and patient camerawork at Iwanami Productions' facility in Tokyo, audiences were able to watch in extreme close-up as the flies laid egg after egg, as larvae emerged from the eggs, as the maggots fed (not for the squeamish) and pupated, and finally as adult flies emerged from their pupae, ready to begin the entire cycle all over again.

Armed with their new knowledge, the members of the "Health Unit" report what they've learned to the school's student council and recommend focusing their efforts on destroying as many eggs or larvae as they can, as that will be far more effective than trying to eliminate flies after they've reached the adult stage. In the intensive cleanup of the school grounds that follows, the children burn piles of garbage where flies had laid their eggs, build covers for the school garbage boxes and panels to seal shut the openings used to clean out the toilet waste tanks, and use insecticide to dispatch larvae wherever they're found. No adults are consulted prior to or present for any of these activities—the process of identifying the problem, studying its causes, and implementing a solution is entirely in the hands of the students themselves. The emphasis on the school-children's independence and ingenuity can certainly be understood as an argument in favor of democratic values and local self-reliance more generally, but it also highlights the value of low-cost, simple interventions against flies and other pests. Having created the conditions that allowed the flies to breed, it was clearly not impossible to correct those mistakes, even for children.

It is only once the scope of the students' concerns expands beyond the school itself that adults begin to play a role. Having dealt with the fly problem at the school, the students begin to notice other places where flies congregate in town, whether at a local dump site, at farms with livestock, or along poorly cleaned side streets. At this point, they enlist the help of one of their teachers, who encourages them to speak with a local public health official. The health official in turn helps them convince the town hall to send its men to clean up the unauthorized dump site and to spray the field nearby, and soon enough the whole town has been mobilized for its first "Fly-Catching Day" (*hae tori dē*) and general cleanup. In time, the schoolchildren notice that the once cluttered side streets traveled by the town's trash collectors have been swept clean, the wooden garbage boxes sealed tight and dusted with insecticide. Even the local fish shop, once a popular destination for the town's flies, invests in new glass windows that keep them at bay.

The closing scenes of "The Town with No Flies" highlight the community's accomplishments but also draw attention to the true scale of the problem it must confront. As at the film's start, at the end it is one of the students who discovers that the flies have returned, this time as a swarm accompanying a delivery of fish from a nearby town. The boy watches as the flies crawl all over trays of fish as they are being unloaded from the back of the truck. The contrast between the pristine, fresh-looking fish on display in the fly-less local shop and these now deeply suspect specimens is striking. As he watches the delivery truck depart, and the camera's line of sight moves for the first time to take in the world outside the town, the student offers this closing exhortation: "Wouldn't it be great if flies were to totally disappear in those other villages and towns too? How are all of you planning on getting rid of flies in your own villages and towns? Let's all think of ways to rid all of Japan from flies!"[48]

THE CAMPAIGN FOR LIVES WITHOUT
MOSQUITOES AND FLIES

The move by the government in mid-1955 to launch a national "people's movement" to eradicate flies and mosquitoes made activities that were already taking place all across the country more legible than they had been. The lack of a single descriptive label likely didn't matter much to the communities pursuing eradication, but Ministry of Health and Welfare officials clearly believed that there was something to be gained by providing one. One official in particular—Hashimoto Masami, director of the ministry's newly established Department of Environmental Sanitation—was instrumental in explaining why mosquito and fly control was a worthwhile national project.

Hashimoto graduated from Osaka University's School of Medicine in March 1940 with plans to become a surgeon, but he spent the next five years as a medical officer in the Imperial Japanese Navy instead. By war's end, he had developed an interest in epidemiology and transferred to the Ministry of Health and Welfare to help monitor the repatriation of Japanese from overseas. He quickly decided to give up on a career as a surgeon and to specialize instead in public health, which, he later recalled, "seemed to me a supreme way of a medical scholar survived the war, to reconstruct a peaceful, welfare nation" (sic).[49] Over the next several years, Hashimoto worked as a public health official in Toyonaka City, just north of Osaka proper. The Toyonaka Health Center was something of an experiment at the time, in that it focused on improving public health through aggressive community-wide education campaigns—women and children were central to its outreach efforts—and emphasized the importance of grassroots engagement in local reform efforts. Hashimoto and his colleagues at the center reported considerable success using these new strategies and were recognized for their efforts by both the prefectural government and American officials.[50]

In late 1952, Hashimoto was appointed director of the newly established Department of Environmental Sanitation in the Ministry of Health and Welfare. His enthusiasm for community-led public health projects carried over into the new job, and he was soon traveling to towns and villages all over Japan to learn more about their anti-fly and -mosquito projects. Hashimoto was impressed by what he saw happening in those locations. Communities participating in the eradication campaigns reported fewer infectious disease cases than before and attributed other improvements in the well-being of local families to reductions in the fly and mosquito populations. Hashimoto carefully documented these results and over the next few years shared his findings in journal articles and eventually a book—*Public Health and Organized Activities* (Kōshū eisei to soshiki katsudō).[51] Press coverage of local eradication efforts before 1955 and of the national campaign thereafter relied heavily on data and arguments that originated with Hashimoto.

When it came to explaining the benefits of getting rid of flies and mosquitoes, for example, it will come as no surprise that Hashimoto flagged reductions in the number of cases of infectious disease as the most important. Writing in 1955 about conditions in Hiroshima Prefecture, he pointed to the differences in the incidence of infectious diseases between communities that had started fly and mosquito eradication campaigns and those that had not. In districts that were part of the prefectural project, Hashimoto reported that the incidence of dysentery in 1953 was 15.2 cases per 100,000 people; in districts that were not part of the anti-fly and -mosquito campaign, the rate was 95.6 cases per 100,000, or more than six times as common. Reports of typhoid fever (0.5 vs 4.7 per 100,000) and Japanese encephalitis (0.5 vs 1.8 per 100,000) showed similarly dramatic disparities.[52] It was not common to be able to compare the effects of the eradication campaign across entire districts the way that Hashimoto was able to do in Hiroshima; far more typical were narratives describing positive change over time in a single community. Hashimoto had numerous examples to draw from in that category, and there too the changes could be dramatic.

In an article he wrote for *Nōgyō sekai* (Agriculture world), for example, Hashimoto described what had happened in two semi-impoverished farming villages. The first, Toyonomura, was not far from Tokyo as the crow flies, but in Hashimoto's telling might just as well have been in another country, or century, entirely. Among its many economic problems, the low-lying, flood-prone village was also plagued by infestations of mosquitoes and flies. In the summer, there were so many that family members had to take turns eating their meals; while some ate, the others tried to shoo the insects away. Insect-borne diseases were widespread. In the spring of 1951, a dysentery outbreak had swept through the village, infecting dozens and leaving five dead. The combination of lost production, fear of future outbreaks, and ill health, Hashimoto reported, had left the community almost without hope.

The second community, Nagaura Village, was in a remote part of Nagasaki Prefecture, and if anything even less well-off than Toyonomura. As of the late 1940s, many of the village's homes were still without electricity, access to a radio, or even a newspaper subscription. Cases of typhoid fever and dysentery were commonplace; hookworm and roundworm infections were endemic.[53]

Both villages' fortunes took a turn for the better after they launched environmental improvement projects, in which fly and mosquito eradication efforts played a major role. In Nagaura, the turnaround began in 1949, when prefectural public health officials began helping residents receive treatment for their parasites and introduced practices that would help prevent reinfection. Fly and mosquito eradication work began in 1951, and according to Hashimoto, within just a few years the community's circumstances had improved markedly. The number of villagers coming down with illnesses like dysentery dropped sharply, a development that had gone hand in hand with the near disappearance of flies and mosquitoes from Nagaura.[54]

Toyonomura's experiences were said to be similar. A local agricultural cooperative in one of the village's hamlets began implementing a series of environmental sanitation improvements after the 1951 dysentery outbreak, to good effect. Those practices were soon taken up by the rest of the village, and by 1954, according to Hashimoto, 97 percent of the households surveyed reported that there were either no flies at all (or perhaps just a very few) in their vicinity. The number of mosquitoes, meanwhile, was said to have been reduced by 95 percent.[55] It is implied, but not spelled out explicitly, that the health of Toyonomura's residents improved as the size of fly and mosquito populations shrank.

Hashimoto also offered concrete evidence of the economic benefits of the antipest efforts. Families were spending much less than they once had on flypaper and mosquito-repellant incense, and on feed for their animals, he noted. Spending on medical expenses was down. In addition—and this is a point that Hashimoto and the press returned to quite frequently in coverage of the eradication campaign—their farm animals had also become more productive since the anti-insect efforts had gotten underway. In Toyonomura's case, that was evident in the 21 percent increase in the number of eggs the village's chickens were providing, but the benefits didn't stop there.[56] A 1956 *Yomiuri* editorial in support of what it called the national campaign to create "A Japan without Even a Single Mosquito or

Fly" (Ka ya hae no ippiki moinai Nihon) cited a recent survey of model districts all over Japan that reported an 18 percent increase in milk production and a 20 percent increase in the number of eggs collected since the start of their eradication efforts.[57] Hashimoto was a strong proponent of using cost-benefit analysis to gauge the value of different public health initiatives. The investments communities were making in their eradication campaigns certainly seemed to be paying off.[58]

Better health and more money were all well and good, but Hashimoto was convinced that getting rid of flies and mosquitoes had the potential to transform Japanese communities in other ways that were in the long run no less important. In his assessment, the fact that so many of the anti-insect projects underway all across Japan in the 1950s had started out as spontaneous, local initiatives was worth celebrating, and fostering where it was possible to do so. Hashimoto was careful to avoid using terms that might be politically fraught—he did not, for example, imply that local anti-fly and -mosquito activities were an expression of communal harmony rooted in Japan's mythic past—but he did return many times to the following ideas.

One was that effective responses to the threats posed by flies and mosquitoes could only come about if communities truly united behind those efforts. Nothing good or permanent could come of efforts in which only some households participated, or that involved only half measures. Neither the insects nor the diseases they carried could be deterred so long as even a single safe haven remained nearby.[59] It wasn't lost on Hashimoto or other observers that the emphasis on community-based responses allowed the state to avoid having to bear the cost of addressing what was obviously a national public health problem. Hashimoto's response, though, was that until Japan had the wherewithal to hook everyone up to clean water supplies and adequate sewerage systems, which might yet take quite some time, then local initiatives like the ones he was writing about were the country's best bets when it came to making progress toward improving the nation's health.[60]

It also mattered that there was a proven correlation between community solidarity and success in the struggle against the mosquitoes and flies. By definition, the towns and neighborhoods that had made progress against the insect pests were those that had overcome their differences, whatever those might be, and united toward a common goal of eradication. Conversely, for those communities that had yet to join the fight against flies and mosquitoes (or those that had done so and maybe fallen short), the implication of Hashimoto's analysis was that they must have failed to transcend whatever divisions stood between them and success. To be clear, Hashimoto only ever framed this calculus in positive terms and not as an opportunity to single out underachieving locales. He comes across as truly enthusiastic about how Japan as a whole might benefit from what was happening in so many different communities all over the country. The proximate positive effects of eradication were one element of those benefits, but so too was the development of a new attention to the well-being of one's neighbors, one's community, and by extension, the nation as a whole.

The idea that the project of eliminating flies and mosquitoes might also be a vehicle for the maintenance of a certain kind of social order surfaced in other venues as well. A few months after the Hashimoto cabinet's launch of the "Campaign for Lives without Mosquitoes and Flies," the Sakura Motion Picture Company (Sakura Eigasha) released its latest film, *The 100 Merry Wives* (*Hyakunin no yōki na nyōbō tachi*). Although nothing about the title hints directly at its subject matter, *Merry Wives* tells the story of how one neighborhood came together to eradicate the flies and mosquitoes that threatened its well-being.[61] The film is based in part on events in Yokohama's Funaichō District, where a local women's group had helped lead a successful effort to clean up their community. Hashimoto Masami was called in to help advise on the film in his capacity as director of the Department of Environmental Sanitation. He arranged for the Ministry of Health and Welfare to endorse the final product; Hashimoto also helped convince one of Japan's largest pesticide manufacturers, Chūgai Pharmaceuticals, to sign on as a sponsor.[62] (The company's Varsan-brand insecticides receive prominent product placement throughout *The 100 Merry Wives*.)

This thirty-minute docudrama was one of two insect-related films to be completed that year by the newly established Sakura Motion Picture Company (Sakura Eigasha). The first was "Goodbye, Mr. Mosquito and Mr. Fly" (Sayonara Ka to Hae San; twenty minutes); its focus was on a successful insect eradication project led by the members of the women's association of the town of Mizuho, on Tokyo's western outskirts.[63] That both films centered on the lives and activism of women is a direct reflection of the inspiration behind the founding of Sakura Eigasha itself. The new company had been created specifically to promote the educational mission of the National Federation of Regional Women's Organizations (Zenkoku Chiiki Fujin Dantai Rennraku Kyōgikai), a left-leaning group formed a few months after the Occupation's end. National Federation members had lobbied hard against efforts to roll back rights granted to women under the new constitution, for example, and also helped lead public campaigns against nuclear weapons testing in the Pacific in the mid-1950s. In 1955, federation leaders from all over Japan helped launch the Sakura Motion Picture Company to give themselves a platform from which to highlight the accomplishments of Japanese women and promote the spread of civic-minded, family-friendly values.[64] *The 100 Merry Wives* was a highly effective vehicle for those ideals.

The movie was filmed almost entirely in Yokohama's Urafunechō, a district at the time considered to be one of the city's poorest. Murayama Eiji, the film's producer, reportedly chose Urafunechō after scouting a number of other communities that had already been singled out for their achievements as model environmental hygiene districts.[65] Yokohama's administration had taken a series of steps since the end of the war to mobilize residents in support of cleanup campaigns, including several that targeted mosquitoes, following a 1948 outbreak of Japanese encephalitis. The city launched its own "Movement to Get Rid of Mosquitoes and Flies" in the summer of 1953, dispatching public health technicians into the neighborhoods, sponsoring lectures, and of course helping to organize large-scale cleaning and environmental improvement projects. The next year, they changed the initiative's name to "The Movement to Create a Clean Yokohama," but eradicating flies and mosquitoes remained one its priorities for some time to come. Civic groups from Urafunechō participated in the campaign right from the start and invested enough effort into it to win recognition for their work creating a "model environmental sanitation site" just two years later. Right around the time that filming for *The 100 Merry Wives* was wrapping up, the *Mainichi Shinbun* announced that the neighborhood was one of the winners of its own Environmental Sanitation Award.[66] Urafunechō's residents were clearly doing something right, and Murayama was impressed both by the "lower city" vibe of the neighborhood and by the enthusiasm of the women's groups and young people he encountered there.[67] He and the film's director drew directly from residents' experiences for some of elements of the movie's plot.[68]

The neighborhood is not identified by name in the film (although observant viewers might have spotted enough clues to place it in Yokohama), and as was the case with "The Town with No Flies," the setting is arguably a stand-in for any number of communities like it throughout Japan. In this case, those would be ones in which the residents were not well-off, where families might share a common water tap in the narrow path behind their row houses, and where during the day at least the neighborhood's only inhabitants were women and children. In one of the earlier scenes, the middle-aged woman who is the film's "star" (played by veteran movie actress Toda Haruko) is shown diligently sweeping rubbish out of the way on a busy city street. She pauses to pick up a street placard that had fallen to the ground, only to discover once she does that it is an advertisement for a nearby nude show; in haste she turns the sign around so that is no longer visible to passersby, leans it against a utility pole, and goes back to her sweeping. That gesture shares something with viewers about the upright character of the "auntie," and it also gestures toward the neighborhood's slightly rough edges.

The plot of The 100 Merry Wives has similarities to that of "The Town with No Flies," in that it too tells the story of a grassroots effort to address the threat that poor sanitation in general and harmful insects in particular pose to the community. It proceeds through similar stages as the earlier film, beginning with the "discovery" of the challenges to the neighborhood's well-being, followed by a careful study of their causes, to showing how the residents of the community eventually overcome the problems they faced by putting their new knowledge into practice and working together for the common good. The 100 Merry Wives differs from the earlier films in that it significantly raises the stakes of the struggle to overcome the hazards that flies represent for local families. Because the stakes are so high and the threat is shown to be so real, the victory over the insects brings the film to an uplifting and perhaps even inspiring conclusion.

Toda Haruko's character is a little older than most of the other women we meet in the film, and unlike most of them, she has no young children of her own. She watches over the boys and girls in the neighborhood even so, and in one of the film's early scenes she is shown scolding a group of children playing dangerously close to the filthy river's edge, chastising them until they reluctantly agree to go have their fun somewhere else. The camera follows them as they start a game of hide-and-seek; one boy climbs inside a recently emptied garbage bin and pulls the lid down over his head to make himself that much harder for his friend to find him out. Others hide under discarded baskets and other refuse in a local empty lot that has been turned into a makeshift dump. Toda's character urges them to wash their hands afterward, but no doubt it would have occurred to audiences that the dump may not be any safer a play space than the riverside.

The plot indeed soon takes a frightening turn. At some point after their game of hide-and-seek, one of the younger neighborhood children falls seriously ill. Toda's character rushes to the mother's side, takes one look at the unconscious boy, and insists on taking him to the hospital without delay. Her decision likely helped save his life, as we later learn that the boy had been diagnosed with dysentery. That determination in turn leads to the dispatch of a public health sanitation team to the neighborhood, where they do two things. Their first action is to spray disinfectant and insecticide near the boy's home; the second is to explain to the local women how it was that the boy likely contracted the disease. One health official, clad in a doctor's white lab coat, points out the many different locations in the neighborhood where flies and mosquitoes bred: household toilet tanks that were open to the air, standing containers of water, piles of uncollected garbage, and so on. The message is clear enough—preventing the spread of infectious diseases like dysentery would have to begin with denying flies and mosquitoes such easy access to food and breeding sites.

Toda's character and one of her friends are the only ones to take up this challenge, at least at first. Their efforts get off to a slow start—they make their way awkwardly from house to house, opening the poorly sealed shutters on their neighbors' toilet tanks and frantically spraying insecticide inside before moving determinedly on to the next one. Along the way they clash with the proprietor of the local fish-paste shop, who complains that their intervention is a violation of people's human rights. The local garbage collector refuses to help clean up the trash in the abandoned field, claiming it wasn't his responsibility. One of their neighbors proudly shows off the assortment of Varsan-brand insecticides she has been using to keep her own house pest free, implying perhaps that she and her family are doing well enough regardless of what the rest of the community might be up to, while a different, wealthier neighbor mistakes Toda's character and her friend for street cleaners. Their attempt to persuade the fishmonger to perhaps do something about the flies his shop attracts is rudely rebuffed. Finally, after convincing several more women from the neighborhood to join them, Toda's character and the others travel to city hall and plead with officials there to clean up their neighborhood, only to be told that the city can't help; it doesn't have the budget for it.

It is at this point that circumstances go from bad to worse for the women and their families. On their way back from their failed effort at city hall, they watch as some of the children play by the side of the river; Toda's character appears about to scold them again as she did earlier, only to decide not to, uncertain perhaps about where to send them that might actually be safer than the riverbank. As the group of women are about to reach their homes, one of the children who had been playing at the river's edge comes running toward them, shouting that his friend had just fallen into the water and disappeared. The entire neighborhood, it seems, rushes to the riverbank, where police and other rescue personnel join them in a desperate but unsuccessful search for the boy. The missing boy's mother is of course inconsolable. In an interesting didactic twist, it was she who had taken such pride in her purchase of insecticides to protect the members of her own household. The message her son's death sends, the film argues, is that it had been a mistake to trust in private, independent responses to hazards that threaten the community at large.

The tragedy is deeply disheartening to almost everyone. Toda's character is the exception, and she begins a single-handed effort to clean up the refuse-strewn field so that the children will finally have a safe space in which to play. At first she struggles alone, but soon the neighborhood children show up and begin cheerfully helping her haul away loads of debris. They are joined by the mother of the boy who drowned, then by other women from the neighborhood, and soon by the garbage collector too. (Newspaper accounts suggest that the cleanup effort began more or less as the film portrayed it, with the efforts of just one local woman working all by herself.[69]) A new women's association is formed, and its members sit for lectures led by experts on how best to control flies and mosquitoes as a community. Eventually even city hall sends help, and the abandoned field's transformation into a pristine playground for the kids, complete with swings, a jungle gym, and other amusements, is soon complete. The film lingers on scenes of the children at play, watched over by Toda's character and the other adults who helped bring the project to fruition.[70]

The film's final scenes draw attention to the community's now ongoing commitment to protecting itself from flies, mosquitoes, and disease. The fishmonger expresses his gratitude toward Toda's character and the other women for helping rid the neighborhood of flies; even the proprietor of the fish-paste shop has come around and has started using Varsan prod-

FIGURE 6.1. Women sweeping in front of their homes. From the 1955 film
The 100 Merry Wives (Hyakunin no yōki na nyōbō tachi).

ucts in his store to keep flies away. But the most powerful expression of
how much has changed comes in the film's closing sequence, which begins
with the image of a single woman, clad in a white apron and white hair
covering, emerging from her home and starting to ring a large handbell,
walking down as the street as she does. Soon other women, identically
clad in white aprons and hair covers, emerge from their doorways, brooms
in hand, and begin sweeping the streets in front of their homes.[71] At first
the camera is at street level, but as the focus pulls back and up, we see
that there are many more women than that initial framing could have
captured. The last scene in *Merry Wives* shows a wide, long boulevard
with houses on the one side and the riverbank on the other, filled almost
as far as the eye can see with white-clad women, sweeping their community clean (fig. 6.1). Their numbers and unity are in marked contrast to
the film's opening images, which were of Toda's character alone on the
side of the road, sweeping, struggling to clean up a community not yet
prepared to accept her help.[72]

ERADICATION RUNS ITS COURSE

The Japan Environmental Sanitation Association (Nihon Kankyō Eisei Kyōkai) was established shortly after the "Campaign for Lives without Mosquitoes and Flies" got underway. Hashimoto Masami chaired the association's first national gathering, which brought some 2,500 community leaders and public health officials to Tokyo in April 1957. The eradication campaign was a central topic of discussion at the assembly, and the enthusiasm around it was expressed in the usual ways—speeches by ministers and politicians, posters, and so on—and in some more original formats too. Anzai Aikō, the star of NHK radio's long-running "The Singing Auntie" (Uta no obāsan) program, appeared onstage at the assembly venue to debut the "Life without Mosquitoes and Flies Song" (Ka to hae no inai seikatsu no uta) for a (presumably) rapt audience.[73] The song's first verse reminds listeners of the many annoyances and harms these two pests inflict—they are "the overseers of a great many sicknesses," accuses one lyric—but the second verse reflects on the benefits of their eradication:

> With mosquitoes and flies no more, horses and cattle get fat
> And that's the truth
> Chickens and milk up by 20 percent
> ooh ooh ooh
> With mosquitoes and flies no more, money can be saved
> And that's the truth
> Mosquito incense and mosquito netting, you won't need either![74]

Recordings of the song were available for purchase for anyone who wished to revisit the experience later or share it with others.

In 1957 the Ministry of Health and Welfare still had ambitious goals for the eradication campaigns, but as had been true since 1955, had only modest proposals for how it planned to achieve them. The overall target the ministry set for itself was to have made the eradication campaign a truly nationwide movement by the end of 1958. Progress toward that goal, officials said, would be reflected in the growth in the number of communities newly designated as model sites each year.[75] At some point, presumably, there would be enough sites dispersed widely enough across Japan to justify describing the anti-insect efforts as a national movement. Exactly what that number might be was left to the public's imagination, and it is unlikely that Hashimoto or his colleagues ever had a specific threshold in mind. What was clear was that however many communities had already committed to eradicating mosquitoes and flies in 1955, the government had concluded that it wasn't enough.

The ministry expected that new communities would sign on to the movement as more people learned about the benefits that were already evident in many of the existing model sites, in the forms of lower rates of communicable disease, increased productivity, and better health all around. Making sure that news of those success stories spread would be an important part of the ministry's work over the next three years. One advantage of that approach was that it didn't require a huge outlay of money, which was a plus for the ministry since it quickly became clear that the anti-insect campaign would have very little in the way of new funding available to it.

In its first year, all the money for the movement had to come out of the current budgets of the Ministries of Education, Labor, and Welfare, with the latter bearing the largest burden by far. The Ministry of Welfare purportedly committed just under 7 billion yen, the Ministry of Labor offered an additional 1.3 billion yen to hire day laborers and the unemployed to work on clearing ditches, cleaning public spaces of refuse, or similarly labor-intensive projects. The Ministry of Education, for its part, agreed to take 10 million yen of its funding for the New Life Movement and spend it instead in support of the anti-insect campaign.[76] The budget the Ministry of Welfare submitted in 1956 included its first request for funds specifically for the anti-insect campaign: the ministry asked for 280 million yen. When only 790,000 yen was actually forthcoming, observers were quick to suggest that such an amount fell far short of what the ministry would need to meet its goals.[77]

Budgets were one indicator of how the movement was doing, but the ministry had other metrics it could turn to. These suggested that the campaign was doing quite well. Officials reported that the number of direct beneficiaries of the movement had reached 6.5 million by the end of 1954, residents of almost 6,500 different model sites all over Japan. The number of sites and of the beneficiaries of the campaign more than doubled the following year, and then doubled again in 1956 (table 6.1).

The ministry kept track of the number of "model districts" active in the anti-insect campaign well into the 1960s. Keeping in mind that there is almost certainly some slipperiness from year to year around what qualified as a new site, the ministry's numbers do attest to steady growth in

TABLE 6.1. Ministry of Welfare Model Districts, 1954–1956

	MODEL SITES	POPULATION
Sites and population through 1954	6,493	6.5 million
New additions in 1955	8,750	8.4 million
New additions in 1956	16,843	15.7 million
Totals as of 1956	32,086	30.7 million

Source: *Kōsei Hakusho*, 1957.

participation. ministry officials counted 64,642 "model districts" in 1958, or roughly twice as many as in 1956. The 91,300 districts on their list in 1963 grew to 150,000 by the end of the following year.[78] According to ministry estimates, that meant that in 1964 roughly six out of ten Japanese resided within the boundaries of one of these model districts.[79]

The press also kept an eye on local anti-fly and -mosquito efforts. The *Yomiuri* continued to offer awards and hold contests in support of the campaign and of course regularly reported on local successes where they could be found. In midsummer 1959, for example, the paper drew attention to the "Big Mosquito and Fly Extermination Parade" (Ka to hae taiji dai parēdo) it had sponsored in Tokyo's Meguro Ward. The parade included city and ward officials, the head of the *Yomiuri*'s Society section, representatives of the local women's associations, several thousand schoolchildren, and members of the Tokyo Metropolitan Fire Department Marching Band. As the speeches came to a close and the band struck up the theme music from *The Bridge on the River Kwai*, the *Yomiuri*'s very own airplane arrived overhead and began showering the delighted crowd below with thousands of handbills. "Let's Get Rid of Mosquitoes and Flies!" they insisted. Soon the parade set off on its winding route through the city, its marchers following behind banners (also provided by the *Yomiuri*) that read "For a Comfortable/Lovely Tokyo without Mosquitoes or Flies."[80]

The paper followed that extravaganza with announcements a few weeks later of the winners of its "Getting Rid of Mosquitoes and Flies" essay and artwork contest for the city's elementary and middle school students. The prize for the best essay by a middle schooler went to a student who related her personal journey from annoyance at having her favorite meal interrupted by a pesky fly (which she promptly dispatched) to realizing the importance of doing away with flies and mosquitoes altogether in time for the Olympics.[81] "The start of the Olympics in five years isn't really that long from now," she wrote. "I believe that if we all rise up as a citizens' movement of Japan (*Nihon no kokumin undō*) we can create a hygienic nation (*seiketsuna kuni*), so that people from all different countries will have spent an enjoyable time here when that day comes, and take away with them an impression of Japan as a pleasant country, shouldn't we all from this day forward set about getting rid of mosquitoes and flies?"[82]

The following year's "Getting Rid of Mosquitoes and Flies" contest appears to have been the *Yomiuri*'s last, but the subject matter was clearly still a popular one. Elementary and middle school students in Tokyo submitted more than seventeen thousand entries in response to the paper's call for posters in support of the campaign.[83] Editors chose selections from among the submissions to help illustrate a ten-part "Life without Mosquitoes and Flies" series it ran that summer. Each of those articles highlighted an individual or group still active in the fight against the insects in the city.[84]

The *Yomiuri*'s emphasis on the continued relevance of its campaign had a paradoxical element to it as well. Several of the cases its reporters looked at in the summer of 1960, for example, were ones in which community groups had been trying for years to control the flies and mosquitoes in their neighborhoods. Some, like the women's association in Meguro Ward or the Ebara Neighborhood Association in Shinagawa, were in positions to claim that their efforts had done some good. In Ebara's case, for example, residents reported that they used mosquito netting now far less often than they had just a few years before and that the incidence of insect-borne diseases had gone down quite a lot.[85]

The paradoxical element to all this is the admission at every turn that mosquitoes and flies remained a problem for Japan. After five years (if not more) of sustained effort, the promise of lives that were fly- and mosquito-free still seemed well out of reach. The first three-year plan hadn't exactly promised that the country would be pest free by the end of 1958, but as we've seen, eradication was presented as a goal that could be achieved so long as everyone did their part. By the early 1960s, that no longer seemed to be true. The campaign's role as an important element of the nation's public health regime and as an opportunity to celebrate what community-minded citizens could achieve had both dimmed. Far fewer accounts of local eradication made their way into the news after 1960, and the number of articles on the anti-mosquito and -fly campaigns appearing in professional journals devoted to public health and sanitation also dropped precipitously around that same time.

The Hatoyama cabinet had endorsed a three-year plan to rid the country of flies and mosquitoes in June 1955. When those three years were up, Kishi Nobusuke's government chose not to commit to another multiyear proposal. There was some discussion among Liberal Democratic Party policy makers about crafting legislation that would make state funding for local pest control and sanitation projects an ongoing thing, but nothing came of it. Ministry of Welfare officials, for their part, continued to identify communities active in the eradication effort and add them to the ministry's list of "model districts" well into the 1960s, as we've seen.

Signs of concerns about the way forward for the whole enterprise were there as the initial three-year plan came to a close. Imogawa Sakuko, one of the leaders who had helped gather support for the campaign in Meguro Ward's Mitanichō neighborhood, expressed her frustration to a reporter from the Yomiuri newspaper in April 1958. For a while it had looked as if the diet might take up what she referred to as the "Mosquito and Fly Campaign Law," a bill that would have provided support to local sanitation organizations and put the antipest movement on a much more secure footing. She and her colleagues had put a great deal of effort into lobbying on behalf of the proposal, visiting LDP and other party officials in person, and had received assurances that the bill's prospects looked good. As it was, however, by April it looked as if the diet was about to dissolve before considering the proposal, which she took to mean that it might never get done.[86] She was correct in that assumption. As one young civil servant from Kanagawa put it in a letter to the Mainichi a few months later, it felt to him as if local groups doing the work of eradicating flies and mosquitoes had hit a wall of sorts when it came to thinking about what to do next and where to direct their efforts. It was clear to him that there was still much to be done: "A great many areas," he wrote, "continue to be afflicted still by mosquitoes and flies."[87] He remained hopeful that a second three-year plan or perhaps even new legislation would eventually chart the way forward and called on the Ministry of Health and Welfare to continue to support local efforts. "The movement must carry on with patient fortitude, passion, and deliberateness," he wrote, "until not a single mosquito or fly is left in Japan, no matter how many years it takes."[88]

The ministry itself acknowledged as early as 1957 that there were limits on what could be accomplished locally so long as sewerage and other infrastructure improvements lagged behind.[89] The passage of the Water Supply Law (Suidōhō) in 1957 and the Sewerage Law (Gesuidōhō) the following year signaled the government's intention to improve access to supplies of clean drinking water and to connect more of the country's homes to sewerage systems. Neither project moved forward all that quickly, but both gathered momentum in the 1960s. In 1955, only 32 percent of the nation's population lived in areas served by regional or municipal water systems; by 1960 that figure had risen to 53 percent, and by 1965 to 70 percent.[90] Eiko Siniawer notes that in 1962, "the usage rate of sewers in Japan's urban areas was 10 percent, compared to 70 to 90 percent in Western countries."[91] In Tokyo, roughly a fifth of all households in the twenty-three wards were connected to a sewer line in 1960; by 1970, over 40 percent were, and by 1980, almost 80 percent.[92]

The Olympics were certainly one reason the Japanese government was willing to commit to such massive investments in sanitation infrastructure. The announcement that Tokyo had been chosen to host the 1964 summer games came in May 1959, and over the next few years the city and the national government poured money and resources into preparing for the occasion. The need to present Japan in the best possible light was acutely felt; even the young girl whose dinner had been ruined by a fly had said as much in her essay for the Yomiuri in 1959. This included making sure that foreigners were spared encounters with unpleasant odors or sights, much less potentially disease-carrying flies or mosquitoes. The Ministry of Health and Welfare launched a new Environmental Cleanup Movement (Kankyō jōka undō) not long after the announcement of Tokyo's selection. The city itself announced the start of a "Capital Beautification Campaign" in early 1962; its Headquarters for the Promotion of Metropolitan Beautification opened its doors later that year.[93] The new beautification campaign incidentally meant the end of the long-standing "City Residents' Movement to Get Rid of Mosquitoes and Flies."[94] Insect control would be part of the beautification effort, naturally, but city officials may well have decided that rallying cries of "Let's get rid of mosquitoes and flies!" sent the wrong message to visitors.

Along these same lines, Tokyo began regularly scheduled garbage collection in the city's center in 1962 and expanded it to all twenty-three central wards the following year. As Siniawer notes, this was also when polyethylene garbage containers began replacing the old-style wooden refuse boxes.[95] These beautification efforts and the infrastructure improvements associated with preparations for the Olympics are credited with significantly reducing the fly and mosquito populations, at least in the areas where those projects were pursued most aggressively.[96] Top-down directives, experts, and economic growth, in other words, seem to have achieved what the "Lives without Mosquitoes and Flies" campaigns of the 1950s could not.

CONCLUSION

In Japan in the 1950s, the presence of flies and mosquitoes in spaces also occupied by humans came to be defined as a problem that could only be solved through communal action and communal solidarity. Those arguments played out in different forms, whether on film or in the analyses of experts like Hashimoto Masami. Where communities were successful against the insects, explanations for their success more often than not focused on the bottom-up activism and the near seamless cooperation among neighbors said to be evident in those locations. As Hashimoto and others pointed out, flies and mosquitoes were useful foils for a public emerging from war and occupation. Their continued presence posed a threat that most everyone would agree needed to be taken seriously. Unlike many of the other challenges that Japan faced in the 1950s, however, getting rid of mosquitoes and flies was something average people could actually do themselves; done well, their efforts produced positive results in short order. Not only were those outcomes worth welcoming, but as Hashimoto and other observers pointed out again and again, it mattered too that the successful prosecution of insect eradication efforts was so closely associated with the act of coming together as a community.

The mosquitoes and flies that made the news after the campaigns of the 1950s often did so in different guises than before. Japan's mosquitoes and flies hadn't disappeared just because the campaigns to eradicate them had faded away. The Ministry of Health and Welfare reported that about half the people it had surveyed in late 1965 complained of being bothered by mosquitoes and flies; more than 90 percent said that both insects were present in their communities.[97] What was different by the mid-1960s, however, was that neither municipal governments nor policy makers in Tokyo (nor the media, for that matter) were inclined to describe the ubiquitous bugs as problems that particularly needed to be solved. One likely reason for this was that diseases like dysentery and typhoid fever had become much less common than they had been when the eradication campaigns first began. More than 6,000 Japanese had died of dysentery in 1955; a decade later, in 1965, only 270 deaths were attributed to the disease. By 1970, that number had fallen to 51.[98] Even though the public was still coming into contact with mosquitoes and flies in the mid-1960s, there were far fewer voices warning about the potentially dire consequences of those encounters. Mosquitoes and flies were moving out of the "harmful insect" column and into the one that described them as just a "nuisance."

And at the risk of stating the obvious, Japan's unprecedented economic growth during the 1960s was transforming the nation, for better and for worse, in ways that would also impact how people thought about the role of insects in their lives. The launch of the Income Doubling Plan in 1960, and the embrace of economic growth as the most meaningful metric for national achievement, put Japan on a path toward affluence and a future full of technological wonders. At some level, developments such as the expansion of access to higher education and the rapid growth in the ranks of the self-described middle class made it possible to think that the mosquito-infested and sewage-filled ponds of the 1950s were a thing of the past. (Indeed, one wonders whether memories of a time when a life without mosquitoes and flies was a goal worth chasing helped fuel that furious growth.)

Instead of opportunities to band together, encounters between humans and flies (and humans and mosquitoes, less often) increasingly entailed deference to experts and negotiating with the by-products of economic growth and rapid urbanization as individuals. Community-based responses gave way to solutions that in many ways facilitated withdrawal from the face-to-face interactions with neighbors that had been so central to earlier successes against harmful insects. The spread of aluminum screening, for example, made simply excluding flies and mosquitoes from their homes an affordable option for most families. Seki Naomi has pointed as well to the growth of the pest control industry—there were 430 such companies in operation as of February 1968—as an indicator of the disassociation of human-insect interactions from community-based solutions.[99] The development of new forms of built environment in the 1960s, especially in urban settings, left people with little choice but to turn to experts for help. High-rises, subways, underground shopping centers, and the like required the services of professionals with the knowledge and tools to cope with unwelcome insects in those spaces.[100]

Finally, and along somewhat similar lines, the need to dispose of the massive volume of household and other wastes that were the by-products Japan's booming economy in the 1960s also led to some rethinking of what the presence of certain insects signified. The "fly riot" (*hae sōdō*) of the summer of 1965, for example, began when massive swarms of the pests made their way from the so-called Island of Dreams (Yume no Shima) in Tokyo Bay to nearby neighborhoods in Kōtō Ward.[101] The "Island of Dreams" was one of the landfill sites that Tokyo relied on to dispose of the many truckloads of waste it generated every day, and conditions there that summer had been especially fly-friendly. For the residents of Kōtō Ward, insecticides and flypaper were all but useless against the onslaught. In the end, "hundreds of personnel from the fire department, the coast guard, Ground Self-Defense Force (Rikujō Jieitai), and Metropolitan Police Department (Keishichō), as well as public health centers were mobilized as part of a scorched-earth policy whereby parts of the artificial island made of trash were doused in oil and set on fire to eradicate the pests."[102]

An insect problem and problem insects that had once seemed within the power of local actors to address had obviously become something different. In the mid-1950s, the nature of the mosquito and fly problem was more or less the same regardless of where in Japan one was. The circumstances of one community and the strategies it developed to deal with the pests were unlikely to vary that much; as we've seen, the preferred solutions all over Japan relied on local, collaborative interventions. What happened in Kōtō Ward that summer, on the other hand, had no obvious precedent, and at least at the time it appeared unique to that one site. Likewise, no one was prepared to argue that the problem was one that local women's associations or anyone else in Kōtō Ward was equipped to address, indiscriminate incineration not being one of their go-to anti-fly practices. Solutions to insect problems on the scale of the "fly riot" required different tools, and offered different lessons about where Japanese society might be headed, than had the concerns of the mid-1950s.

NOTES

1. Kurosawa, *Ikiru*.

2. There are a great many varieties of flies and mosquitoes in Japan. The primary targets of the eradication campaigns discussed here included common houseflies (*bae*; *Musca domestica vicina*), lesser houseflies (*hime bae*; *Fannia canicu-*

laris), blowflies (*kuro bae*; *Calliphora latta*), and "flesh flies" (*senchi niku bae*; *Sarcophaga Boettcherisca peregrine*). Among the sixty-some varieties of mosquito found in Japan, the common house mosquito (*ka*; *Culex pipiens*), and *Kogata* (*ka*; *Culex tritaeniorhynchus*) are vectors for Japanese encephalitis; *Shina hamadaraka* (*Anopheles sinensis*) was the primary vector for vivax malaria. Suzuki and Ogata, *Nihon no Eisei Gaichū*, 117–19, 137–39, 146–48.

3. *Kōsei Hakusho*, 1966.

4. Gordon, "Managing the Japanese Household."

5. Neitzel, *The Life We Longed For*.

6. Efforts to control flies and other pests in the United States, on the other hand, have had historians' attention for some time. Biehler's *Pests in the City*, for example, shows how the political, class, and racial tensions endemic to American cities had a profound effect on whose private and public spaces became the targets of vermin removal projects, and with what results. While those same tensions do not map directly onto the Japanese experience, this chapter shows how pest eradication efforts there, too, were shaped by ongoing rural and urban reform projects and the politics of high-speed growth.

7. Gordon, "Managing the Japanese Household," 246.

8. Although, as Katō Mutsuo pointed out in 1960, some of the infrastructure improvements associated with the New Life Movement inadvertently created new breeding sites for mosquitoes and flies. Katō, *Hae ka no hasseigen to seikatsu kaizen*.

9. Human-insect interactions have been left out of most of the narratives we've constructed about Japan's modern history. There are a few exceptions to that general rule, of course; Brett Walker's work on the advent of pesticides and anti-insect campaigns in Meiji Japan is one. Eiko Siniawer's *Waste*—which does touch on the anti-fly and -mosquito campaigns of the '50s—is another. See Walker, "Sanemori's Revenge," and Siniawer, *Waste*. One might also add Igarashi Yoshikuni's analysis of the first *Mosura* film to that list: "Mothra's Gigantic Egg." There is a larger body of work in Japanese: Mizutani, "Nihon no eisei chūgai bōjoshi"; Seki, "Sengo Nihon no 'ka to hae no inai seikatsu undō'"; Setoguchi, *Gaichū no tanjō*; Sawada, "Sengo Nihon ni okeru 'Ka to hae no inai seikatsu' jissen undō no tenkai"; Yamanaka, "Sengo nanyo ni okeru 'Ka to hae no inai seikatsu' no tenkai."

10. *Kōshū Eisei*, *Shisei*, *Kōsei*, and *Nōgyō Seikai*, among others.

11. Setoguchi, *Gaichū no tanjō*, 126; *Yomiuri Shinbun*, August 20, 1927.

12. Westerners writing about their experiences in Japan around the turn of the century could be counted on to remark on the abundance of flies, mosquitoes, fleas, and other insects they encountered in their travels and on the fact that most Japanese appeared to take the presence of these pests as a given. See, for example, Bird, *Unbeaten Tracks in Japan*, 219–20, 225–27; Setoguchi, "Control of Insect Vectors in the Japanese Empire," 168.

13. Setoguchi, *Gaichū no tanjō*, 11–12.

14. Setoguchi, *Gaichū no tanjō*, 100–101, 120.

15. In his 1908 encomium on the Japanese Army's medical facilities and expertise, which he observed firsthand during the Russo-Japanese War, the American military surgeon Louis Seaman was especially effusive in his praise of the care taken to keep flies (and thus disease) at bay. In Seaman's assessment, the striking differences between the prevalence of typhoid fever and dysentery among the troops during this campaign and the one fought a decade before, over much of the same territory, was due largely to the army's heightened attention to hygiene, which included practices that specifically sought to deny flies opportunities to breed. Seaman, *The Real Triumph of Japan*, 166.

George Chandler Whipple (1866–1924), in his 1908 treatise on typhoid fever, accepted Seaman's explanation, while noting that he "graphically depicts the little Japanese soldiers turning themselves into an army of fly-catchers, with ingenious devices for catching them. Apparently, the soldiers had been taught to realize that the catching of flies was as much an act of patriotism as the shooting of a Russian." Whipple, *Typhoid Fever*, 198.

For a useful analysis of Japanese efforts to curtail the spread of malaria in Taiwan, see Setoguchi, "Control of Insect Vectors in the Japanese Empire."

16. Setoguchi, "Control of Insect Vectors in the Japanese Empire," 174; Mizutani, "Nihon no eisei chūgai bōjoshi," 56.

17. By the 1930s, Japan was the world's leading producer (and exporter) of pyrethrum. Ota, "Historical Development of Pesticides in Japan," 26.

18. Ota, "Historical Development of Pesticides in Japan," 27.

19. Setoguchi, *Gaichū no tanjō*, 124.

20. Anti-fly campaigns in the United States predated Japan's by a few years and overlapped thereafter. Samuel J. Crumbine's "swat-the-fly" campaigns, for example, were underway in the United States by 1915. See Rogers, "Germs with Legs."

21. Setoguchi, *Gaichū no tanjō*, 125–26. See also *Asahi Shinbun*, August 16, 1925; September 3, 1925; August 24, 1926; July 19, 1928; July 24, 1932; July 23, 1935.

22. *Asahi Shinbun*, October 4, 1938.

23. Setoguchi, *Gaichū no tanjō*, 130.

24. Setoguchi, *Gaichū no tanjō*, 129.

25. Aldous, "Transforming Public Health?"

26. For more on this era, see Hirano, *Mr. Smith Goes to Tokyo,* and Nornes, *Forest of Pressure*.

27. "The Winged Scourge," Walt Disney Studios, 1943, available at https://archive.org/details/gov.archives.arc.47063; "How Disease Travels," "Insects as Carriers of Disease," and "Cleanliness Brings Health" were among the other Health for the Americas series that ended up being shown in Japan. All three films were originally released in 1945. See "Insects as Carriers of Disease," Walt Disney Studios, 1945, available at https://archive.org/details/76154InsectsAsCarriersOfDiseases; "Cleanliness Brings Health," Walt Disney Studios, 1945, available at https://archive.org/details/HealthForTheAmericasCleanlinessBringsHealth.

28. Igarashi, *Bodies of Memory*, 66–67.

29. Igarashi, *Bodies of Memory*, 68–72.

30. As quoted in Igarashi, *Bodies of Memory*, 69.

31. Domestic production began in 1947. Ota, "Historical Development of Pesticides in Japan," 26; Aldous, "Transforming Public Health?" 11–12.

32. One reason for BHC's popularity was that by the mid-1950s, some varieties of insect had become resistant to DDT's effects. *Yomiuri Shinbun*, April 11, 1958.

33. Newly developed organophosphates like parathion and methyl parathion, meanwhile, entered the Japanese market in the very early 1950s as imports. So effective were these products against rice borers in particular that they were credited with helping bring about the dramatic increases in Japan's agricultural productivity that began in the late 1950s. Unlike DDT and BHC, these early organophosphates were highly toxic to mammals, and their use led to dramatic increases in the number of deaths and injuries from pesticide poisoning in Japan. Parathion remained popular with farmers for many years until its use as a pesticide was finally banned in 1971, replaced in part by "safer" organophosphates like malathion and diazinon. Ota, "Historical Development of Pesticides in Japan," 34, 37–38. See also Mizutani, "Nihon no eisei chūgai bōjoshi."

34. Quoted in Russell, *War and Nature*, 170.

35. Quoted in Russell, *War and Nature*, 170.

36. Quoted in Russell, *War and Nature*, 171.

37. See Aldous and Suzuki, *Reforming Public Health in Occupied Japan*, 107.

38. Aldous and Suzuki, *Reforming Public Health in Occupied Japan*, 107–9.

39. Hashimoto, "Ka to hae no inai toshi no kensetsu," 64.

40. Seki, "Sengo Nihon no 'ka to hae no inai seikatsu undō,'" 2; Mizutani, "Nihon no eisei chūgai bōjoshi," 56.

41. Ikeno, "Sengo Nihon no Nōson kaihatsu ni okeru nōson shakaigakutekina shiya," 87; Hashimoto, "Ka to hae no inai seikatsu," 315. For an early example of a local effort in Miyagi Prefecture, see *Yomiuri Shinbun*, June 23, 1951.

42. Yamanaka, "Sengo nanyo ni okeru 'Ka to hae no inai seikatsu' no tenkai," 42.

43. Hashimoto, "Ka to hae no inai seikatsu," 315; Hashimoto, *Kōshūeisei to Sōshiki Katsudō*, 135.

44. *Asahi Shinbun*, June 11, 1954.

45. *Mainichi Shinbun*, October 13, 1954.

46. Nornes, *Forest of Pressure*, 16.

47. The film is reproduced in its entirety on a DVD that accompanies this volume: Fujise, "'Hae no inai machi' o tsukutta goro," 21.

48. "The Town with No Flies" was a success for Iwanami Productions. The Ministry of Education singled it out for an award, and likely more importantly for the studio, the film was a popular one with schools. It became the best-selling film in Iwanami Productions' initial foray into the education market, handily outperforming the studio's subsequent additions to its Compendium series. Fujise, "'Hae

no inai machi' o tsukutta goro," 25–26; Nakamura, "Mieru mono kara Mienai mono e," 85.

49. Hashimoto, "Forty Years of My Public Health Study," 2.

50. As the SCAP official in charge of improving Japan's public health infrastructure, Dr. Crawford Sams seldom missed an opportunity to highlight the superiority of US methods. Aldous, "Transforming Public Health?" In this instance, however, Sams's 1951 visit to the Toyonaka center left him with a favorable impression of the facility and its methods. "General Sams was very much pleased," Hashimoto recalled, "and told his friend boastingly the success of health center in post-war Japan" (sic). Hashimoto, *Kōshūeisei to sōshiki katsudō*, 4; for Sams's account of the visit and a photograph featuring Sams, Hashimoto, and the health center staff, see Sams and Zakarian, "*Medic*," 74.

51. Hashimoto, "Ka to hae no inai machi o iku," "Ka to hae no inai mura zukuri," "Ka to hae no inai seikatsu," "Ka to hae no inai toshi no kensetsu," *Kōshūeisei to sōshiki katsudō*, "'Ka to hae no inai seikatsu' jisen undo no genjō."

52. Hashimoto's data were for conditions in 1953. Hashimoto, "Ka to hae no inai seikatsu," 316.

53. Hashimoto, "Ka to hae no inai mura zukuri" and *Kōshūeisei to sōshiki katsudō*, 345–70.

54. Nagaura was designated an "Environmental Hygiene Model Village" in 1951.

55. Hashimoto, "Ka to hae no inai mura zukuri," 74.

56. Hashimoto, "Ka to hae no inai mura zukuri," 74, and "Ka to hae no inai seikatsu," 316.

57. *Yomiuri Shinbun*, June 27, 1956. Similar numbers appear in a report in the same paper in February 7, 1954, which also points to reduced medical expenses as another side effect of the eradication campaign.

58. Hashimoto, "Forty Years of My Public Health Study," 6.

59. Hashimoto, "Ka to hae no inai mura zukuri," 75.

60. Hashimoto, "Ka to hae no inai toshi no kensetsu," 67–68.

61. The film was released in November 1955. See Aoyama, "Hyakunin no yōki na nyōbō tachi."

62. Sawada, "Sengo Nihon ni okeru 'Ka to hae no inai seikatsu' jissen undō no tenkai," 37.

63. Copies of this film may still exist, but I have not yet been able to access one for viewing.

64. The early 1950s popularity of films like *Teen-Ager's Sex Manual* (Judai no seiten, 1953) and its sequels was also a factor in the federation's decision to support moviemaking on its own terms. See Zenkoku Chiiki Fujin Dantai Renraku Kyōgikai, *Zenchifuren 30-nen no ayumi*, 47.

65. Sawada, "Sengo Nihon ni okeru 'Ka to hae no inai seikatsu' jissen undō no tenkai," 37.

66. Sawada, "Sengo Nihon ni okeru 'Ka to hae no inai seikatsu' jissen undō no tenkai," 35; the *Mainichi Shinbun*'s profile of the neighborhood on the occasion of the award appeared on November 11, 1955.

67. Sawada, "Sengo Nihon ni okeru 'Ka to hae no inai seikatsu' jissen undō no tenkai," 37.

68. *Asahi Shinbun*, October 9, 1955, evening edition, p. 3, relates some of the actual events later depicted in the film.

69. *Asahi Shinbun*, October 9, 1955, evening edition, p. 3.

70. There is an interesting but perhaps unintentional reminder of the stinky pond, Watanabe's crusade, and the construction of the playground in *Ikiru*.

71. This scene, too, reflects practices the neighborhood had adopted as part of the cleanup effort; a group of some two hundred women and children assembled early in the morning on the first, tenth, and twentieth of every month for a collective cleanup and sweeping of the streets. *Asahi Shinbun*, October 9, 1955, evening edition, p. 3.

72. *Merry Wives* won a long list of awards. Some were from education film industry groups, but others originated with NHK, the *Asahi Shinbun*, and the Ministry of Welfare. Zenkoku Chiiki Fujin Dantai Renraku Kyōgikai, *Zenchifuren 30-nen no ayumi*, 49.

73. Gomi mondai no rekishi, Dai-ni shō, "Eisei taisaku to gomi shori," 11, www.l-env.net/data/pdf/9/history_figure_vol02.pdf, accessed January 2, 2023. Attendees were also treated to the performance of a contemporary dance piece specially commissioned to accompany the new campaign anthem. Hashimoto himself left the Department of Environmental Sanitation right around the same time as the assembly for a position in the Institute of Public Health, where he spent the remainder of his career.

74. The third verse continues, "Without mosquitoes and flies, a bright Japan; and that is the truth; hamlets and towns are pretty; shining, shining, shining; without mosquitoes and flies, a paradise of culture; and that is the truth; Well then, let's all get rid of mosquitoes and flies!" Images of the song's lyrics and related materials are on a Rakuten blog post dated August 12, 2007: https://plaza.rakuten.co.jp/yamashi1966/diary/200708120000.

75. *Kōsei Hakusho*, 1956.

76. *Mainichi Shinbun*, June 22, 1955.

77. *Mainichi Shinbun*, January 25, 1956. Later reports cited a higher figure of 1.5 million yen in funding but were no less critical of the government's failure to properly support the movement. *Yomiuri Shinbun*, June 27, 1956.

78. Yoshimoto, "Chiku soshiki katsudō no yoru eisei gaichu kujō," 360; *Kōsei Hakusho*, 1957.

79. The ministry's 1966 white paper was the last to reference the number of districts participating in the movement.

80. *Yomiuri Shinbun*, July 17, 1959.

81. *Yomiuri Shinbun*, August 26, 1959.

82. *Yomiuri Shinbun*, August 26, 1959.

83. *Yomiuri Shinbun*, June 19, 1960.

84. The first in the series appeared on July 4, 1960, the tenth and final install-ment on July 14, 1960.

85. *Yomiuri Shinbun*, July 6 and July 7, 1960.

86. *Yomiuri Shinbun*, April 22, 1958.

87. *Mainichi Shinbun*, September 26, 1958.

88. *Mainichi Shinbun*, September 26, 1958.

89. *Kōsei Hakusho*, 1957.

90. Kōseishō 50 Nen Shi Hensan Iinkai, *Kōseishō 50 nen shi*, 736.

91. Siniawer, *Waste*, 83.

92. Calculations based on data from *Tokyo Statistical Yearbook, produced by the Tokyo metropolitan government, for the years* 1960, 1970, 1980. The yearbooks are avail-able at www.toukei.metro.tokyo.lg.jp/tnenkan/tn-eindex.htm.

93. Siniawer, *Waste*, 79, 83.

94. Oyama, "Tokyoto ni okeru chiku eisei sōshiki no ka to hae kujo," 364.

95. Siniawer, *Waste*, 81–82.

96. *Asahi Shinbun*, April 18, 1964; Mizutani, "Nihon no eisei chūgai bōjoshi," 58.

97. *Mainichi Shinbun*, October 16, 1966.

98. Typhoid fever fatalities declined from 105 in 1955 to 9 in 1965 and then to just 3 in 1970. The number of cases of Japanese encephalitis fluctuated considerably in the 1950s and the first half of the 1960s but dropped precipitously after 1966. Kōseishō 50 Nen Shi Hensan Iinkai, *Kōseishō 50 nen shi*, 714–21.

99. Seki, "Sengo Nihon no 'ka to hae no inai seikatsu undō,'" 3.

100. Oyama, "Tokyoto ni okeru chiku eisei sōshiki no ka to hae kujo," 366.

101. Siniawer, *Waste*, 84–85.

102. Siniawer, *Waste*, 85.

PART THREE

The Institutionalization of Entomology in Twentieth-Century China

SEVEN

Circumscribing China with Insects

A MANUAL OF THE DRAGONFLIES OF CHINA AND THE INDIGENIZATION OF ACADEMIC ENTOMOLOGY IN THE REPUBLICAN PERIOD

Daniel Burton-Rose

Entomologists do not lightly bestow the superlative of their best day collecting in the field. John Henry Comstock (1849–1931) declared of Fort Reed on the Johns River in Florida, "This is the richest field I have ever worked."[1] He did so in 1876, six years before founding the first department of entomology in the United States at Cornell University. Comstock's student and colleague James G. Needham (1868–1957) bestowed his lifetime distinction upon a field site half a century and half a world away: the saturated stretch of land joining urban Suzhou and the low-lying hills adjacent to Lake Tai in Jiangsu Province, China, in April of 1928. The insects were different—crickets and grasshoppers for Comstock, dragonflies and damselflies for Needham—but the enthusiasm was the same. Of "a collecting trip by canal westward" from the Soochow University campus, just inside the eastern walls of the city, to "Seven Sons Hill" (Qizishan), Needham wrote, "I enjoyed one of the best collecting days of my life."[2]

The intervening fifty years between the bestowal of superlatives by teacher and student witnessed the widespread acceptance and institutionalization of entomology in the United States. In 1881, Comstock served in the recently created capacity of chief entomologist of the United States Department of Agriculture in Washington, DC. The existence of such a position reflected a trend in Western Europe and North America of linking knowledge of insect lifecycles and behaviors with state power. The impetus to do so was due to the economic impact of insect blights, the incidence of which increased with the accelerating integration of markets across vast distances. Needham completed his PhD at Cornell under Comstock in 1898 and returned as a faculty member in 1907. He then went on to serve as chair of the Cornell Entomology Department from 1914 to 1936. These were also crucial years for the establishment of scientific careers and institutions in the nascent Republic of China (1912–49): a process with close ties to the Cornell community.[3]

In China in the 1910s and '20s, Cornell and its faculty reprised the central role they had played in the establishment of entomology as a discipline in the late nineteenth-century United States. In this process, Needham filled the role of distinguished disciplinary patriarch that Comstock had earlier assumed. The reason lay in the centrality of Cornell in the export to China of a culturally bounded form of science that grew directly out of European experience but at the time was treated by its advocates as universalist. For nearly forty years, the distinctly American impact on the Republic of China in the fields of sociology, biology, chemistry, genetics, economics, agriculture, geology, public health, and medicine has been at the forefront of scholarly inquiry.[4] Entomology, however—as a subset of biology or zoology and on its own terms—has received little attention in the secondary literature.[5]

Much of the financing for efforts to transform Republican China into a modern nation-state under the tutelage of the United States came from American-controlled foundations, with the Rockefeller Foundation the most prominent among them.[6] The China Foundation for the Promotion of Education and Culture was of a different model. Initiated in 1924 with the second remission of the United States' portion of the Boxer Indemnity, from the start it featured both American and Chinese officers.[7] The China Foundation worked closely with a group of overseas students who had founded the Science Society of China (Zhongguo Kexue She) in Cornell in 1914.[8] Due to his crucial role in the pedagogy of the life sciences at Cornell, many of these men regarded Needham as their teacher.[9] When they returned to China—the society itself relocated to Nanjing in 1918—they instituted their vision through the founding of the first research institute dedicated to biology in China: the Biology Institute at National Southeastern University in Nanjing in 1922.[10]

The first director of the Biology Institute was Bing Zhi (1886–1965), an ethnic Manchu who earned a raised scholar (juren) degree in 1903, shortly before the abolition of the civil service examinations in 1905. In 1909, Bing began studying at Cornell as part of the first group of Chinese students funded by the relinquished Boxer Indemnity.[11] He completed his Bachelor of Science Degree in biology from Cornell in 1913, then embarked on his PhD in entomology under Needham, which he completed in 1918. He was one of the founding members of the Science Society of China and a frequent contributor to its Chinese-language journal *Science* (Kexue).[12] Bing is the likely reason that Needham received an invitation from the China Foundation to serve as a visiting professor in China during the academic year of 1927–28 in order to propagate knowledge of the discipline of biology.

Bing's hosting of Needham is an example of the indigenization of the discipline of academic entomology in Chinese scientific culture in the early twentieth century. Indigenization in this context refers to the translation into the Chinese language—concurrent with the construction of a physical institutional infrastructure and professional networks—of concepts and practices related to the knowledge of insects inspired by the Euro-American tradition, *not* the Sinophone one.

In examining the textual record of knowledge of insects from the vista of the Republic of China in the 1920s, it is evident that human categories of administration and taxonomic systems relating to nonhuman species were equally fluid. It is a story of shared human agency between teachers and students, Americans and Chinese, rather than a positivistic celebration of the advance of human knowledge of insect species. While problematizing the cultural impetus of treating nonhuman species as the possessions of human political entities through taxonomic discourse, this chapter concurrently examines how culturally bounded bodies of knowledge shifted from relevance, to irrelevance, and back again in tandem with political changes expressed through claims about science.

WHY DRAGONFLIES? THE ORIGINS OF NEEDHAM'S MANUAL

Needham was an expert in Odonata, the order primarily constituted by the suborders Anisoptera (dragonflies) and Zygoptera (damselflies). Dragonflies were the topic of his 1898 dissertation from Cornell, and he began publishing articles on the subject in 1901.[13] This material paved the way for *A Handbook of the Dragonflies of North America*, which he coauthored with

Hortense Butler Heywood (1884–1977); completed at the time Needham departed for China, it was published in 1929.[14] Considering that Needham had already spent three decades exploring the Odonata on offer in North America, the opportunity to visit southeastern Eurasia must have been immensely attractive.

From the perspective of an American odonatologist with no knowledge of the Chinese language and little more in the way of familiarity with Chinese culture, China was a vast spot on the map waiting to be filled in with reliable information. What information did exist was contained in two forms: (1) European-language taxonomical treatises and (2) specimen collections. The first body of work began with the publication in 1758 of the tenth edition of the *Systema Naturae* of Carl Linnaeus (1707–1778), which included one species of dragonfly found in China,[15] and continued with the first monograph dedicated exclusively to insects in China: Edward Donovan's (1768–1837) *The Insects of China*, which included six species, illustrated on hand-colored plates. Specimens gathered in China were held in collections both public and private in the United States and China. A personal visit to China provided Needham with the opportunity to expand existing knowledge in both groups by collecting new species in the field and publishing on them. This he did piecemeal in a journal article and comprehensively in *A Manual of the Dragonflies of China: A Monographic Study of the Chinese Odonata*, which summarized his findings.

Needham's own account of the origins of the *Dragonflies of China* is as follows:

> Chinese dragonflies first caught my attention in 1927, when I received
> an unanticipated invitation to spend a year in China visiting and confer-
> ring with departments of Biology in the Universities of that country under
> the auspices of the China Foundation for the Promotion of Education and
> Culture. I looked about for aids to the study of the local dragonflies and
> found there were none. There were only bare descriptions of the adults of
> many species, printed in half a dozen languages, and well scattered through
> the zoological literature of the world. Nothing was known of the immature
> stages.
>
> Since I was invited to lend what aid I might to the study of biology in
> China, I conceived the idea that by supplying a manual for the study of the
> one group of insects with which I already had some practical acquaintance
> at home, I might help Chinese students in the study of their local fauna.

Indeed, I was quite sure that such aid might be more real and the results more lasting.[16]

Needham arrived in Shanghai in September of 1927. There he was greeted by Bing, who had been sending Needham specimens for identification for the past several years. Bing welcomed Needham by sharing with him a new catch of Odonata he had recently collected in Amoy (Xiamen). Bing then escorted Needham to the Shanghai Museum, which possessed what Needham characterized as "the first considerable lot of new specimens I got on my arrival in Shanghai." The bulk of these consisted of specimens collected in Fujian Province by the museum's late in-house taxidermist, Tong Wong-wong.[17] Arthur de Carle Sowerby (1885–1954)—a vigorous explorer of North China, Mongolia, and Manchuria who acted as the curator of the museum—lent the specimens to Needham as he proceeded to Peking (Beijing).

In the northern capital, Needham received a "large, important consignment of specimens" from Fujian provided by Claude R. Kellogg, an *apis* expert based at the Fukien Christian University in Foochow (Fuzhou).[18] Chinese colleagues at Yenching and Tsing Hua Universities shared specimens from around their campuses, as well as ones collected separately in Suzhou. In February of 1928, Needham traveled to Tianjin, where his colleague Tsi-tung Li shared specimens from the Biological Laboratory at Nankai University and escorted Needham to the more sizable collection held by Musée Hoangho Paiho (Huanghe Baihe Bowuguan). As Sowerby had done at the Shanghai Museum, curator Émile Licent (1876–1952) loaned the relevant specimens to Needham.

Needham had arrived too late in the previous year to do any collecting himself. This situation was remedied in Jinan, Shandong, in April, when he scoured streams as soon as they had thawed to collect nymphs.[19] He soon moved south, spending the remainder of April and much of May in Nanjing, where Peter Buck and others provided him access to the Biological Laboratories at the College of Agriculture at the University of Nanking. Needham had occasion to briefly visit Hangzhou and Suzhou, then returned to the United States. Beyond the collecting opportunities provided in the countryside outside a handful of cities on the eastern seaboard, Needham was entirely reliant on others to send him samples from the vast expanses he included under the rubric "China" in his manual.

One of the major accomplishments in regards to the institutionalization of biology in China was enabled by Needham's visit but not brought about by Needham himself. After Needham had accepted the invitation of the China Foundation for the visiting professorship, Needham's former students Bing Zhi and Zou Bingwen composed a letter to the China Foundation proposing the creation of an institute of biology in Peiping (present-day Beijing). Having consolidated their profession in Nanjing— along with the new professional identity of scientist—they wished to extend north the Euro-American model of institutions devoted to biological research that they had successfully realized in Nanjing. The northern city itself was not yet under the same political control as Nanjing; when that occurred in 1928, the name of the city changed from Needham's "Peking" to "Peiping" ("Northern Peace"). It is the latter name that appears on the title of Needham's monograph.

Needham's visit to China provided the occasion for Bing and Zou to request funding for such an institute. Their request was granted. The resulting institute was named after Fan Yuanlian (1875–1927; cognomen Jingsheng), an esteemed educator whose reformist credentials dated back to fleeing to Japan after the failure of the Hundred Days Reforms in 1898.[20] Along with John Dewey and other notables in Republican politics such as V. K. Wellington Koo, Alfred Sao-ke Sze, and V. K. Ting, Fan was one of the original fifteen trustees of the China Foundation appointed in 1924.[21] The Fan Memorial Institute of Biology (Jingsheng Shengwu Diaochasuo) was founded in 1928; Bing served as its first director, dividing his time between Peiping and Nanjing. Two years later, the institute published Needham's *Dragonflies of China*. Provided that Bing is the figure whose assistance Needham most frequently acknowledged in his manual, we can assume that Needham was well aware of how his presence was used to further the goals he shared with his students.

To a certain extent, Needham fits the profile described by Margherita Zanasi of the human agents of League of Nations–sponsored knowledge transfers to China in the early 1930s: "The new experts in international development were not 'China hands' and had no previous knowledge of the Chinese language or the country's history and current circumstances."[22] Needham was certainly no Sinologist: at no place in his writings does he exhibit any serious engagement with the language or culture. But he was clearly on board with the movement in the 1920s to build up the capacity of Chinese professionals and institutions to practice science themselves free of Euro-American mentorship.

In imagining how Needham might have understood the relationship between scientific education and national revitalization in China in the 1920s, a programmatic essay published in 1921 by Columbia University professor John Dewey (1859–1952) provides a contemporaneous perspective from a fellow East Coast educator. The article was inspired by Dewey's conversations with the student activist Hu Shi (1891–1962), who had attended Cornell and participated in the Chinese Science Society there before beginning his studies at Columbia.[23] Dewey paraphrased the radical Chinese student's charge that "American missionary education has failed to develop independent, energetic thought and character among even its most distinguished graduates. It has produced rather a subservient intellectual type, one which he [Hu] characterized as slavish." Without endorsing Hu's unqualified condemnation of missionary schools, Dewey articulated the type of education he perceived the Chinese as desiring from the United States: "They want Western knowledge and Western methods which they themselves can independently employ to develop and sustain a China which is itself and not a copy of something else." From this perspective, "what China most needs from the West . . . [is] scientific method and aggressive freedom and independence of inquiry, criticism and action." On an emotional note, he added: "They are touchingly grateful to any foreigner who gives anything which can be construed as aid in this process."[24]

Needham's China visit—six years after the publication of Dewey's essay—was part of a successful effort to transmit scientific knowledge with the stated aim of laying the groundwork for the Chinese professionals themselves taking the reins. Needham wanted participation from Chinese students in the cocreation of new knowledge: an impulse driving the creation of his manual was that "such aid might be more real and the results more lasting, than any that might come from merely lecturing to them."[25]

MUTABLE BOUNDARIES, MUTABLE SPECIES: THE MUTUAL CONSTITUTION OF POLITICAL AND BIOLOGICAL NOMENCLATURE

Dragonflies of China describes 266 species, 58 of which were "new to science," in 89 genera, one of which was new.[26] The terminology of the manual exhibits a slippage between nonhuman species that occur within a human politico-cultural unit—"Dragonflies *of* China"—and ones that belong to that unit: "Chinese Odonata." Dragonflies can exist in "China" as a noun; they are possessed by the adjective "Chinese." The agenda of Needham's China visit and his manual was to strengthen the Chinese nation through science. Examining his literature review, however, what is striking is that the *political* nomenclature employed by Needham and his predecessors is as mutable as the *biological* nomenclature. For example, nowhere did Needham acknowledge that the majority of articles he cited were composed during the Qing dynasty (1644–1912), a multiethnic empire ruled by the Northeast Asian Manchus that vastly extended the territory of their predecessors into Central and Northeast Asia. As for biological nomenclature, the class Odonata was not stabilized until the early twentieth century, coinciding with the fall of the Qing and the first time in history that "China" was used in the name of a nation-state.[27] In the earlier sources cited by Needham, what he considered Odonata were classified under the order Neuroptera, which currently exclusively designates lacewings.[28]

In order to relate "the progress of systematic knowledge of the dragonfly fauna of China" up to 1928, he provided an alphabetical list of "Describers of Chinese Dragonflies." Due to the nomenclatural practice of including the surname of the first identifier of a species in the scientific literature following the Linnaean binomial, all these "authorities" remained in play in the late '20s synthesis of Needham's manual.[29] Despite stretching back 170 years to the tenth edition of *Systema Naturae*, Needham's list featured only thirty-five names, including his own.[30] The national affiliations of the describers indicate the geopolitical map of the first two centuries of odonatology. All were Europeans of the metropole, with the exception of F. C. Fraser, a major in the Indian Medical Service who described an Indian species, and two Japanese entomologists, whose presence confirmed in the entomological register Japan's success after the Russo-Japanese War (1904–5) in obtaining peer status with the Western powers. The first of these, Matsumura Shōnen (1872–1960), was the father of Japanese colonial entomology (with an identification of 1911). He established Japan's first course on entomology at Hokkaido University and named over twelve hundred species of Japanese insects. In 1926, he founded the entomological journal *Insecta Matsumurana*, which continues publication to this day. His Japanese-language *6000 Illustrated Insects of Japan-Empire* (Nihon konchū daizu kan) of 1931 is the summa of Japanese colonial entomology.[31] Between J. O. Westwood's 1842 revision of Donovan's *Insects of China* and Needham's 1930 manual, there were no other monographs dedicated to insects generally or a particular group of insects in China. Needham closed his brief historical survey with citations of eight short articles in English and German dating from 1894 to 1925.

Beyond universal claims inadvertently calling forth localist ones, did any of the early entomological authors object to mapping emerging national or imperial and colonial boundaries onto species that predated such distinctions by tens of millennia? Robert McLachlan (1837–1904 or 1845–1926) did. He opened his study of winged insects of the Portuguese and Spanish Atlantic islands of Madeira and the Canary Islands with a discursus on the arbitrary nature of conflating administrative and biological boundaries:

> It has always appeared to me that attempts to work out, group by group, the fauna or flora of special countries or districts are duties to which the attention of naturalists should be especially directed. It is by means of such attempts that we are enabled, little by little, to grasp broad generalizations on the probable origins of the productions of certain districts, to ascertain the geographical distribution of species, and to form some idea of the possible means whereby, through a process of evolution, certain forms have acquired their existing characteristics as distinguishing them from others to which they are most closely allied.
>
> If this be true regarding the value of local monographs for countries or districts separated arbitrarily by political frontiers, or physically by mountain-ranges, &c., such monographs become of far greater value when they concern small islands, or groups of islands, separated from the nearest mainland by wide distances and great depths of sea or ocean.[32]

Needham authored hundreds of pages enumerating minute differences among odonate species using criteria such as wing venation and the shape of mandibles, but he never defined his key terminology "China" and "Chinese."[33] *Dragonflies of China* thus reveals a tension between geographic and politico-administrative terminology; due to the political muteness of the author, his precision as a scientist is undermined.

This tension between geography and political unit is evident in the manual's "Annotated List of Chinese Species." Needham employed the abbreviations N, S, E, W for the cardinal directions, complemented by "G" for general, "C" for central, "F" for Formosa and "H" for Hainan.[34] Needham did not address the fact that "Formosa"—the island of Taiwan—had been ceded by the Qing Empire to the Japanese in the resolution of the

Sino-Japanese War of 1894–95; at no time had it been a possession of the Republic of China, and it would not become one until after World War II. Though not formally colonized by a rival power, Hainan Island was nearly as remote from the administrative control of Republican officials as Taiwan.

Needham's reluctance to address the changing *political* nomenclature of the period covered by his studies left a blurriness in his terminology related to *entomological* nomenclature. He identified a habitat for each of the enumerated species, but his terminology veered without explanation from the geographical to the political. Attempts at geographical objectivity included South, Central, and North China, as well as "China Plain" (presumably the North China Plain).[35] Administrative units sowed greater confusion. Needham employed the names of provinces alongside those of cities. The habitat for *Ictinus fallax Selys* is identified as "Kwangsi [Guangxi], and Shanghai"; that Shanghai is located in the province of Jiangsu—which is northeast of and noncontiguous with Jiangxi—was not communicated to the reader.[36] The orthography for a city Needham spent considerable time in is likewise not consistent: "Peiping" appears on the cover page, but "Peking" and "Peping" appear in the body of the manual.[37] The entry for *Gomphidia krugeri Martin* reads "Fukien [Fujian], Tonkin."[38] The logical implication would have been that Tonkin was a Chinese province; in actuality, it referred to the Red River Delta Region of northern Vietnam and was the term for the northernmost colonial administrative division of French Indochina.

Needham used the term "China" repeatedly but made a concession to the vagueness of this designation over space and time by putting it in scare quotes in one instance.[39] Geographic designations that overlap with administrative-political terminology include "Manchuria" and "Thibet [Tibet]," neither of which were under the control of the Nationalist government at the time Needham was writing.[40] "Hongkong southward" is a designation clearly indicating that Needham used "China" in a broad cultural sense, as Hong Kong was obviously a British colonial possession.[41] A more confusing example is the inclusion of Sylhet—a city in present-day northeastern Bangladesh, well beyond a broad cultural or narrow political definition of China—as the sole habitat designation of *Allogomphus smithii Selys*.[42]

INSECTS IN THE SCHEMA OF CIVILIZATIONAL
UNITS; OR, DIFFERENTIATING THE UNIVERSAL
AND THE PARTICULAR

The literature review in *Dragonflies of China* contains an implicit dichotomy familiar in Euro-American natural science encounters with the rest of the world over the preceding several centuries: laments of the extent of local ignorance combined with acknowledgment of reliance on local guides. To be "known to science" was to be textualized and circulated within the international community of scientists; vernacular knowledge needed to be translated into textual form in a (Western) European language in order to be validated.[43] The difference between China and what was, in the 1920s, just beginning to be reimagined as a potentially *postcolonial* world, was the extent and quality of its written record.

Broader contours of the civilizational units came into contact in Needham's manual, as evident in the study of insects.[44] The Western tradition dated back to Aristotle and Pliny the Elder's (ca. 23–79 CE) book on insects in his *Naturalis historia*.[45] On the Chinese side, early records include Wang Chong's (27–ca. 97 CE) meditation on the semantic range of *chong* in *Balanced Discourses* (Lunheng) and the pharmacopoeia tradition that began with *Shennong bencao* (Divine Husbandman's materia medica; first century BCE–first century CE).[46] Dragonflies were not well represented in these early sources. Fuller representation is evident in the major pharmacopoeia that bracketed the sixteenth century: *Imperially Mandated Essential Information, Arranged in Grades, on Materia Medica* (Yuzhi bencao pinhui jingyao) of 1505 and Li Shizhen's (1518–1593) *Comprehensive Materia Medica* (Bencao gangmu) of 1596.[47] *Essential Information, Arranged in Grades* has color illustrations but did not circulate widely. However, its illustrations provided the basis for at least two painted color works that did not include the textual entries: *Supplement to Master Thunder's Conveniently Arrayed Instructions for Processed Materia Medica* (Buyi Lei gong paozhi bianlan), an imperial manuscript dated 1591,[48] and Wen Shu's (1595–1634) *Forms of the Natural World* (Jinshikunchongcaomu zhuang), which was copied between 1617 and 1620 (i.e., the last years of the Wanli reign [1572–1620]).[49] The former continued within the pharmacological genre, but the latter is a work of literati painting.[50] Taken together, Li's *Comprehensive Materia Medica* and the two illustrated works based on *Essential Information, Arranged in Grades* provide a vivid window into Chinese knowledge of insects at the precise moment when intellectual contact with Europe was reaching an unprecedented intensity through Jesuit missionaries.[51]

Li's *Comprehensive Materia Medica* has attracted the lion's share of scholarly attention. The author's invaluable three decades of peripatetic fieldwork and innovative systematization of the written tradition was rewarded with frequent publication in and beyond Ming (1368–1644) and Qing China.[52] Soyoung Suh and Federico Marcon, writing on Chosŏn dynasty (1392–1897) Korea and Edo period (1600–1868) Japan, respectively, have shown how pharmaceutical study and natural history, driven in part by Li's work, developed a similar early modern register of concerns for differentiating the local *qua* emergent national from the broader classical language unit (in Classical Chinese as opposed to Latin).[53] A similar phenomenon was happening concurrently in the British Isles, with Linnaeus's universal system calling into existence local inventories of nonhuman species.[54] When modern scientists decided—after the late Qing and early Republican period interregnum—that the Sinophone textual corpus mattered again, *Comprehensive Materia Medica* was one of the first works to which they turned.[55] In a series of six volumes published from 1931 to 1941, Bernard E. Read (1887–1949), a professor at the Peking Union Medical College, produced a detailed translation published by the *Peking Natural History Bulletin*.[56] Thus, during the time Needham was in China, Read was engaged in mining the Chinese textual tradition of natural science as a foundation for modern globalizing science.[57]

The *Comprehensive Materia Medica* follows a standardized rubric for its approximately 1,895 entries.[58] It begins with etymology and then evaluates claims in previously written works with Li's field experience. Dragonflies are described as belonging to five or six types, with the distinguishing characteristics color (red or green) and size (big or small). While undoubtedly a humble number compared to the 266 species belonging to five families in two suborders enumerated by Needham, Li's "five or six" was similar in spirit to the seven dragonflies differentiated by Linnaeus in *Systema Naturae* nearly two centuries later.[59] In its vagueness, Li's description was qualitatively no different from eyewitness reports by untrained Europeans accepted by metropole scholars as late as the late nineteenth century. For example, McLachlan reconciled textual knowledge obtained in places such as "the rich library of the Royal Geographic Society" with insect samples sent by informants from locales spanning the entirety of Eurasia, from western Sichuan to the Canary Islands off the African mainland.[60] Needham cited two articles by McLachlan as among only eight published "local lists" bridging the comprehensive ambitions of the 1854 revised edition of Donovan's *Insects of China* and Needham's own manual.[61] In his 1882 survey of the Neuroptera of Madeira, McLachlan cited "a curious little book" published anonymously and dated 1815 that constituted the earliest reference to Neuroptera on the intriguing islands.[62] Regarding dragonflies, it declared, "There are several kinds, and the largest sort 3 inches long." From this McLachlan surmised, "*Anax formosus* in all probability."[63]

Additionally, the *Comprehensive Materia Medica* included information on behavior that could have been of interest to Needham, such as the swarming over the Bohai Sea that continues to this day.[64] Li's work also included ethnographic data beyond the scope of Needham's *manual*, such as on the indigenous (non-Han) peoples who periodically ate dragonflies.[65]

As a palace production, *Essential Information, Arranged in Grades* hardly circulated, with the significant exception of when an official carried it with him to Suzhou, where Wen Shu was able to copy it.[66] Immediately preceding Li's innovative ordering of all known materials from the simplest (rocks and minerals) the most advanced (humans), *Essential Information, Arranged in Grades* and the works based upon it had a scattershot approach to classification. In contrast to Li's three-fold differentiation of the *chong* ("insects") category—oviparous (forty-five kinds; *j.* thirty-nine to forty), metamorphizing (thirty-two kinds; *j.* forty-one), and water-born (twenty-two kinds plus supplementary species; *j.* forty-two), the *Essential Information, Arranged in Grades* had one undifferentiated category that placed snakes, clams, and hedgehogs alongside wasps, cicadas, and mantises. Yet unlike the crude wood-block illustrations of the early editions of the *Comprehensive Materia Medica*, the high-quality illustrations of the *Essential Information, Arranged in Grades* and the works based upon it stand out for their cutting-edge verisimilitude.[67] In the dragonfly illustration of Wen's *Forms of the Natural World* (fig. 7.1), for example, the terminal appendages can be clearly distinguished on the upper of a pair of dragonflies, and pterostigma are evident on the wings of both of them.

Such accurate illustrations did not remain the baseline in Chinese depictions of dragonflies. One example is the Qing painter Nie Huang's *Oceanic Complexities, Illustrated* (Haicuo tu), featuring some three hundred creatures. Nie explained that the dragonflies observed off the coast of Fujian were the adult stages of shrimp.[68] He added valuable behavioral detail by commenting that the swarming observed in Bohai also occurs in

蜻
蛉

FIGURE 7.1. The detailed wing venation of dragonflies, including pterostigma, as well as terminal appendages of the top dragonfly. From Wen Shu's (1595–1634) *Forms of the Natural World* (Jinshikunchongcaomu zhuang, 1617–20), based on a 1505 imperial pharmacopoeia.

Fujian but came no closer to comprehending the life-cycle development from nymphs to adults. In supporting his textual case with illustrations, Nie stuck with Li's broad color schema by providing a green and a red dragonfly, each of them next to a shrimp of the same color. In order to highlight the morphological analogy, rather than distinct double prongs of cercus and epiproct, the dragonflies are depicted with crustacean-evoking tail fins. Similarly, a green dragonfly in a painting dating from 1812 to 1824 commissioned by John Reeves (1774–1856) from a Canton painter depicts an apparent tumorous lump at the base of the abdominal segments and a biologically inconceivable three prongs at the hind tip.[69] These examples warn us away from expecting a clear progression of depictional accuracy for the purposes of contemporary criteria of taxonomic identification and differentiation and demonstrate the value of devoting greater attention to earlier depictions (Yuan [1271–1368] and Ming instead of Qing, in this case).

Due to his impulse to systemize the physical manifestations of all of the known world, Li is sometimes termed "the Chinese Linnaeus," but given Li's priority, Linnaeus should obviously be "the Swedish Li Shizhen." The tenth edition of Linnaeus's *Systema Naturae* placed all dragonflies and damselflies in one genus (*Libellula*) and contained one species occurring in China: *Neurobasis chinensis*.[70] Of this damselfly, Needham enthused, "It is one of the most beautiful insects in the world, having hind wings of a wonderful metallic green whose shimmering surfaces reflect every tint of the rainbow." He acknowledged an awareness of what Sarah Easterby-Smith termed, in her exploration of the role of commerce in eighteenth-century Anglo-French botany, a "bias towards the beautiful," continuing, "It was sure to be collected as soon as discovered and to be taken to Europe by those who gather things curious and beautiful."[71]

As with Li's *Comprehensive Materia Medica*, the very comprehensiveness of Linnaeus's *Systema Naturae* produced a dialectal impulse to delineate the particular. As mentioned above, the first monograph dedicated exclusively to insects in China was Donovan's *Insects of China*. Needham described each of the six dragonfly species identified by Donovan with poetic gusto, concluding, "This was a bevy of beauties. Surely they were the sort of insects to be collected first."[72]

Donovan acknowledged Chinese expertise over their own flora and fauna. In a passage quoted by Needham, he wrote, "The Chinese are well acquainted with the natural productions of their empire, and zoology and botany in particular are favorite studies among them." Jumping ahead chronologically half a century to J. O. Westwood's preface to the expanded 1842 edition, Needham proceeded to quote Westwood on the redundancy of insect samples shipped primary from pre–Opium War (1839–42) "Old Canton" to London: "There is such an absolute monotony in these arrivals that it is almost impossible to discover in an quantity of these boxes a single species that is not contained in all the rest."[73] Another remark by Westwood demonstrates that Needham must have been aware of the Chinese depictional tradition of insects. Westwood observed that "numerous beautiful drawings of insects upon rice paper [were] brought to Europe in great quantities" but that unfortunately "many of these figures are, however, evidently fictitious, although some are occasionally found accurately correct and most elaborately pencilled."[74]

Scholarship on technical illustrations in imperial China has stressed intentions other than verisimilitude on the part of those who produced and disseminated such images. Yet the question remains as to what extent wood-block illustrations and "China trade" paintings and drawings could and did provide information to European taxonomists. In regards to natural history sketches produced by Chinese artisans for European consumers in the nineteenth century, historian of science Fa-ti Fan has warned that convincing details were not a guarantee of biological accuracy: "Although the carefully executed details gave the paintings an air of observational realism, and the artists' skill carried persuasive power, the subjects were nonetheless often imaginary. A plant might be decorated with flowers of striking colors, resembling no existing plant, all with a deceptive vividness. A butterfly might be a hybrid of the features of two or three different species or be an entirely fanciful invention."[75]

In her work on the Guangzhou painters Ju Lian (1828–1904) and his student Gao Jianfu (1879–1951), however, art historian Lisa Claypool makes a strong case against dismissing out of hand the entomological value of the "flowers and insects" motifs. Ju and Gao continued and adapted depictional methods that dated back to the popular Qing Kangxi-reign (1661–1722) *Manual of the Mustard Seed Garden* (Jieziyuan huapu) and beyond to China's first high age of mimetic realism, the Northern Song (960–1127).[76] The way in which they contributed to human knowledge of insects in a Chinese cultural context across the premodern-modern divide deserves further attention. Certainly one important task for the emerging field of Chinese insect humanities is to engage the millennia-plus of images of insects produced in the Sinophone world with precise questions grounded in present-day biological knowledge of species endemic to these areas.

CONCLUSION

Consideration of what James G. Needham considered relevant knowledge begs the question: how did the rich tradition of natural history relating to dragonflies in the Chinese-language cultural sphere abruptly become irrelevant at the particular moment in the early twentieth century in which Needham produced his manual? Part of the answer is: it didn't. Or rather, it became so only for a narrow sector of Euro-American professional scientists who could not read Chinese. At the time of Needham's use of the laboratory facilities at the Peking Medical Union, Bernard Read, a faculty member there, was combining the philological skills of academic Sinology with the interests of the life sciences by systematically translating Li Shizhen's *Comprehensive Materia Medica*. He published the section on *chong* as "Insects Drugs" in 1941. European or American professionals working in China without knowledge of the language had access to the expertise of Chinese students and colleagues. Claude R. Kellogg, Needham's correspondent in Fuzhou, is an example of an American entomologist who spent a prolonged period in China and who clearly delighted in the temporal length and informational breadth of the Chinese written record. Kellogg used his Chinese students to comb through and translate primary sources on topics such as the earliest records of beekeeping in China and records of locust disasters.[77] On the latter topic, his awe at the extent and detail of the Chinese record provides echoes of Jesuit missionaries centuries earlier who were shaken by textual evidence that China had escaped the Flood of Genesis.[78] Kellogg did not publish his essays on entomological subjects drawing on Chinese-language sources until the 1960s, but they clearly drew on material he collected much earlier and could possibly have discussed with Needham.[79]

As a young man, Bing Zhi, Needham's primary host throughout his term in China, had mastered two entirely distinct bodies of knowledge: the civil examination system curriculum, then Euro-American biology. He clearly had the ability to access Sinophone knowledge on human-insect relations but prioritized the institutionalization of science along Euro-American lines as a crucial step in national strengthening. The task of mining the Sinophone literature for entomological information was taken up by another of Needham's one-time Cornell students: Zou Shuwen (1884–1980). In 1958, Zou began publishing a series of articles reading descriptions of animals in pre-Han texts in the light of taxonomic categories prevailing in the 1950s. Of particular interest to Zou as a starting point was the "Monthly Regulations" (Yue ling) chapter of *The Book of Rites* (Liji), in which the modern field of entomology and the abandoned civil service examination curriculum could find common ground.[80] From this starting point, Zou dedicated his energies to the construction of a comprehensive chronology, organized in the conventional annalistic dynastic format, of indigenous Sinophone entomological knowledge from the founding of the Zhou dynasty (1046–256 BCE) to the late Qing. *History of Chinese Entomology* (Zhongguo kunchongxue shi) was published only posthumously in 1982, but much of its content circulated earlier to interested experts. The rush of nativistic pride that followed in the wake of the 1949 Communist revolution enabled Zou's synthesis of imported categories and native sources; Zhou Yao (1912–2008) performed the same task in his *Initial Study of Entomology in Early China* (Zhongguo zaoqi kunchongxue yanjiu shi: Chu gao), first published in 1957. Zhou initially took a species-based approach, starting with those best documented, such as silkworms and honeybees. He, too, dedicated the remainder of a long career to combing the Sinophone textual record for entomological information relevant to the present.

Viewed in light of the accomplishments of his students and their colleagues in the Republic of China and the People's Republic of China, with his Odonata manual Needham achieved precisely what had set out to do. He summarized the body of textual knowledge that he was familiar with, while expanding with biological information available through collaboration with Chinese professionals who had studied abroad and Americans and Europeans with careers in China. The publication of Needham's manual is perched on the edge of two momentous developments: the emergent capacity of Chinese institutions to train experts in biology and the mapping of flora and fauna within claimed political boundaries that were as of yet largely aspirational.

NOTES

The author would like to thank the following individuals for feedback that has improved this chapter: David A. Bello, Alexandra Cook, Prasenjit Duara, Frank N.

Egerton, David Gilmartin, Wilt Idema, Nancy Jacobs, Lijing Jiang, and Heather Martel. William Ma also gave generously of his time, orienting the author in the scholarly literature at the intersection of art history, technical and scientific illustration, and animal studies.

1. This passage is from a letter Comstock wrote to his future wife Anna Botsford Comstock. See her posthumously published autobiography, *The Comstocks of Cornell*, 87–88. Needham quoted the same passage: Needham, "The Lengthened Shadow . . . —I," 145.

2. Needham, *A Manual of the Dragonflies of China* (hereafter MDC), 2.

3. Needham, "The Lengthened Shadow . . . —II," 225–26.

4. For example, Furth, *Ting Wen-Chiang*, esp. 34–69 (on geology, paleontology, and anthropology); Chiang, "Social Engineering"; Haas, "Gist Gee"; Lee, "Geological Sciences"; Reardon-Anderson, *The Study of Change*; Sheng, "The Origins of the Science Society"; and Spence, *To Change China*. A new generation of scholarship on biology in Republican China is initiated in Jiang, "Retouching the Past."

5. The only entomological field addressed in the Science and Civilisation in China series is pest control (Huang, "Plants and Insects in Man's Service"). The only survey of the discipline of entomology in China in any language is Zhou, Wang, and Xia, *Er shi shiji Zhongguo de kunchongxue*. While invaluable for its detail, this work is a nationalistic celebratory history of pioneers and landmarks, rather than a critical history. On the formation of entomology as a distinct academic discipline, see Egerton, "History of Ecological Sciences, Part 45," and Clark, *Bugs and the Victorians*.

6. On the Rockefeller Foundation, see Bullock, *An American Transplant* and *The Oil Prince's Legacy*. On the expression of American power in China through the register of science, see Buck, *American Science and Modern China*.

7. On the China Foundation, see T. Yang, *Patronage of Science*.

8. On the Science Society, see Z. Wang, "Saving China through Science."

9. Major figures in Republican science who regarded themselves as Needham's disciples included Zou Shuwen (on whom see below), Chen Zhen (1894–1957), Hu Jingfu (1896–1972), Liu Chongle (1901–1969), Zhu Yuanding (1896–1986), Wu Fuzhen (1898–1996), Zou Bingwen (1893–1985), Guo Tanxian (1886–1929), Qian Tianhe (b. 1893), and Jin Bangzheng (1886–1946) (Hu, *Jingsheng shengwu diaochasuo shigao*, 9).

10. National Southeastern University became National Central University in 1928, after several name changes during the 1927–28 partial occupation of the campus by Nationalist troops. For the name changes, see Schneider, *Biology and Revolution*, 55n2.

11. On the first remission of the indemnity and its allocation for study in the United States, see Hunt, "The American Remission of the Boxer Indemnity."

12. For Bing's original contributions, see Bing, *Bing Zhi wencun*. For a brief English-language profile, see Li and Kang, "Bing Zhi."

13. See, for example, Needham, "A Genealogic Study of Dragon-fly Wing Venation." Given the dramatic absence of women in the field of entomology at this time,
it is notable that Needham's only two credited collaborators were women: Heywood
and Elsie Broughton. On the latter, see Needham and Broughton, "The Venation of
the Libellulinae (Odonata)." This too could be considered a Comstockian legacy, as
Comstock collaborated closely with his wife, the scientific illustrator Anna Botsford
Comstock, with whom he also cofounded a publishing company.

14. The *Handbook* was a forerunner of the detailed textbook, authored with
Minter J. Westfall, *A Manual of the Dragonflies of North America (Anisoptera), Including the Greater Antilles and the Provinces of the Mexican Border*, which was published
by the University of California Press in 1955 and which has been revised in two
subsequent editions after Needham's passing, those of 2000 and 2014.

15. I will continue to refer to the tenth edition because it is the accepted baseline
of the modern taxonomic system. For this reason, it is the edition Needham cited
in MDC.

16. Needham, "Observations on Chinese Gomphine Dragonflies," 145.

17. Also transliterated "T'ang Wang-wang." A photograph of Tong appears
following page 4 in Sowerby, *China's Natural History*, 4. Insects in the museum's
collection are detailed on pages 87–97 of the same work, which includes four color
plates of butterfly and moth specimens.

18. Kellogg sent two more shipments later in the year. Needham had further occasion to consult specimens Kellogg had provided to the Smithsonian Institution
in Washington, DC. On Kellogg's collection of *apis* in Fujian, see Cockerell, "Bees
Obtained." Kellogg also published on Massachusetts species: for example, Kellogg
and Asquith, "Preliminary Studies" and Kellogg et al., "Variations in the Size of
Wings." Needham referred to the Smithsonian as the "United States National
Museum" (MDC, 4), a name that was officially changed in 1811.

19. MDC, 1.

20. A third signatory was the botanist Hu Xiansu (1894–1968). The letter is
reproduced in full in Hu, *Jingsheng shengwu diaochasuo shigao*, 9–11.

21. *The China Foundation*, 4.

22. Zanasi, "Exporting Development," 144.

23. Hu was designated in the article only as "A Chinese student who is now
in this country and who was an active leader in the Students' Revolt in 1918 in
Peking." Dewey, "America and Chinese Education," 77.

24. Dewey, "America and Chinese Education," 78–79.

25. Needham, "Observations on Chinese Gomphine Dragonflies," 145

26. For an overview of changes in Odonata nomenclature since the publication
of MDC, see Trueman, "A Brief History of the Classification and Nomenclature of
Odonata."

27. Zhonghua, the term used in the Chinese name of both the "Republic of
China" (Zhonghua minguo) and the "People's Republic of China" (Zhonghua

renmin gonghe guo) literally means "central florescence." The term grew out of the classical culture of the North China plains and floated free from its geographical moorings over time to indicate "culture" itself in the Sinophone world. See the discussion in H. Clark, "What's the Matter with 'China'?" The term "central flores-cence" was claimed by Chosŏn and Edo intellectuals during the Qing conquest: see Y. Wang, "Manchu-Chosŏn Relations" and Mervart, "The Point of the Centre."

28. The last use of Neuroptera to include Odonata was in 1853: see Newman, "Proposed Division of Neuroptera into Two Classes." Needham cited an 1833 article by Newman in MDC (p. 301) but not this one. On historical change in the taxon Neuroptera, see Kluge, "Circumscriptional Names of Higher Taxa in Hexapoda," 40–41.

29. See the discussion in Cook, "Plant Technology and Science."

30. Needham's offering was the most recent identification: one of 1928.

31. The English title is that provided on the spine. Chapter 20 of this work is devoted to odonates (pp. 1428–63). Matsumura's posthumously published Japa-nese-language autobiography *Memoiren Matsumuras* (1968) bears a dragonfly on the front and back covers. The second Japanese entomologist cited by Needham was Kan Oguma (identifications of 1922 and 1926).

On the establishment of entomology as a discipline concurrent with the cre-ation of Japanese empire, see Setoguchi, *Gaichū no tanjō*, and the English-language version of chapter 2, "Control of Insect Vectors in the Japanese Empire." For a present-day survey of insect diversity conflated with Japanese borders, see Tojo et al., "Species Diversity of Insects in Japan."

32. McLachlan, "The Neuroptera of Madeira and the Canary Islands," 149–50.

33. In this geographical vagueness, Needham was echoing Linnaeus himself, who consistently conflated India and China in plant identifications. See the dis-cussion in Cook, "Linnaeus and Chinese Plants," 123–24. Linnaeus's students, how-ever, made a clear distinction between India and China in consistently identifying the latter (the Qing Empire) as, in Lisbet Koerner's words, "an ideal cameralist state." See the discussion in Koerner, *Linnaeus*, 98–101.

34. MDC, 286n2.

35. "China Plain" (21), "N. China" (33), "Northern China" (37).

36. MDC, 23.

37. "Peking" (MDC, 29), "Peping" (57).

38. MDC, 26.

39. For *Allogomphus Sommeri Selys* (MDC, 36). Examples of "China" as the sole habitat designation appear on pages 23 and 26.

40. MDC, 34.

41. MDC, 73.

42. Needham elaborated in a manner that did not clarify his reason for inclu-sion: "One male, the type, from Sylhet, in the British Museum; another reported by Fraser from Sikkim." MDC, 35.

43. On this process, see Jacobs, *Birders of Africa,* and the contributions to the workshop "Colonial Sciences and Indigenous Knowledge Systems in South Asia," organized by Minakshi Menon at the Max Planck Institute for the History of Science, June 10, 2016.

44. The problematic and essentializing terminology of "civilization" is employed here in the heuristic manner described by Arun Bala and Prasenjit Duara, in which civilization is treated as "an open-ended and evolving sphere of inter-referential ideas and practices" that "nonetheless, can draw from—often unacknowledged—sources outside the sphere." Bala and Duara, "Introduction," 1.

45. Book 11. The two most thoroughly annotated translations are Pliny, *Natural History, Volume III,* and Pline l'Ancien, *Histoire naturelle. Livre XI.* Illustrated volumes of *Naturalis historia* were a major source of insect imagery from the mid-fifteenth century on. See, for example, the first page of book 1 of the Nicolas Jenson edition of 1472, held by the British Library. Reproduced in McHam, *Pliny and the Artistic Culture of the Italian Renaissance,* 146.

46. On the materia medica tradition up to the sixteenth century and its relationship to other developments in medicine, see Unschuld, "Prologomena," in *Ben Cao Gang Mu, Volume VIII,* 25–39.

47. *Buyi Lei gong paozhi bianlan,* 2:227 (dragonflies). On Master Thunder texts more broadly, see Bian, *Know Your Remedies,* 40–44.

48. A color reproduction of *Buyi Lei gong paozhi bianlan* is available in the 2012 edition prepared by Zheng Jinsheng.

49. PDF of Taiwan National Museum exemplar. The edition of *Jinshikunchongcaomu zhuang* published by Sichuan Daxue Chubanshe is incomplete compared to the Taiwan National Museum exemplar.

50. On *Jinshikunchongcaomu zhuang* and the social network in which it was embedded, see Li Xiaoyu, "Cong Huangjia yaodian dao 'zhenqi zhi chu.'" On the works' relationship with the *Bencao pinhui jingyao,* see Cao, *Bencao pinhui jingyao,* 728–31.

51. Q. Zhang, *Making the New World Their Own.*

52. Métailié, "Le *Bencao gangmu*" and Nappi, *The Monkey and Inkpot* are important starting points for the study of Li's work.

53. Suh, "Herbs of Our Own Kingdom" and Marcon, *The Knowledge of Nature.*

54. English entomology was a relatively late manifestation of this phenomenon, which was closely related to the emergence of a modern national identity. Clark observed, "Nineteenth-century entomology was part of the systemization of nature that underpinned the emergence of modern Britain." Clark, *Bugs and the Victorians,* 12.

55. Benjamin Elman argues convincingly that the Qing defeat in the Sino-Japanese War of 1894–95 was the critical event in late nineteenth and early twentieth-century "denigration of traditional Chinese natural sciences." See the discus-

sion in Elman, "From Pre-modern Chinese Natural Studies to Modern Science in China," 53–65.

56. According to the title page, Read was also associated with the Henry Lester Institute of Medical Research in Shanghai. I have relied upon the reprint by the Southern Materials Center, Inc. (Taipei: 1977). The entry for dragonflies is on pp. 72–73. Read is mentioned briefly in Bullock, *An American Transplant*, 20, 88, and 223–24.

57. The volume titled *Insect Drugs* was published in 1941.

58. For an insightful discussion of Li's taxonomic rubric, see Métailié, "The *Bencao gangmu* of Li Shizhen."

59. MDC, 14.

60. McLachlan, "The Neuroptera of Madeira and the Canary Islands," 150.

61. The two articles cited by Needham are McLachlan, "On Two Small Collections of Neuroptera from Ta-Chien-Lu in the Province of Szechuan, West China, on the Frontier of Thibet" and "On Odonata from the Province of Szechuen in Western China, and from Moupin in eastern Tibet."

62. Confusingly, despite the title of his article, McLachlan referred to odonates as "Pseudo-neuroptera" in the text itself: McLachlan, "The Neuroptera of Madeira and the Canary Islands," 155 and 176–83. "Pseudo-neuroptera" is an antiquated term that referred to insects with reticulated wings, as in the Neuroptera, but which also had an active pupal stage. See *Webster's Revised Unabridged Dictionary* (C. & G. Merriam Co., 1913).

63. McLachlan, "The Neuroptera of Madeira and the Canary Islands," 151. The work cited is *The Traveller's Guide to Madeira and the West Indies* (Haddington).

64. Feng et al., "Nocturnal Migration."

65. Métailié, "Aperçu de l'entomophagie en Chine," 79.

66. Li Xiaoyu, "Cong Huangjia yaodian dao 'zhenqi zhi chu.'"

67. On technical illustrations in late imperial China, see Bray, Dorofeeva-Lichtmann, and Métailié, *Graphics and Text*. For an account of European insect illustrations from the sixteenth to nineteenth centuries, see Ball, *The Art of Insect Illustration* and Engel, *Innumerable Insects*. For European zoological illustration in the same period, see Sleigh, *The Paper Zoo*.

68. For a recent annotated edition, see Zhang, *Hai cuo tu biji*. On a related precocious work of oceanological zoography sometimes attributed to Nie, see Greenberg, "Weird Science." Greenberg tentatively dates this work to 1688 and does not discuss Nie in the essay.

69. Reproduced in Magee, *Chinese Art and the Reeves Collection*, 88. The caption for this illustration reads, "The Reeves' drawings form one of the finest natural history collections of the nineteenth century. Artistic merit and scientific accuracy is present in almost all the drawings, including the one shown here, and reveal the excellent draughtsmanship and observational skills of the artists." In this catalog

insects are the only category of fauna depicted for which Magee does not venture Latin names, indicating the extent to which natural historical studies of entomology still lag behind those of botany and zoology.

70. Needham used the common name "Green-wing"; that prevailing today is "stream glory." It is currently classified in the odonate family Calopterygidae.

71. Easterby-Smith, "Cross-Channel Commerce," 218; MDC, 6.

72. The six species are *Neurobasis chinensis, Ictinus clavatus, Rhyothemis variegata, Palpopleura sexmaculata, Crocothemis servilia,* and *Neurobasis fulvia.* The quote appears in MDC, 5.

73. MDC, 6. Citing this same passage from Westwood's preface, Fan comments, "The Chinese had no idea of Western entomology; they collected and arranged the insects according to their brilliant coloration. Despite the erratic juxtaposition of kinds, these specimens gave Western naturalists some basic ideas concerning China's insects." See his *British Naturalists in Qing China,* 28.

74. Donovan, *The Insects of China, n.p. (iii).*

75. F. Fan, *British Naturalists in Qing China,* 51; see also the discussion of the above-quoted Westwood comment on 190n58.

76. Claypool, "Beggars, Black Bears, and Butterflies," 29–38.

77. Kellogg, *Aborigines.* In his preface, Kellogg wrote, "Most emphatically I express my deepest gratitude to the zoology students at the university for the inspiration received from association with them and for their help in parts of the book. They were able to find interesting references in Chinese literature for which they deserve credit" (iii).

78. On Jesuit exploration of early Chinese dynastic histories, see Standaert, "Jesuit Accounts of Chinese History and Chronology and Their Chinese Sources."

79. Kellogg's bear titles such as "Insects in Chinese History, Medicine, and Agriculture," "Locusts in Chinese History," "The History of Silk in China," and "Honey in Chinese History" (in Kellogg, *Aborigines*). Kellogg, *Aborigines,* 16–20A, 21–25, 31–35, and 73–76, respectively.

80. The monthly ordinances share material with the *Lü shi chunqiu* and *Huainanzi.*

EIGHT

The Dialectics of Species

CHEN SHIXIANG,

INSECT TAXONOMY,

AND THE "SPECIES PROBLEM"

IN SOCIALIST CHINA

Lijing Jiang

At present, general zoology textbooks published in China and in the United States are quite similar in structure and content. They usually start with an introduction of the cell as the unit of life and then give an overview of evolutionary principles before delving into systematic classifications of animals. Research method, however, is emphasized to a greater degree in Chinese zoology books, such as the opening sentence of the 2014 edition of *Zoology* (Dongwuxue), published by Fudan University Press, which invokes "holistic perspective" (*zhengti de guannian*), "unity of the opposites" (*duili tongyi*), "regularities" (*guilü*), and "dialectical materialism" (*bianzheng weiwu zhuyi*).[1]

By the early 2000s, an emphasis on dialectical method may have already sounded like a cliché to domestically educated biology students who had gone through similar openings of some science textbooks in middle and high schools. The emphasis on dialectical method, however, was quite uneven in its appearances among textbooks—it could not be so easily found in textbooks on other subjects, such as molecular biology, for example. The heavy load of dialectics in zoology textbooks actually had a specific lineage of invoking such tropes from zoologists themselves.

The formation of dialectical thinking in entomology and taxonomy was led by Chen Shixiang (1905–1988). As an entomologist interested in classifications of individual species and taxa beyond the species level, Chen tried in the Socialist period to follow major international debates about the species problem in the world as much as he could using the limited literature sources available, including ample works from the Soviet Union and pre-Soviet Russia. What has been known as the "species problem" consisted of a series of dissensions from a Linnaean "species essentialism" that depicted species as real, unchanged, and sharing a particular set of common essential properties. In the 1930s and 1940s, while leading biologists discussed how genetics could explain evolution, a congregation of ideas that was later depicted as "modern evolutionary synthesis," some taxonomists started to take Darwinian evolution seriously for their classificatory work. The question of how evolution should be incorporated exactly to taxonomic practice, however, has been a point of contention.[2] After the 1950s, Chen's readings in Soviet biology, dialectics, modern evolutionary and molecular biology, and eventually, the works of Mao Zedong (1893–1976) offered him sources of inspiration for his innovative solution to the species problem from a unique perspective.

Chen justified entomological works across different periods and how he explained a dialectical method over time for taxonomy of insects, the animal kingdom, and beyond. How did the experience in the Republican and Socialist periods square with his taxonomic research and administrative work? In what ways was his dialectical method a borrowing from Marxist philosophy and Socialist ideology, and in what ways was it an independent philosophical and methodological intervention? How effective was it for addressing the species problem and for carrying out daily research? Why did insects become particularly fruitful for such intervention in Socialist China?

Historians have shown the multifarious meanings and practical modes insects have offered for modern biology and agriculture. *Drosophila melanogaster* was made into a foundational experimental organism in modern genetics and, as historian of science Robert E. Kohler argued, facilitated a new moral economy organizing the ways scientists exchanged materials, examined them, formed allies, and distributed favors and credits.[3] Entomology, as a field, not only offered much for genetics, systematics, and ecology but also contributed to agricultural developments well funded by post–World War II nations, carrying the prevalent discourse about politics and science into its practice.[4] Historians of science Tania Munz and Sigrid Schmalzer both have shown that highly dictatorial, ideological regimes could inspire scientific contributions that are not necessarily reflective of the usual problematic distortions of the regime.[5] Cases of ethologist Karl von Frisch's discovery of the bee dance's meanings and entomologist Pu Zhelong's (1912–1997) innovation in insect control via the use of ducks, for example, were not about the racialized pseudoscience under Nazi rule or a blind, anti-intellectual appropriation of indigenous methods in 1950s China but were genuine entomological insights inspired by the state's priority in agriculture. The versatility of the insects was not lost in the more theoretical realms of systematics and evolutionary biology. In fact, as Chen's heuristics of dialectical relations developed, his work in insect classification balanced the opposing emphases in geographical or historical dimension in taxonomy, and it proliferated via multiplications of texts for further taxonomical education.

NEW INSECTS FOR THE NEW REPUBLIC

During the Republican period (1912–49), not only were a large number of entomologists working in China, they also had firmly established the importance of the field for both its practical benefits in agriculture and its potential in generating prestige for emerging domestic academic research. With the great popularity of agricultural science among the students who went to study in the United States in the early twentieth century, especially with students and associates of the Cornell entomologist and limnologist James G. Needham, entomology probably had attracted the largest number of professional biologists by the late 1930s.[6] They argued for the importance of discovering new species for gaining shortcuts to international fame at a time when science in China met with a number of obstacles such as lack of sufficient funding and technological infrastructure. Officials of local entomological bureaus that were responsible for insect monitoring and control frequently appeared at academic events, sponsoring research and consulting about local issues.[7]

Although trained in Europe, Chen belonged to this generation of entomologists and worked along with them after his study abroad. Born in 1905 in Jiaxing County, Zhejiang, he first studied biology in Fudan University in Shanghai, then traveled to France to study at University of Paris and obtained his PhD in 1934. His dissertation was on the species within a subfamily of the leaf beetle, Chrysomelinae (Yejiayake) in Vietnam and China. In the same year, he returned to China to work at the Institute of Zoology and Botany of Academia Sinica.

It was a peak time for species collection work in China. By the late 1920s, as Chiang Kai-shek consolidated extensive political power and started to plan for Academia Sinica, biologists seized the opportunity to establish more institutional support for extensive field collections. In the process, biological specimens became representatives of the new republic, its history, and its economic future.[8] Thus, Chen immediately had a rich variety of insect specimens to work with, including those from foreign missionary scientists and an increasing amount amassed by his Chinese colleagues. While describing different species, Chen occasionally mentioned the geographical variation of morphology of a single species. His overall work, however, stressed the distinctiveness of morphological features of different species, which was almost unavoidable as Chen and other taxonomists focused on surveying particular types of species in a region to publish lists of them. Their efforts can be seen as a kind of classical Linnaean taxonomical work whose very nature encouraged the attention to the discontinuity, discreteness, and ontological reality of species.[9]

From 1937, with Japan's invasion of China, the Institute of Zoology relocated several times inland, further from the coast and Japanese occupation. It first moved from Nanjing to Yueyang, Hunan, in August 1937 and then to Yangshuo in Guangxi and stayed there for one year, before reaching Chongqing by the end of 1938. The multiple relocations of the institute enlarged the research scope of entomology and elevated its relative research importance in the eyes of the government. First, entomology was useful for solving pest issues that plagued the areas to which the Guomindang government moved: correct identification of the species of pests was crucial for designing effective ways to contain them. Second, entomological research required less of the pricey and heavy equipment than studies of mammals usually required. New collections of insects were made along the moving route. In addition, proximity to the field in the interior gave Chen more opportunity to observe nature directly. It was also during wartime that Chen started to consider how the metamorphosis of different insects affected the way insects should be classified, a topic that would become a crucial consideration in his dialectical method later.[10] These publications, however, did not articulate specific concerns about the precise definition of species, a topic later known as the "species problem."

At this stage, Chen was more concerned with the use of the Chinese language for naming species or higher taxa. At the time when an overhaul of Chinese natural knowledge was underway, how to properly translate taxonomic language from Latin binomial nomenclature became an important issue. In *Science* (Kexue), the flagship journal of science in China, Chen published an article to suggest several general translational principles.[11] He made the recommendation of naming higher taxa using the representative Chinese character already used for either the type genus or the genus that was most prevalent in China. Other modifications of taxa names can be adapted from parts of the vernacular names, such as those that denote habitats or hosts. For example, Pediculidae—the genus of sucking lice—can be translated as "*shi* family" (*shi ke*), and *Pediculus humanus* (head and body lice) can be rendered as "human lice" (*renshi*). To increase the number of Chinese characters suitable for entomological use, Chen also recommended constructing new characters with the radical *chong* in them.

Overall, Chen rejected the idea of transliteration based on sound, arguing the resulting names would appear nonsensical for nonexperts. These suggestions emphasized the daily usage of the Chinese language and practical aspects of taxonomy, which may make Chen almost sound like a nominalist, a taxonomist who did not care much about the reality of species but only the practical use of their names. Yet, to standardize terms for academic fields was one of the priorities of the burgeoning academic biology in general at the time. Chen's fixation on terms probably revealed little about his deeper-seated philosophy regarding insect species.

AN ENTOMOLOGIST FACES SOCIALISM

In the wake of the Communist Revolution in China, the study of biology went through a period of significant change. What is most well-known among these changes was the sharp downturn in genetics as the Communist Party reorganized natural sciences following the Soviet Union. As the Soviet agronomist Trofim Lysenko (1898–1976) was in disagreement with classical genetics, many Chinese geneticists were criticized for their work and had to abandon the subject altogether from 1950 to roughly 1956.[12]

However, as genetics was not often referred to in taxonomy at the time, Lysenkoism's influence in taxonomy was of a more peripheral nature. In the end, the major priorities of entomology in the early years of Socialist China were similar to those of the Republican period, with its emphasis in agricultural insect control.[13] The overall learning of Marxism-Leninism, along with Soviet works in biology then circulating, however, affected the teaching and research philosophy of taxonomy and biology in general. Above all, a dialectical approach was incorporated into the fabric of related biological discourse. Through such incorporation, Chen gave an innovative response to a global debate about the ontology and definition of species, although this response is less known to scientists working in Europe and North America. Chen's evolving interpretations of taxonomy through evolutionary and dialectical perspectives was one telling case of how such incorporation can be fruitful and can eventually legitimate the continued use of the dialectical language in teaching and research.

In the 1950s, dialectical thinking's reach in biology was more generally felt in biological education, with accounts of various organisms' malleability and connectivity and the regularities hidden behind their manifest diversity. Following Soviet educators, pro-Communist philosophers, biologists, and teachers published essays to discuss how natural dialectics was the most progressive philosophy to guide biological education. Whether the most significant feature of the living world was diversity or regularity mattered a great deal to properly inculcate the dialectical view. As anatomist Lu Yudao (1906–1985) noted, to start a textbook with a depiction of biological diversity would give the false impression that living organisms were separated from each other, and it encouraged an isolationist, static view about species. Instead, he suggested starting the textbook with an emphasis on regularity, such as "Biology is a scientific subject that studies the regularities of biological development; only after we master these developmental regularities, can we change these organisms."[14] As a result, new editions of textbooks were published throughout the 1950s with emphasis on dialectics, hands-on experience, and the malleability of organisms. One of the most prominent role models was Gu Qiaoying (b. 1923), whose teaching plan about species and evolution at Shanghai Middle School in the 1950s became published as a blueprint for course development elsewhere.[15]

For Chen, learning from the Soviets in the 1950s meant, first and foremost, learning from Soviet entomology. He extensively studied entomological research done in Soviet and Tsarist Russia. In the first quarter of the twentieth century, both institutionally and intellectually, entomology was one of the most developed biological disciplines in Russia, with a dozen journals and local research communities throughout the Russian Empire. There, a dynamic concept of species called physiological species, which means that morphologically identical organisms might belong to different species due to their divergent physiological features, emerged in Russia as early as 1905, which challenged the notion that morphology alone could ensure correct classification. The arguably most important player in the modern synthesis, the Ukrainian-American population geneticist Theodosius Dobzhansky (1900–1975), from whose earlier definition Ernst Mayr derived the biological species concept, had worked as an entomologist studying beetle populations between 1917 and 1927 in Kiev and Saint Petersburg. As Nikolai Krementsov pointed out, Dobzhansky's significant work for the modern evolutionary synthesis could not be separated from the population thinking in the Russian school of entomology.[16]

At the time, Chen became quite active in organizing scientific exchange and collaboration with the Soviet Union, organizing a collaborative expedition in Yunnan and publishing articles to advocate further learning of Soviet science.[17] In his own research, he also started to consider the reality and definition of species, a question that had been concerning evolutionary studies, taxonomy, and philosophy of biology. Simply put, if every individual organism is different from one another, and intraspecies variations are widespread, species may not be real groups. They may be continuous individuals that we recognize as groups due to our brain's tendency to divide, instead of seeing the complexity of the real nature out there. The center questions are thus: Is species real? If so, what is species?

Before he addressed these more general questions, Chen considered the problem of the origin and evolution of insects as a class. During the Republican period, Chen already held great interest in the evolution of insects, publishing short articles to analyze the formation of larva and insect metamorphosis.[18] In the 1950s, when genetics was under scrutiny for its alleged idealist ideology, evolutionary studies were greatly encouraged in China. Soviet discussions in evolution were translated and disseminated for scientists to study and discuss. In a 1955 article, Chen articulated what he considered the "major contradiction" in insect evolution, citing his inspiration from a translated version of *General Introduction to Darwinism* (Osnovy darwinizma), a textbook for ninth graders in the Soviet Union published in 1951. Particularly, he quoted the two major evolutionary paths of animals suggested by evolutionary morphologist Aleksey Nikolaevich Severtsov (1866–1936) that the organization and functionality of animals would become more complex over time and that usually, animals would gain a new path to adapt to new living conditions without general change in their organizations.

Claiming the new inspiration, Chen set out to systematically review the evolutionary process of the class Insecta, pointing out the importance of dealing with three problems integrally: the origin of insects as a class, the origin of wings, and the origin of holometabolism (complete metamorphosis). Although previous scientists had usually discussed them individually, he noted that their interrelationship and mutual connection were crucial for solving these questions in proper historical context. For example, the crucial step for the class Insecta to take shape was the formation of the locomotory center, which offered the space for wings to develop and evolve. This step became the basis for the origin of wings, linking the first problem to the second. The possession of wings afforded insects wider space on land and in the air but also brought "a definite contradiction" between the larva and adult life in their "living conditions," linking the latter two problems. The article analyzed previous publications in Europe about insect evolution in regard to how these three problems should be understood individually as well as a whole. Although at this point Chen avoided explicit reference of dialectics, his appropriation of terms such as "contradiction" and "living condition" were apparently borrowed from recent biological tropes in the Soviet Union.[19]

In the same year, Chen gave speech at the occasion of China's celebration of the centennial of the birth of the Russian (and Soviet) geneticist Ivan Vladimirovich Michurin (1855–1935). It was published as an article the following year, entitled "Wuzhong jiegou yu wuzhong xingcheng," in which he started to address the more general issue of species. In the article, Chen discussed how the structure of a species, reflected in the characteristics of populations and subspecies within it, was a reflection of the historical process that had shaped the species. This time, he was more articulate in an emerging philosophical and methodological view about viewing species and their evolution. In the article, he defined species as breaks in the process of continuous development of organisms. Thus, the study of species formation entails unveiling how a continuous evolutionary history could produce these discontinuities manifesting as species.[20] The definition would be further revised in the 1960s, after Chen consulted more literature in modern synthesis and debates about species and speciation.

Again, he named a few disparate processes as major "contradictions" in species formation. The continuity and discontinuity in the organismal characteristics within a species, for one, was regarded as one contradictory pair. The other pair was the interbreeding between populations and isolation of individual populations within a species. With interbreeding between different populations within a species, the continuity and a relative uniformity of a single species can be ensured. With isolations of species, the relative uniformity would be broken down and pave a way for differentiation within species, which may eventually lead to the formation of new species. Thus, studying interbreeding and isolation events that took place in evolutionary history would be crucial for pinpointing the major processes that led to species formation. Chen cited both Michurin's and Gregor Mendel's (1822–1884) research on hybridization to discuss this view in the same paper.[21] Regarding Michurin's view that hybridization would enhance the living force of organisms and increase variability, Chen noted that although hybridization between populations increases the level of variation within species, it nevertheless also decreases the variation between populations and actually keeps the species as a whole more uniform. Similarly, Mendel's hybridization experiments that crossed the round, yellow pea with wrinkled, green pea indeed introduced more variations. However, the hybridization also reduced the dissimilarity between the original two types by introducing intermediate types. Given the converging points of Michurin and Mendel, two scientists whose theories had been often depicted as ideologically antagonistic in the debate of genetics in the Communist bloc, Chen noted that "we can thus see the similarity between Michurian theories and Mendel's principles."[22]

To learn from the Soviets did not mean only adopting the language of dialectics or simply making due reference to Michurin's theories. As a field that has high relevance for insect control in agriculture and beyond, entomology was a hot spot for reform under the Communist regime, under the direct effects of slogans or movements such as "Theories combined with practices" and "Collaborate with the masses."[23] Although Chen's longer-term legacy in entomology was his dialectical interpretations of species and species formation, with major contributions in insect evolution, he also had engaged in a series of work for classification related to insect control since the late 1950s. In 1957, to commemorate the fortieth anniversary of the October Revolution, Chen published an article praising the features of entomology in the Soviet Union. Carrying out scientific research programs based on the nation's practical needs was the first feature that Chen praised about Soviet entomology, followed by its dialectical thought as the second commendable feature.[24] He soon coauthored the first volume of *The Encyclopedia of Chinese Economic Insects* (Zhongguo jingji kunchong zhi) in 1958, whose later volumes continued to be published until the late 1990s.[25]

A CHINESE RESPONSE TO THE SPECIES PROBLEM

To a practitioner of insect classification, or any casual reader in taxonomy or evolution, Chen's characterization of species may well sound like a tentative response to a global question about the ontology of species, later known as "the species problem." Against the backdrop of the biological modern synthesis that began to take shape in the 1930s and 1940s in which leading biologists discussed how genetics could explain evolution, taxonomists began to feel compelled to take Darwinian evolution as a crucial consideration for their classificatory work.[26] For them, it was clear that the earlier typological understanding of species was no longer sufficient for guiding their work.

Historically, Linnaean taxonomy made the assumption of a "species essentialism" that depicted species as real, unchanged, and sharing a particular set of common essential properties. For example, mammals are distinguished by their possession of mammary glands. Yet the category was problematic: due to sexual dimorphism, not all individuals of mammals have well-developed mammary glands. Some philosophers therefore rejected the ontological reality of species altogether, while others sought alternative solutions. In the 1930s and 1940s, many challenged the typological mode of classification by devising novel methods or theories. There were numerical taxonomists who assigned values to measure the degrees of phenotypical difference for proper classification and the cladists (taxonomers who classify according to shared common ancestry) who insisted relations in evolutionary history should be the only yardstick for classification. Others tried to reconcile the cladistic approach, which focused on historical lineage, and the numerical approach, which analyzed manifest difference between species now. In other words, middle-ground solutions were sought after regarding ways to take both the historical and the geographical accounts of species into consideration.

Ornithologist Ernst Mayr's (1904–2005) biological species concept was one proposed definition that emphasized that the reproductive barrier resulted from isolation of populations or genetic restructuring. Although he firmly defended Darwinian evolution, publishing the book *Systematics and the Origin of Species* in 1942 to account for how factors such as mutation, population change, and natural selection could lead to speciation and biological diversification, Mayr intentionally eliminated the historical dimension from his formal definition of species to avoid unnecessary complications.[27] In addition, as new tools and new modes of thinking added to the repertoire of measurements that could potentially aid classification, such as population biology, ecology, protein profiling, or chromosomal banding, among evolution-minded systematists, what counted as most important for distinguishing one species from another became ever more contentious. The resulting species problem, as philosopher Richard A. Richards succinctly summed it up, was the fact that "there are multiple, inconsistent ways to divide biodiversity into species on the basis of multiple, conflicting species concepts."[28] As these discussions continued well into the 1960s in the Western world, Socialist China offered a different set of textual, heuristic, and ideological resources for consideration when Chen began to tackle the problem from his own practical and theoretical milieu.

Chen's formal entry to explicitly address the species question started with his consideration of a debate that attacked Lysenko's understanding of species and species transformation in the Soviet Union that began in late 1952. Reacting to Lysenko's article, "New Developments in the Science of Biological Species" (Novoe v nauke o biologicheskom vide), a number of Soviet scientists published a series of articles to dispute Lysenko's definition and the "proofs" of species transformation in the *Botanical Journal* (Botanicheskii zhurnal). Several Lysenkoites rejected these objections via their own articles. This debate became the beginning of the downfall of Lysenko as a theorist.[29]

The translation of this series of "speciation debates" eventually took place in China, and by 1956, eighteen volumes of translations of related discussion were published.[30] A few established Chinese biologists soon followed up with their own commentaries on the issue. In 1957, Chen published an overall clarification of philosophy and method of taxonomy, heralding his more systematic discussion of these issues later in 1961, along with commentaries about Lysenko's work.[31] Regarding Lysenko's definition of species that stated "a species is a distinct, qualitatively definite state of living matter," Chen interpreted that the "living matter of certain quality" had a relatively correct emphasis on the kind of disruption of continuity that species represent. After this graceful interpretation, however, he criticized Lysenko's denial of the existence of intermediate types and the existence of intraspecies competition or mutual aids. According to Chen, these latter views not only contradicted known scientific facts but also resembled Linnaeus's static view and were in contradiction with the dialectics that Lysenko himself had advocated.

The speciation debate offered an opportunity for Chen to voice his systematic view about taxonomy. It was a time that the Communist Party leaders started to reassess Lysenko's influence in Chinese academic biology, as his ideas were refuted after the death of Stalin. When a genetics symposium was held in the resort town Qingdao in 1956, Chen and other biologists—some of whom had been forced into silence in the early 1950s at the height of Lysenkoism—voiced their views regarding Lysenko's biological ideas. Chen's criticisms of Lysenko in his speech were similar to those in his 1957 paper.[32] Along with the hotly debated problem of speciation, the revisit to Lysenkoism's harmful effect and a national effort to revamp biology afforded Chen a timely opportunity to present his views and push forward his vision about a new taxonomy. This was an opportune time for doing so also because academic scientific research and discussion revived to an unprecedented level from 1956 onward, until the Cultural Revolution ended most forms of academic practice in 1966.[33] This open atmosphere can be also reflected by the fact that Chen's philosophical and methodological views were challenged by colleagues at the time, and he would write further clarification and rebuttal to further the discussion.[34]

In the early 1960s, Chen's overall philosophy and method of animal classification via considerations of dialectical pairs began to mature. Among the contradictory forces that played roles in evolution that he had considered, commonality and distinctiveness and continuity and discontinuity became the two major pairs Chen focused on. In a 1961 article, he formally subscribed to a set of philosophical and practical considerations for animal taxonomy.[35] According to Chen, the double features of commonality and distinctiveness provided the foundation for classification so that individual animals could be grouped into different categories to begin with. Because biological individuals are alike to a certain degree while distinguishing themselves with their differences, it provided the basis for classification across space in the contemporary world. Yet, across time, each group changed while maintaining a certain continuity to their previous generations, and the continuity/discontinuity pair offered a parallel basis for studying the process of species formation, different stages of such formation, and how they connect and divide original forms in the contemporary world and in fossil records. Thus, the two major pairs of contradiction formed a "dialectical principle" underlying taxonomic work that combined both spatial and chronological dimensions.

Chen made connections of these features to Chinese language and Marxist historical understanding. He noted that the character *lei* (類; "kind") contains meanings richer than the English term "type." To explain it, he offered the following formula: "*lei* = populations + distinct features + evolutionary stages" ("類" = 類 [群體] + 型 [特性] + 段 [階段]).[36] This formula connected the concrete existence of species in populations to their more abstract distinct features distributed in space as well as in time (i.e., their evolutionary stages). He also compared the temporal dimension of the formula to the historical stages in Marxist philosophy of history from the slave society to the ultimate Communist society. These seemingly far-fetched linguistic and ideological connections probably added the needed gravitas to his ideas to be accepted by students and fellow experts who had cultivated particular political affinities in the Socialist milieu.

In reality, however, Chen was probably much more affected by the newly stirred debates about the species problem in the United States as they were reflected in Mayr's publications. What are species? How to deal with the vast difference in variability within species and the quagmire given existence of intermediate type? Are species real, or are they simply human constructs for the sake of sorting out the world? These were the questions that concerned Mayr and his contemporaries. In response to these questions, Mayr himself had given a definition based on interbreeding populations and reproductive barriers between species, and others emphasized the evolutionary process and defined a species as a basic evolutionary unit that ran through time. Thus, the biological species concept and cladistic species concept do not always agree with each other in terms of their exact divisions of taxa. For many, these, along with other competing definitions, were contradictory criteria and rather demonstrate the impossibility of a classification system that reflects biological reality.

Citing Soviet biologist Vladimir Leontyevich Komarov (1869–1945), Chen regarded species as real. The definition of species Chen gave, however, directly derived from the biological species concept given by Mayr and his own consideration of dialectics. In the two-part definition Chen gave, the first part stated the dialectical relations between discontinuity and continuity: "Species is a basic link in the chain of development in the organismal world. They are the basic form of breaks that unify the discontinuity and continuity. The organismal world develops through the form of species, and speciation is a basic link in its development." The second part, although it could have alluded to the commonality/distinctiveness pair, actually was adopted directly from Mayr's definition, stating that in sexually reproductive organisms, "species are groups of actually or potentially interbreeding natural populations, which are reproductively isolated from other such groups."[37] By attaching the additional part to Mayr's definition at the beginning, Chen considered he had added the much-needed time dimension to Mayr's species definition.

The 1961 article was by nature a synthetic piece that summarized what Chen viewed as the proper way of approaching classification, a philosophical and methodological exposé. After reviewing the definition of species, modes of evolution, types of taxa in a classification system, and types of classification systems, Chen started to discuss concrete ways of applying philosophical thinking to practice. He pointed out that the major tasks of taxonomists were to differentiate the breaks from the continuities of characteristics of organisms, and such breaks should be identified not in individuals but in populations. A significant example Chen gave to further illustrate the advantage of his emphasis on the break in continuity was the classic case of whether the ancestral bird should be classified among the reptiles or grouped into the class of birds. According to the cladistic analysis in German entomologist Willi Hennig's (1913–1976) phylogenetic (cladistic) systematics, because the ancestor of birds had a close evolutionary relation to crocodiles' ancestor, even closer than between crocodiles and lizards, or between crocodiles and turtles, the ancestral birds should be grouped as an order under the class reptiles, however absurd it may seem. Chen regarded the conundrum as easily solved by differentiating discontinuities that reflected different evolutionary stages from others that rather reflected specializations or diversifications. In such new "stage phylogenetic systematics," as Chen called it, because ancestral birds display features that characterize a higher evolutionary stage, these features should exempt them from being classified simply according to a cladistic principle, and they should be singled out into a separate class.

Based on his definition, Chen highlighted that striving to understand historical continuity between species should be an important task for taxonomists, although what taxonomists usually sought were discrete characteristics that show discontinuity. For Chen, the combination of perspectives of discontinuity and continuity of species was essential and desirable for doing taxonomy with an evolutional perspective. Although the tinge of dialecticism was palpable, before the Cultural Revolution he used the exact term "dialectics" only sparingly.

ARTICULATING POLITICAL INSPIRATIONS

During the early Cultural Revolution, Chen and other leading biologists at the Institute of Zoology were condemned as counterrevolutionaries. Chen was particularly condemned for his earlier collaboration with the Soviet "revisionists." In the late 1970s, when some scientific research resumed, Chen's articulation of dialectical method became more explicit, and his quotations of Mao became lengthy. This rearticulated set of ideas about taxonomy expressed in dialectical language became widely adopted in the reemerged science manuals and textbooks after the end of Cultural Revolution.

Along with the explicit quotations from Communist leaders, such as from Mao's 1937 essay "On Contradiction" (Maodun lun), Chen also started to use simpler terms to describe dialectical pairs in biological processes and to incorporate more recent molecular biology to support his arguments. It was a time when he started to use "change" (*bian*) to parallel "unchanged" (*bu bian*), which was more easily understood colloquially than commonality/distinctiveness as a basic dialectical pair in evolution and speciation. Thus, evolution was interpreted a "process that unifies the contradictions between change and the unchanged."[38] Reading more recent developments in molecular biology, Chen was greatly provoked by molecular biologist Jacob Monod's (1910–1976) 1970 book *Chance and Necessity* (Le hasard et la nécessité) and found it amusing that the book raised "constancy" and "purposefulness" as biological bodies' "strange properties." Chen found it odd that Monod, a scientist who understood the basic knowledge of DNA, still invoked the concept of constancy and immutability in life. DNA's modes of function in heredity, for Chen, rather showed a mix of changes and constancy through the process of molecular replication and mutation that involved the dynamic movement of molecules through their unwinding and base pair matching or mismatching.

With the unlikely combination of new sources, an understanding of how DNA replicates and mutates—Monod's book, Soviet discussion of species, and Mao's "On Contradiction"—Chen constructed his dialectics of evolution and final resolution of the ontological problem of species. In 1975, in the paper "The Dialectics of Biological Evolution" published in *Chinese Science Bulletin* (Kexue tongbao), Chen noted that across change, variation, and the nonexistence of change, the unchanged, or constancy, made the major pair of contradiction for evolution.[39] Thus, classification work should consider both their "changed" and "unchanged" characteristics. Chen concluded that the existing debate among evolutionary biologists about whether species were real entities or not was due to the neglect of either the changing or the unchanging part of the dialectics in viewing the problem: the debate no longer made sense if the debaters could encompass the whole dialectic. Furthermore, Chen noted that the "unchanged" corresponded to the understanding of the discontinuity of species, while the changing parts linked to continuity. Thus, the debate about continuity and discontinuity of species was also solved with this dialectical view. For taxonomical work, this dialectical understanding implied that the morphological similarity and the infertility of inter-breeding demonstrate particular species' "unchanged" characteristics, which provide the criteria for classificatory work.

Perhaps to appeal to a general readership, the paper no longer delved into the specifics of entomological classifications to explain the advantages of this particular interpretation. Instead, it invoked newer discoveries in modern molecular biology as well as historical observations by Chinese scholars about biological changes, along with quotes from Mao's "On Contradiction." First, the major body of the text illustrated the "inner cause" of "changed" and "unchanged" via DNA replication and mutation that supplied the underlying source of stability and change and how sexual reproduction provided additional variations. Second, Chen cited legalist scholars, such as Guan Zhong (ca. 720–645 BCE), to point out that the notion about gradual change in organisms has been continually expressed by scholars in history.[40] He also sprinkled citations of Mao in verbatim, sometimes at unnecessary length, about how to understand coexistence of contradictory forces, how such pairs work together to make changes, and the corresponding patterns of historical development. Citing Mao in such a profuse way and invoking China's long history as a source of wisdom and insights followed a pattern of publication during the Cultural Revolution, when books often displayed Mao's adages as epigrams and included some indigenous knowledge. However, the copious exposition regarding how recent molecular biological research, such as that of the function of DNA, could support the dialectical understanding of evolution nevertheless attests to the reemerging appeal of international scientific research during the later years of the Cultural Revolution.

CONCLUSION

In the 1980s, adages similar to the statement "Species evolve through the contradiction of change and the unchanged and that of discontinuity and continuity" proliferated in zoology textbooks published in the People's Republic of China. This discourse of dialectical view as desirable and important for studying zoology and evolution had continued uninterrupted since the 1950s, when dialectics was introduced to the teaching of general biology. Its continuation into the 1980s, however, was legitimized by academic work such as Chen's, which continued to take dialectics as useful theoretical reference. This process transformed the understanding of species from discrete, diverse entities into dialectical beings. The flourishing field of entomology—through its virtues in aiding agricultural development, offering excellent biodiversity, and connecting to local languages and records and, later, to Soviet academic works—offered a fertile ground for legitimizing and maintaining the related discussions.

With the Cold War obstacles for more open intellectual exchange between the Eastern and Western blocs, the postwar hierarchical understanding of national scientific achievement, and the language barriers, Chen's innovative reply to the global debate on the species problem has been little known outside China. Chen's contribution nevertheless constitutes a Socialist response to the debate about the ontology and definition of species that was separated from the specific confinement of ideology but became methodically liberating and pedagogically useful. The process through which his ideas evolved also showed that "learning from Soviets" (*xuexi Sulian*) and "Marx-Leninism and Mao's Thought" (*Makesi Liening zhuyi he Mao Zedong sixiang*) had indeed occasionally inspired Chinese scientists and educators. Despite their ideological tinge, and the later wholesale reintroduction of recent Western science, these Maoist-era taxonomic innovations have continued to reverberate with their epistemological impact in today's classrooms.

NOTES

1. Fu, *Dongwuxue*, 4. The introduction includes such a paragraph: "When we study animals in nature, we have to start from a holistic perspective. To deal with the relation of animals with their environments through views of 'unity of the opposites,' [we have to] reveal regularities of change through experimentation and field observations. Therefore, when conducting research, we need to use the dialectical materialism as a guidance." All translations by the author unless otherwise noted.

2. Richards, *The Species Problem*.

3. Kohler, *Lords of the Fly*.

4. Schmalzer, *Red Revolution, Green Revolution*; Palladino, *Entomology, Ecology and Agriculture*.

5. Munz, *The Dancing Bees*; Schmalzer, *Red Revolution, Green Revolution*.

6. Burton-Rose, "Circumscribing with Insects" in this volume.

7. Burton-Rose, "Circumscribing with Insects"; Jiang, "Retouching the Past."

8. Jiang, "Retouching the Past."

9. For example, see Chen Shixiang, "The Chinese Species of the Genus *Chreonoma*."

10. Chen Shixiang, "Youchong de fenxing xueshuo," 3, 80; Chen Shixiang, "Quanbiantai kunchong," 5, 142.

11. Chen Shixiang, "Kunchong zhi Zhongwen mingming wenti."

12. Schneider, "Michurinist Biology."

13. Chen Shixiang, "Wei wancheng quanguo nongye fazhan gangyao."

14. Xin Jiaoyu She, *Zhongxue shengwu jiaoxue de gaizao*, 50.

15. Huadong Shifan Daxue Yanjiu he Zongjie Shanghai Zhongxue Shengwu Jiaoxue Xianjin Yanke Yanjiu Xiaozu, *Gu Qiaoying de shengwu jiaoxue*.

16. Krementsov, "Dobzhansky and Russian Entomology."

17. Chen Shixiang, "Renzhen di xiang xianjin de Sulian kexue xuexi."

18. Chen Shixiang, "Youchong de fenxing xueshuo" and "Quanbiantai kunchong."

19. Chen Shixiang, "Kunchonggang de fazhan lishi," 1.

20. Chen Shixiang, "Wuzhong jiegou yu wuzhong xingcheng."

21. Chen Shixiang, "Wuzhong jiegou yu wuzhong xingcheng," 53.

22. Chen Shixiang, "Wuzhong jiegou yu wuzhong xingcheng," 53.

23. A recent monograph by historian Sigrid Schmalzer shows the spectrum of how scientists and the masses translated these slogans into practical modes of work and, sometimes, creative innovations in entomology, crop genetics, and other agricultural endeavors. Schmalzer, *Red Revolution, Green Revolution*.

24. Chen Shixiang, "Renzhen di xiang xianjin de Sulian kexue xuexi."

25. Chen, Xie, and Deng, *Zhongguo jingji kunchong zhi*.

26. Smocovitis, *Unifying Biology*.

27. Mayr, *Systematics and the Origin of Species*, xxvii–xxviii, 120.

28. Richards, *The Species Problem*, 5.

29. Mikulak, "Darwinism, Soviet Genetics, and Marxism-Leninism," 371.

30. Huang and Luo, "Jieshao 'Sulian guanyu wuzhong yu wuzhong xingcheng wenti de taolun' lunwenji."

31. Chen Shixiang, "Guanyu wuzhong wenti."

32. Schneider, "Michurinist Biology." Chen's speech at the Genetics Symposium can be found in Li et al., *Baijia zhengming*, 253–63, which is a report of the 1956 Qingdao Genetic Symposium.

33. Z. Wang, "The Chinese Developmental State during the Cold War."

34. Chen Shixiang, "Guanyu fenleixue."

35. Chen Shixiang, "Fenleixue."

36. Chen Shixiang, "Fenleixue," 323.

37. Chen's definition was so close to the original wording of Mayr's definition of biological species that I quote the original definition in Mayr, *Systematics and the Origin of Species*, 120.

38. Chen Shixiang, "Shengwu jinhua," 349.

39. Chen Shixiang, "Shengwu jinhua."

40. The emphasize on *bian*, change or transformation, has been a major theme in the pharmacological literature since the Ming dynasty: see Nappi, *The Monkey and the Inkpot*. However, materia medica seemed not to have been one of Chen's main sources of reference at the time.

GLOSSARY OF CHINESE, JAPANESE, AND KOREAN TERMS

An Chong-su 安宗洙
An'ŭi-ŭp 安義邑
ao 夭
Aojuku 青熟
Araya 新屋

Bai hu tong 白虎通
bailu jie 白露節
bian 變
biandan 扁担
bianfu 蝙蝠
bianzheng weiwu zhuyi 辯證唯物主義
bingbao huangnan zai 冰雹蝗蝻災
bu bian 不變

"Cao chong" 草蟲
cao mu 草木
Ceke 車克
chaerae 在來
chai 薑
Chamŏpkwa 蠶業課
Chamsang ch'waryo 蠶桑撮要
chan 蟬
chang 廠
Chang díng 昌鼎
chang ji 長脊
Chang Myŏn 張勉
Chen Zhen 陳楨
chi 跐
Chi Sŏk-yŏng 池錫永
Ch'ŏlwŏn-ŭp 鐵原邑
chong 蟲
chong ming 蟲螟

Ch'ŏnghakkwan 靑鶴館
Chōsen Sangyōrei 朝鮮蠶業令
chou wei bie xie 醜爲龜蟹
Chunri 春日
chunxiong 純雄
chwabusŭngji 左副承旨

"Da tian" 大田
Dai De 戴德
danchi 団地
dao xie 稻蟹
Densenbyō yobōhō 伝染病予防法
"Di guan situ" 地官司徒
diaolang 蚏螂
"Dong guan kaogongji" 冬官考工記
"Dong shan" 東山
dongwu 動物
"Du renshi" 都人士
duili tongyi 對立統一
Dung Tiyan Gi 董天機
dunzi mazha 墩子螞蚱
duo shi yu niao shou cao mu zhi ming
　　　多識於鳥獸草木之名

eisei kumiai 衛生組合

Fan Yuanlian 范源廉
fantizi 繁體字
fei zhe 飛者
feng 蜂
feng fen jian jun chen 蜂分見君臣
feng you junchen zhi li 蜂有君臣之禮
fengcai diequ 蜂猜蝶覷

fengchen 蜂臣
fengdie 蜂蝶
fengdie yi gui xian guan jing 蜂蝶已歸絃管靜
Feng'er 蜂兒
fengkuang dieluan 蜂狂蝶亂
fengmei dieshi 蜂媒蝶使
fengmi diecai 蜂迷蝶猜
fengmi dielian 蜂迷蝶戀
fengwang 蜂王
fengwang tai 蜂王臺
fu 蝮
furyō 不良
fuyou 蜉蝣
fuzhong 阜螽

gaichū 害虫
Gan Yi 甘怡
Gao Jianfu 高劍父
Gensanshu Seizōsho 原蠶種製造所
Gesuidōhō 下水道方
Gu Qiaoying 顧巧英
Guan Zhong 管仲
guilü 規律
Guo Pu 郭璞
Guo Tanxian 過探先
guo zhi suoyi xing zhe, nong zhan ye 國之所以興者，農戰也
guoguo 蟈蟈
guojun min zhi fumu 國君, 民之父母

hae sōdō ハ工騒動
hae tori dē はえとりデー
hai chong 孩蟲
Haicuo tu 海錯圖
Hakuryū 白龍
hanchan 寒蟬
hanhuang 旱蝗
"He Zizhan 'Mijiu ge'" 和子瞻蜜酒歌
hou 後
Hu Jingfu 胡經甫
Hu Shi 胡適
Hu Xiansu 胡先驌
Huainanzi 淮南子
huang 蝗
huang chong 蝗蟲
huang lei ye 蝗類也
Huanghe Baihe Bowuguan 黃河白河博物館
huangnan zai 蝗蝻災
Huashu 化書
hui 虫
huise zhameng 灰色蚱蜢
huiyi 會意
hŭngwang 興旺
hunwei gu yu guanyao 閽衛固乎管鑰
Hushang 湖上
hyangjik 鄉織
Hyŏng sang 荊桑

Ichihara 市平
Iletu 伊勒圖
Im Han-ryong 林漢龍
Imsil-ŭp 任實邑
in'gong yangjam 人工養蠶
Ipchŏn 立廛
Itō Hirobumi 伊藤博文

ji 脊
"Ji feng" 記蜂
Jia Gongyan 賈公彥
jiaguwen 甲骨文
jiangfeng 將蜂
jiantizi 簡體字
jiao mazha 叫螞蚱
jie chong 介蟲
jie wu 介物
Jieziyuan huapu 芥子園畫譜
Jin Bangzheng 金邦正
jinfang 金房
Jingang jing 金剛經
Jingsheng 靜生
Jingsheng shengwu diaochasuo 靜生生物調查所

Jiyuan Hanshi 濟源寒食
Ju Lian 居廉
jun ru ze chen si 君辱則臣死
juren 舉人

Ka to hae no inai seikatsu no uta
　蚊とハエのいない生活の歌
Ka to hae no inai seikatsu undō
　蚊とハエのいない生活運動
Ka to hae o nakusu undō
　蚊とハエおなくす運動
Ka to hae taiji dai parēdo
　蚊とハエ退治大パレード
kairyō 改良
Kang P'il-ri 姜必履
Kangyō Mohanjō 勸業模範場
Kankyō eisei moderu chiku
　環境衛生モデル地区
Kankyō jōka undō 環境浄化運動
Keishichō 警視庁
Kexue 科學
Kexue tongbao 科學通報
Kŏch'ang-ŭp 居昌邑
Koishimaru 小石丸
kŭmmun 禁紋
Kun 坤
kun chong 昆蟲
kun chong wan wu 昆蟲萬物
Kungbang 宮房
Kwŏn Chae-hyŏng 權在衡
Kwŏn Chung-hyŏn 重顯
kyōdo 郷土

laotao 老饕
Li ji 禮記
"Li yun" 禮運
liangmin 良民
lin wu 鱗物
Linhai yiwu zhi 臨海異物志
Liu An 劉安
Liu Chongle 劉崇樂
Liu Meng 劉猛

Lü shi chunqiu 呂氏春秋
Lu Yudao 盧於道
Lunheng 論衡
Lunyu 論語
luo wu 贏物

Maeil sinbo 每日申報
mai chong 貍[埋]蟲
Makesi Liening zhuyi he Mao Zedong
　sixiang 馬克思列寧主義和毛澤
　東思想
mao 毛 (feathers)
mao 蝥
mao wu 毛物
Mao Zedong 毛澤東
Maodun lun 矛盾論
Matamukashi 又昔
"Mi fu" 蜜賦
"Mifeng fu" 蜜蜂賦
mimu 蜜母
ming 螟
ming zhong zhi shu ye 螟蚣之屬也
minghuang 螟蝗
mipi xin cai lai feng chen
　蜜脾新採賴蜂臣
Miyahara Tadamasa 宮原忠正

Nagaoka Tetsuzō 長岡哲三
namgyŏng yŏjik 男耕女織
nan 蝻
nanzi 蝻子
Neige 內閣
Nezumigaeshi 鼠返
niao 鳥
niao shou 鳥獸
Nie Huang 聶璜
Nihon kankyō eisei kyōkai
　日本環境衛生協会
Nihon no kokumin undo
　日本の国民運動
Nōgyō sanji 農業三事
Nongjŏng sinp'yŏn 農政新編

Nongnim Chŏnmun Hakkyo
農林專門學校
Nongnim Hakkyo 農林學校

Oju yŏnmun changjŏn san'go
五洲衍文長箋散稿
Okumura Enshin 奥村圓心
Okumura Ioko 奥村五百子

Pak Che-ga 朴齊家
Pian-ŭp 比安邑
Pibyŏnsa 備邊司
"Pifu fu" 蚍蜉賦
pinwu 品物
Pu Zhelong 蒲蟄龍
pusa 府使

"Qi yue" 七月
Qian 乾
Qian Tianhe 錢天鶴

qiju zhu ce 起居注冊
qin 禽 (birds; fowl)
qin 蟟 (cicada)
qin 擒 (to catch with a net)
Qin Guan 秦觀
"Qiu Guan Sikou" 秋官司寇
qin shou 禽獸
Qiu Yuexiu 裘日修
qiuchan 秋蟬
Qizishan 七子山
"Qu Li" 曲禮

ren 人
renshi 人蝨
Rikujō Jieitai 陸上自衛隊

San sang 山桑
Sanbyō yōbōhō 蠶病豫防法
Sangju-ŭp 尚州邑
Sangyō Shikensho 蠶業試驗所
sanmin 三眠

Sansho kensahō 蠶種檢查法
saranŭngdan 紗羅綾緞
seiketsuna kuni 清潔な国
shaji 莎雞
Shanfeng ying mi ru ying jia
山蜂營蜜如營家
shen 神
shen er hua zhi 神而化之
Shen Ying 沈瑩
Shen Qiliang 沈啟亮
Shennong 神農
Shennong bencao 神農本草
"Shi chong" 釋蟲
shi ke 蝨科
"Shi yu" 釋魚
Shinshū Ōtani-ha 真宗大谷派
shou 獸
shui 水
shui chong 水蟲
Sinsa yuramdan 紳士遊覽團
Sŏ Myŏng-sŏn 徐命善
sogŏm kŏch'i 昭儉祛侈
Sŏngch'ŏn-ŭp 成川邑
Sŏnjŏn 縇廛
Suidōhō 水道法

Tae-Han Cheguk In'gong Yangjam
Hapcha Hoesa 大韓帝國人工養蠶
合資會社
tai 胎
tang 蟷
Tangjik 唐織
te 螣
Terauchi Masatake 寺内正毅
Tianzi zuo min fumu yiwei Tianxia
wang 天子作民父母以爲天下王
tiao 蜩
tiben 題本
tong 同
tongda 東茶
Toyama Kametaro 外山亀太郎
Tsuda Sen 津田仙

tu 土
tu mazha 土螞蚱
tuo/ta 它

Uta no obāsan 歌のおばあさん

wan wu 萬物
wan wu kun chong 萬物昆蟲

Wang Chong 王充
Wang Ling 王令
wangye zhi genben 王業之根本
wei 蜼
Wŏnjam 原蠶
wu 物
Wu Fuzhen 吳福楨
wu xing 五行

xiang xing 象形
xiangfeng 相蜂
xiao chong 小蟲
xiaoshao 蟏蛸
"Xiaowan" 小宛
xiezi 蠍子
xing zhi zhi ran 行豸豸然
xiong 兄
xishuai 蟋蟀
xuexi Sulian 學系蘇聯
Xunzi 荀子

yajam 野蠶
Yao Chong 姚崇
Yejiayake 葉甲亞科
Yenggišan 尹繼善
Yi Kyu-kyŏng 李圭景
Yi Tŏk-ri 李德履
Yi Tong-hyŏng 李東馨
Yi U-kyu 李祐珪
yifeng 一蜂
Yijing 易經
yin yang 陰陽
yin yang zhi wu 陰陽之物

yinshen 引伸
Yinyang bianhua lu 陰陽變化錄
yiren 一人
Yōkaichi 八日市
you du 有毒
you gong 有功
yu 羽 (feathers)
yu 魚 (fish)
yu 蚘 (likely graphic variant)
yu chong 魚蟲
Yu Kil-chun 俞吉濬
yu wu 羽物
yuan 蝯
Yuancan 原蠶
"Yue ling" 月令
Yugŭijŏn 六矣廛
Yume no shima 夢の島
yumun 有紋
Yun Ch'i-ho 尹致昊
Yunggui 永貴
yushi 玉室
yuxi 羽檄

zei 賊
zha 蜡
zhameng 蚱蜢
zhe 蟄
zhe chong 蟄蟲
zhenchong 貞蟲
zhengming 正名
zhengti de guannian 整體的觀念
zhi 豸
zhi chong 鷙蟲
zhi wu 植物
zhong 眾 (crowd)
zhong 眾/衆
"Zhong si" 螽斯
Zhongguo Kexue She 中國科學社
Zhonghua 中華
Zhonghua Minguo 中華民國
Zhonghua renmin gonghe guo
    中華人民共和國

zhongsi huangchong zhi lei er 螽斯蝗
  蟲之類耳
Zhu Xi 朱熹
Zhu Youran 朱逌然

Zhu Yuanding 朱元鼎
zi 子
ziwen bao xue 恣蚊飽血
Zou Bingwen 鄒秉文

BIBLIOGRAPHY

ABBREVIATIONS

GQZ *Gongzhong dang Qianlongchao zouzhe* (Palace Memorial Archives, Qianlong court memorials). Edited by Guoli Gugong Bowuyuan 國立故宮博物館. 75 vols. Taipei: Guoli Gugong Bowuyuan, 1982–88.

MDC Needham, James George. *A Manual of the Dragonflies of China: A Monographic Study of the Chinese Odonata*. Peiping: The Fan Memorial Institute of Biology, 1930.

QJW *Qing jingshi wenbian* 清經世文編 (Collected writings on statecraft from the Qing dynasty). Edited by He Changling 賀長齡 and Wei Yuan 魏源. 3 vols. 1826. Reprint, Beijing: Zhonghua Shuju, 1992.

QSL *Qing Shilu* 清實錄 (Veritable records of the Qing). 60 vols. Reprint. Beijing: Zhonghua Shuju, 1985–87.

SKQS Siku Quanshu 四庫全書 (Complete works of the four treasuries), Wenyu-ange exemplar.

ARCHIVAL COLLECTIONS AND INSTITUTIONAL DOCUMENTS

Grand Secretariat database, Institute of History and Philology, Academia Sinica, Taipei.

Manchu imperial diaries and veritable records, National Palace Museum Library, Taipei.

Manchu palace memorials file copies, First Historical Archives, Beijing.

PRIMARY SOURCES

Primary sources are defined by the way in which the contributors employed them, rather than by a purely chronological criterion. All translations into European languages are listed under secondary sources.

A-dun 阿頓. *Tongwen guanghui quanshu* 同文廣彙全書/*Tung wen guwang lei cio-wan šu* (Broadly collected complete text in the standard script). First published 1693. Nanjing: Tingsong Lou, 1702.

Agūi 阿桂. "Zou bao du bu huangnan qingxing zhe" 奏報督捕蝗蝻情形摺 (Memorial report concerning the circumstances of supervising locust capture). 1763. In GQZ 18:344a–43b.

———. "Zou bao gongtong dongban pubu huangnan ji fangfan deng yuanyou zhe" 奏報公同董辦撲捕蝗蝻及防範等緣由摺 (Memorial report concerning the rationale for joint supervision of locust capture, prevention, etc.). 1763. In GQZ 18:441b–43a.

———. "'Zou fu soubu huangnan ji jieyu zizhong qingxing zhe" 奏覆搜捕蝗蝻及借予籽種情形摺 (Memorial in reply concerning the circumstances of locust detection and capture, as well as those of seed loans). 1763. In GQZ 18:564b–66a.

An Chong-su. *Nongjŏng sinp'yŏn* (Agrarian administration, newly compiled). N.p., n.d. National Library of Korea exemplar.

Aoyama Michiharu, dir. "Hyakunin no yōki na nyōbō tachi," collected in *Showa 30 nendai no Nihon kazoku no seikatsu, Tōkai no kurashi hen*. Tokyo: Kinokuniya Shoten, 2006. DVD.

Bai Juyi 白居易. "Xianyuan dushang" 閑園獨賞 (Enjoying an overgrown garden all by myself). In *Bai Juyi ji* 白居易集 (Collected writings of Bai Juyi), 32:730. Annotated by Gu Xuejie 顧學頡. Beijing: Zhonghua Shuju, 1988.

Ban Gu 班固. *Hanshu* 漢書 (History of the [former] Han). Annotated by Yan Shigu 顏師古. Beijing: Zhonghua Shuju, 1962.

Bing Zhi 秉志. *Bing Zhi wencun* 秉志文存 (Extant works of Bing Zhi). Edited by Zhai Qihui 翟启慧 and Hu Zonggang 胡宗剛. Beijing: Beijing Daxue Chubanshe, 2006.

Bird, Isabella L. *Unbeaten Tracks in Japan: An Account of Travels in the Interior, Including Visits to the Aborigines of Yezo and the Shrine of Nikko*. [Auckland, NZ]: Floating Press, 2009.

Butler, Charles. *The Feminine Monarchie: or The Historie of Bees*. London, 1634.

Buyi Lei gong paozhi bianlan 補遺雷公炮制便覽 (Master Thunder's conveniently arrayed instructions for processed materia medica, supplemented). Manuscript dated 1591. Collated by Zheng Jinsheng 鄭金生. Shanghai: Shanghai Cishu Chubanshe, 2012.

Cai Bian 蔡卞. *Mao shi mingwu jie* 毛詩名物解 (Explanation of names and things in the Mao recension of *The Book of Poetry*). SKQS ed.

Chen Chongdi 陳崇砥. *Zhihuang shu* 治蝗書 (Manual on locust control). Baoding: Lianchi Shuju, 1874.

Chen Fangsheng 陳芳生. "Bu huang fa" 補蝗法 (Methods of catching locusts). Ca. 1776. In QJW, 2:1070b–73a.

Chen Hongmou 陳宏謀. "Chutu nanzi zecheng dianhu souchu xi" 出土蝻子責成佃户搜除檄 (Announcement instructing tenants to find and eradicate locust nymphs when they emerge from the ground). 1760. In QJW, 2:1080a–b.

Chen Huan 陳奐. *Shi Mao shi zhuan shu* 詩毛氏傳疏 (Subcommentary on the Mao tradition of *The Classic of Poetry*). 1847. Facsimile reprint. Jinan: Shandong Youyi Shushe, 1992.

Chen Li 陳立, annot. *Baihu tong shuzheng* 白虎通疏證 (Subcommentary and analysis of the *Comprehensive Discussions in the White Tiger Hall*). Beijing: Zhonghua Shuju, 1994.

Chen Shixiang 陳世驤. (Chen, Sicien H.) "Fenleixue de ruogan jiben gainian" 分類學的若干基本概念 (A few basic concepts in taxonomy). *Kunchong xuebao (Acta entomologia Sinica)* 10, nos. 4–6 (1961): 321–38.

———. "Guanyu fenleixue de ruogan jiben gainian de taolun" 關於分類學的若干基本概念的討論 (Discussion on the basic conceptions of animal taxonomy). *Kunchong xuebao (Entomologica Sinica)* 13, no. 6 (1964): 889–94.

———. "Guanyu wuzhong wenti" 關於物種問題 (About the problem of species). *Kexue tongbao*, no. 2 (1957): 33–42.

———. "Kunchong zhi Zhongwen mingming wenti" 昆蟲之中文命名問題 (The issue of naming insects in Chinese). *Kexue* 24, no. 3 (1940): 182–200.

———. "Kunchonggang de fazhan lishi," 昆蟲綱的發展歷史 (The origin and evolution of the class Insecta). *Kunchong xuebao*, no. 5 (1955): 1–43.

———. "Quanbiantai kunchong zhi qiyuan yu yanhua" 全變態昆蟲之起源與演化 (The origin and evolution of the homometabolous insects). *Kexue*, no. 29 (1947).

———. "Renzhen di xiang xianjin de Sulian kexue xuexi" 認真地向先進的蘇聯科學學習 (Seriously study progressive Soviet science)." *Kunchong zhishi*, no. 6 (1957): 246–48.

———. "Shengwu jinhua de bianzhengfa" 生物進化的辯證法 (The dialectics of biological evolution). *Kexue tongbao*, no. 8 (1975): 348–57.

———. "The Chinese Species of the Genus *Chreonoma*." *Chinese Journal of Zoology*, no. 2 (1936): 163–69.

———. "Wei wancheng quanguo nongye fazhan gangyao suo fuyu de renwu er nuli." 為完成全國農業發展綱要所賦予的人物而努力 (Strenuous support for those entrusted with completing the countrywide agriculture development outline). *Kunchong zhishi* (1956): 2, 49–50.

———. "Wuzhong jiegou yu wuzhong xingcheng" 物種結構與物種形成 (The species structure and species formation). *Shengwuxue tongbao (Bulletin of biology)*, no. 12 (1956): 51–54.

———. "Youchong de fenxing xueshuo" 幼蟲的分型學說 (On the morphology of insect larva). *Kexue*, no. 29 (1947): 80.

Chen Shixiang, Xie Yunzhen 謝蘊貞, and Deng Guofan 鄧國藩, eds. *Zhongguo jingji kunchong zhi* 中國經濟昆蟲誌 (Encyclopedia of Chinese economic insects). Vol. 1. Beijing: Kexue Chubanshe, 1959.

Chen Yuanlong 陳元龍 et al., comp. *Yuding lidai fu hui* 御定歷代賦彙 (Imperially approved compendium of rhapsodies throughout the ages). SKQS ed.

Chi, Sŏk-yŏng. "Sangjam mundap" (A conversation on sericulture). *Tae-Chosŏn tongnip hyŏphoe hoebo*. February 6, 1897.

Chŏngjo sillok (Veritable records of the Chŏngjo reign). https://sillok.history.go.kr/search/inspectionMonthList.do?id=kva.

Chōsen Sōtokufu Kangyō Mohanjō Sangyō Shikenjō, ed. *Sangyō shikenjō jyūnenbo* (The last decade of the Sericulture Experiment Lab). Keijō (Seoul): Chōsen Insatsu Kabushiki Kaisha, 1922.

Comstock, Anna Botsford. *The Comstocks of Cornell: John Henry Comstock and Anna Botsford Comstock*. Edited by Glenn W. Herrick and Ruby Green Smith. Cornell, NY: Comstock Publishing Associates, 1953.

Da Dai Liji jinzhu jinshi 大戴禮記今註今譯 (New commentary and new explanations for *The Book of Rites of the Elder Dai*). Annotated by Wang Pinzhen 王聘珍, commentary and explanations by Gao Ming 高明. Taipei: Taiwan Shangwu Yinshuguan, 1977.

Da Qing huidian shili 大清會典事例 (Collected statutes and precedents of the Great Qing). 1899. Reprint. Beijing: Zhonghua Shuju, 1991.

Dai Biaoyuan 戴表元. "Yi feng xing" 義蜂行 (Lay of righteous bees). In *Yuan shi xuan* 元詩選 (Selected poems from the Yuan dynasty), compiled by Gu Sili 顧嗣立, 8:22a–23a. SKQS ed.

Dewey, John. "America and Chinese Education (1921)." *Schools: Studies in Education* 3, no. 1 (2006): 77–82.

Donovan, Edward. *The Insects of China: Natural History of the Insects of China, Containing Upwards of Two Hundred and Twenty Figures and Descriptions*. First published 1798. Expanded edition London: Henry G. Bohn, 1838. Z. P. Metcalf exemplar, North Carolina State University Special Collections.

Duan Chengshi 段成式. *Youyang zazu* 酉陽雜俎 (Miscellaneous morsels from Youyang). Beijing: Zhonghua Shuju, 1981.

Duan Yucai 段玉裁. *Shuowen jiezi zhu* 説文解字注 (Commentary on *Explaining Characters and Analyzing Graphs*). Shanghai: Shanghai Guji Chubanshe, 1981.

Ershisi xiao tuzan 二十四孝圖讚 (Twenty-four filial paragons, with images and encomiums). Shanghai: Yihua Tang, 1873.

Erya zhushu 爾雅注疏 (Commentary and subcommentary of *Approaching Elegance*). Annotated by Guo Pu 郭璞 and Xing Bing 邢昺. In *Shisanjing zhushu* 十三經注疏 (Commentaries and subcommentaries of the Thirteen Classics). Edited by Ruan Yuan 阮元. First published in 1797. Beijing: Beijing Daxue Chubanshe, 2000.

Fang Guancheng 方觀承. "Zou wei yanxing canzou Jiaohe xian zhixian Gan Yi huini nanzai zhe" 奏為嚴行參奏交河縣知縣甘怡諱匿蝻災摺 (Memorial concerning official notification of the serious crime of Jiaohe District magistrate Gan Yi for concealing a locust nymph outbreak). 1763. In GQZ 18:229a–30a.

Fang Yue 方岳. *Qiuya ji* 秋崖集 (Collected writings of [Fang] Qiuya). SKQS ed.

Ge Quansheng 葛全胜, ed. *Qingdai zouzhe huibian: Nongye, huanjing* 清代奏折匯編：農業，環境 (Compilation of Qing memorials: Agriculture and environment). Beijing: Shangwu Yinshuguan, 2005.

Gu Yewang 顧野王. *Yupian jiaoshi* 玉篇校釋 (Jade folios, *collated and annotated*). Shanghai: Shanghai Guji Chubanshe, 1989.

Guan Yinbao 觀音保. "Zou bao chakan nannie pubu jinjing zhe" 奏報查勘蝻孽撲捕盡淨摺 (Memorial report of an inquest into the concluding assault on the locust nymph scourge). 1763. In GQZ 18:554b–55a.

———. "Zou xie ming congkuan mian qi ge ren reng zhuce zhe" 奏謝命從寬免其革任仍註冊摺 (Memorial in gratitude for a decree of leniency allowing retention in office and to remain registered). 1763. In GQZ 18:505a–b.

Han-i araha Manju gisun-i buleku bithe (Imperially commissioned mirror of the Manchu language). Beijing: Wuying Dian, 1708.

Han-i araha Ši ging bithe (Imperially commissioned edition of *The Classic of Poetry*). National Palace Museum Library (Taipei) exemplar. 故滿 001016–35. Beijing, 1655.

Hashimoto Masami. "Forty Years of My Public Health Study." *Kōshū eiseiin kenkyū hōkoku* 33, no. 1 (1984): 1–16.

———. "Ka to hae no inai machi o iku." *Kōsei* 8, no. 7 (1953): 44–46.

———. "Ka to hae no inai mura zukuri." *Nogyō seikai* 50, no. 8 (1955): 73–75.

———. "Ka to hae no inai seikatsu." *Taiiku no kagaku* 5, no. 8 (1955): 315–17.

———. "'Ka to hae no inai seikatsu' jisen undo no genjō." *Nippon Koshu eisei zasshi*, nos. 3–4 (1956): 172–77.

———. "Ka to hae no inai toshi no kensetsu." *Shisei* 4, no. 8 (1955): 64–68.

———. *Kōshū eisei to sōshiki katsudō*. Tokyo: Seishin Shobō, 1955.

Hayata Teruhiro and Teramura Masao, eds. *Daishin zensho: Zōho kaitei, tsuketari Manshūgo, Kango sakuin* (Expanded and emended edition of *Complete Book of the Great Qing*, with appended Manchu and Chinese indexes). Fuchū: Tōkyō Gaikokugo Daigaku Ajia Afurika Gengo Bunka Kenkyūjo, 2004.

Hu Baoquan 胡寶瑔. "Zou fu buhuang jingguo qingxing zhe" 奏覆捕蝗經過情形摺 (Memorial in reply concerning circumstances relating to the conclusion of locust catching). 1752. In GQZ 3:138a–39b.

Hu Jixuan 胡吉宣. Yupian *jiao shi* 玉篇校釋 (Jade folios, corrected and explicated). Shanghai: Shanghai Guji Chubanshe, 1989.

Huadong Shifan Daxue Yanjiu he Zongjie Shanghai Zhongxue Shengwu Jiaoxue Xianjin Yanke Yanjiu Xiaozu 華東師範大學研究和總結上海中學生物教學先進驗科學研究小組, eds. *Gu Qiaoying de shengwu jiaoxue* 顧巧英的生物教學 (The biological teachings of Gu Qiaoying). Shanghai: Xinzhishi Chubanshe, 1958.

Huang Huaixin 黃懷信, Zhang Maorong 張懋鎔, and Tian Xudong 田旭東, annot. *Yi Zhoushu huijiao jizhu* 逸周書彙校集注 (Remaining Zhou documents: Assembled collations and collected notes). Shanghai: Shanghai Guji Chubanshe, 1995.

Huang Hui 黃暉, annot. *Lunheng jiaoshi* 論衡校釋 (*Doctrines Weighed* collated and explained). Beijing: Zhonghua Shuju, 1990.

Huang Zongzhen 黃宗甄 and Luo Jianlong 羅見龍. "Jieshao 'Sulian guanyu wuzhong yu wuzhong xingcheng wenti de taolun' lunwenji" 介紹蘇聯關於物種

與物種形成問題的討論論文集 (Introducing the essay collection of "Soviet Discussion on the Problem of Species and Speciation"). *Shengwuxue tongbao* (Bulletin of biology), no. 5 (1956): 12, 59–60.

Ihing 宜興. *Qingwen buhui* 清文補彙/*Manju gisun be niyeceme isabuha bithe* (Manchu collected, supplemented). Apparently privately published copy held at Capital Library, Beijing, with the call number *yi · yi* 乙 · 一 46. 1786.

Jiang Tingxi 蔣廷錫 et al., comps. *Qinchong dian* 禽蟲典 (Canon of fauna). Shanghai: Shanghai Wenyi Chubanshe, 1998.

Jin shu 晉書 (Jin history). Compiled by Fang Xuanling 房玄齡. Jinling Shuju edition accessed through the Scripta Sinica database of Academia Sinica. http://hanchi.ihp.sinica.edu.tw/ihp/hanji.htm.

Katō Mutsuo. *Hae ka no hasseigen to seikatsu kaizen*. Tokyo: Nihon Kankyō Eisei Kyōkai, 1960.

Kellogg, Claude R. *Aborigines: Silkworm, Honeybees and Other Insects; Entomological Excerpts from Southeastern China*. Claremont, CA: Claremont Manor, 1968.

Kellogg, Claude R., and Dean Asquith. "Preliminary Studies in the Physical Characteristics of Some Massachusetts Honeybees." *Journal of Economic Entomology* 27, no. 3 (1934): 641–47.

Kellogg, Claude R., et al. "Variations in the Size of Wings of Some Massachusetts Honeybees." *Journal of Economic Entomology* 32, no. 5 (1939): 665–66.

Kong Guangsen 孔廣森. *Da Dai Liji buzhu* 大戴禮記補註 (*The Book of Rites of the Elder Dai*, supplemented and with commentary). Punctuated and corrected by Wang Fengxian 王豐先. 1752–86. Beijing: Zhonghua Shuju, 2013.

Kong Yingda 孔穎達, annot. *Mao shi zhengyi* 毛詩正義 (Correct meanings of the Mao recension of *The Classic of Poetry*). Beijing: Beijing Daxue Chubanshe, 1999.

———. *Shangshu zhengyi* 尚書正義 (Correct meanings of *The Classic of Documents*). Beijing: Beijing Daxue Chubanshe, 1999.

———. *Zhouyi zhengyi* 周易正義 (Correct meanings of the Zhou *Classic of Changes*). Beijing: Beijing Daxue Chubanshe, 1999.

Kōsei Hakusho. Tokyo: Ōkurashō Insatsukyoku, 1956.

Kōsei Hakusho. Tokyo: Ōkurashō Insatsukyoku, 1957.

Kōsei Hakusho. Tokyo: Ōkurashō Insatsukyoku, 1966.

Kōseishō 50 Nen Shi Hensan Iinkai, ed. *Kōseishō 50-Nenshi: Shiryō Hen*. Tokyo: Kōsei Mondai Kenkyūkai, 1988.

Kurosawa Akira, dir. *Ikiru*. New York: Criterion Collection. 2003. DVD.

Kwŏn Chae-hyŏng. "Nongsanggongbu chamŏpkwa sŏlch'I rŭl ch'ŏngham," in *Kuksa tŭngnok kŭndaep'yŏn* (Documents at ministries and branches, the modern era). Kakpu ch'ŏngŭisŏ chonan 17. https://db.history.go.kr.

"Kwŏn Chung-hyŏn." *Han'guk minjok munhwa taebaekkwa* (Encyclopedia of Korean culture). http://encyclopedia.aks.ac.kr.

Li Fang 李昉 et al., comp. *Taiping yulan* 太平御覽 (Imperial readings from the Taiping reign era). Taipei: Dahua Shuju, 1977.

Li Shizhen 李時珍. *Bencao gangmu* 本草綱目 (Comprehensive materia medica). First edition 1596. SKQS ed.

Li Yanji 李延基. *Qingwen huishu* 清文彙書/*Manju isabuha bithe*. First published 1750. Facsimile reproduction in *Gugong zhenben congkan* 故宮珍本叢刊 vol. 719. Beijing: Yinghua Tang, 2001.

*Liji zhengyi*禮記正義 (Correct meanings of *The Book of Rites*). Annotated by Zheng Xuan 鄭玄 and Kong Yingda 孔穎達. In *Shisanjing zhushu* 十三經注疏 (Commentaries and subcommentaries of the Thirteen Classics). Edited by Ruan Yuan 阮元. First published in 1797. Beijing: Beijing Daxue Chubanshe, 2000.

Lu Jia 陸賈. *Xinyu* 新語 (New tales). Taipei: Taiwan Shangwu Yinshuguan, 1968.

Lu Shiyi 陸世儀. "Chu huang ji" 除蝗記 (Notes on locust eradication). In QJW, 2:1073b–75a.

Luo Zhenyu 羅振玉. *Mao shi cao mu niao shou chong yu shu xin jiaozheng* 毛詩草木鳥獸蟲魚疏新校正 (New critical edition of *Commentary on the Flora and Fauna in the Mao Recension of the Classic of Poetry*). In *Luo Zhenyu xueshu lunzhu ji* 羅振玉學術論著集 (Anthology of the scholarly works of Luo Zhenyu), edited by Luo Jizu 羅繼祖 and Wang Tongce 王同策, 4:223–70. Reprint. Shanghai: Shanghai Guji Chubanshe, 2011.

Matsumura Shōnen 松村松年. *Memoiren Matsumuras*. N.p.: 1968. Exemplar of Metcalf Collection, North Carolina State University.

———. *Nihon konchū daizu kan* 日本昆蟲大圖鑑 (6000 illustrated insects of Japan-Empire). Tokyo: Tōkō shoin, 1931.

McLachlan, Robert. "On Odonata from the Province of Szechuen in Western China, and from Moupin in Eastern Tibet." *Annals of Natural History, or Magazine of Zoology, Botany, and Geology* 6, no. 17 (1896): 365–74.

———. "On Two Small Collections of Neuroptera from Ta-Chien-Lu in the Province of Szechuan, West China, on the Frontier of Thibet." *Annals of Natural History, or Magazine of Zoology, Botany, and Geology* 6, no. 13 (1894): 421–36.

———. "The Neuroptera of Madeira and the Canary Islands." *Zoological Journal of the Linnean Society* 16, no. 90 (1882): 149–83.

Mei Yingzuo 梅膺祚. *Zihui* 字彙 (Collection of characters). Expanded by Wu Renchen 吳任臣. Shanghai: Shanghai Cishu Chubanshe, 1991.

Meng Jiao 孟郊. *Meng Dongye shi ji* 孟東野詩集 (Collected poems by Meng Dongye). Beijing: Renmin Wenxue Chubanshe, 1984.

"Miyahara Tadamasa," *Zai Chōsen naichijin shinshi meikan* (Biographic dictionary of prominent Japanese in colonial Korea), p. 508. Han'guk kŭnhyŏndae inmul charyo. https://db.history.go.kr/item/level.do?itemId=im.

Miyahara Tadamasa, Nagaoka Tetsuzō, and Im Han-ryong. "Chōsen zairai sanshu shīku seiseki." In *Kangyō mohanjō hōkoku* (A report of agricultural experiment station). Suwŏn: Chōsen Sōtokufu Kangyō Mohanjō, 1912.

Nagaoka Tetsuzō. "Chōsen zairai sansho" (Korean native silkworm strains). *Chōsen sōtokufu geppō* 4, no. 5 (1914): 1–13.

Needham, James George. "Genealogic Study Dragonfly Venation." *Proceedings of the U.S. National Museum*, no. 26 (1903): 703.

———. "Observations on Chinese Gomphine Dragonflies." *Bulletin Museum Comparative Zoology*, no. 94 (1944): 145–63.

———. "The Lengthened Shadow of a Man and His Wife—I." *Scientific Monthly* 62, no. 2 (1946): 140–50.

———. "The Lengthened Shadow of a Man and His Wife—II." *Scientific Monthly* 62, no. 3 (1946): 219–29.

Needham, James George, and Elsie Broughton. "The Venation of the Libellulinae (Odonata)." *Transactions of the American Entomological Society* 53, no. 3 (1927): 157–90.

Needham, James George, with Hortense Butler Heywood. *A Handbook of the Dragonflies of North America*. Springfield, IL: C. C. Thomas, 1929.

Needham, James George, with Minter J. Westfall. *A Manual of the Dragonflies of North America (Anisoptera), Including the Greater Antilles and the Provinces of the Mexican Border*. First published 1955. Berkeley: University of California Press, 1975.

Newman, Edward. "Proposed Division of Neuroptera into Two Classes." *Zoologist: A Popular Miscellany of Natural History*, no. 11 (1853): clxxxii–cciv.

Peng Dayi 彭大翼. *Shantang sikao* 山堂肆考 (Extended investigations from the mountain hermitage). SKQS ed.

Pibyŏnsa tŭngnok (Records of the Border Defense Council). http://db.history.go.kr.

Qian Qianyi 錢謙益. *Muzhai chuxue ji* 牧齋初學集 (A beginner's primer from the shepherd's studio). Shanghai: Shanghai Guji Chubanshe, 2002.

Qian Rucheng 錢汝誠. "Zou fu qinwang chakan Dacheng nannie shi xi jinjing zhe" 奏覆親往查勘大城蝻孽實係盡淨摺 (Memorial in reply concerning a personal inquiry into the facts of the actual eradication of the locust nymph scourge in Dacheng). 1763. In GQZ, 18:524b–26a.

Read, Bernard E. *Insect Drugs*. First published 1941. Reprint. Taipei: Southern Materials Center, Inc., 1977.

Ruan Yuan 阮元, ed. *Mao shi zhengyi* 毛詩正義 (Correct meaning of the Mao tradition of *The Classic of Poetry*). Facsimile. Yingyin Ruan ke *Shisanjing zhushu* fu jiaokan ji 影印阮刻十三經注疏附校勘記. Taipei: Qiming Shuju, 1959.

Sams, Crawford F., and Zabelle Zakarian. *"Medic": The Mission of an American Military Doctor in Occupied Japan and Wartorn Korea*. Armonk, NY: M. E. Sharpe, 1998.

Sangge 桑額, ed. *Man-Han leishu* 滿漢類書/*Man han lei šu bithe* (Manchu and Chinese, divided into sections). S.l.: Zixing Zhai, 1700.

"Sanshi hōkokusho" (A report on silk threads). July 16, 1898. *Chū Kan Nippon Kōshikan Kiroku* (Documents of the Japanese Embassy in Korea) http://db.history.go.kr.

Shanghai Shifan Daxue Guji Zhengli Zu 上海師範大學古籍整理組, annot. *Guoyu* 國語 (Tales of the states). Shanghai: Shanghai Guji Chubanshe, 1978.

Shao Bao 邵寶. "Fengzhong tan" 蜂塚嘆 (Lament on the grave of the honeybees). In *Rongchuntang ji: xuji* 容春堂集續集 (Collected writings from the Vernal Hall. Second collection), 1:406. Shanghai: Shanghai Guji Chubanshe, 1991.

Shao Shuqi 邵叔齊. "Pu hudie" 撲蝴蝶 (To the tune of striking the butterfly). In *Meiyuan* 梅苑, compiled Huang Dayu 黃大輿 (The plum garden), 4.14a–b. SKQS ed.

Shen Bingcheng 沈秉成. *Can sang jiyao* 蠶桑輯要 (Essence of sericulture). 1871. Beijing: Nongye Chubanshe, 1960.

Shen Cai 沈彩. "Da linmei" 答鄰妹 (In reply to the young girl next door). In *Chunyulou ji* 春雨樓集 (Collected writings from the Spring Rains Belvedere). Qianlong period woodblock ed., 6:5b.

Shen Shouhong 沈受宏. "Bu huang shuo" 捕蝗說 (On catching locusts). In QJW, 2:1068b–69a.

Shimamura Dengorō. *Tsūzoku yōsan hihō* 通俗養蚕秘方 (The secrets of sericulture). N.p.: Bunkōdō, 1882. National Diet Library exemplar.

Shi Mao 史茂. "Jing chen bu huang shi yi shu" 敬陳捕蝗事宜疏 (A memorial that respectfully lays out the circumstances of locust catching). 1759. In QJW, 2:1076a–b.

Shi zhuan daquan 詩傳大全 (Complete works on *The Classic of Poetry*). SKQS ed.

Sima Qian 司馬遷. *Shiji* 史記 (Records of the grand historian). Beijing: Zhonghua Shuju, 1959.

Sowerby, Arthur de Carle. *China's Natural History: A Guide to the Shanghai Museum (R.A.S.)*. Shanghai: Royal Asiatic Society, North China Branch, 1936.

Su Zhe 蘇轍. *Su Zhe ji* 蘇轍集 (Collected writings of Su Zhe). Beijing: Zhonghua Shuju, 1990.

Sun Yirang 孫詒讓, annot. *Mozi xiangu* 墨子閒詁 (Interlinear annotations on the *Mozi*). Beijing: Zhonghua Shuju, 2001.

Sŭngjŏngwŏn ilgi (The daily records of royal secretariat of Chosŏn dynasty). http://sjw.history.go.kr.

Terauchi Masatake. "Chōsen sōtokufu kunrei dai-11-go." *Chōsen sōtokufu kanpō* (Official gazette of government general of Korea) dai-460-go, March 12, 1912.

Wang Rongbao 汪榮寶, annot. *Fayan yishu* 法言義疏 (*Exemplary Figures* with glosses and subcommentary). Beijing: Zhonghua Shuju, 1987.

Wang Yucheng 王禹稱. *Xiaochu ji* 小畜集 (Collected writings of [Wang] Xiaochu). Taipei: Taiwan Shangwu Yinshuguan, 1968.

Wen Shu 文俶. *Jinshikunchongcaomu zhuang* 金石昆虫草木状 (Forms of the natural world). Taiwan National Library exemplar. https://new.shuge.org/view/jin_shi_kun_chong_cao_mu_zhuang.

Wu Zhizhen 吳之振, comp. *Songshi chao* 宋詩鈔 (Draft compilation of Song poetry). Shanghai: Shanghai Guji Chubanshe, 1993.

Xu Guangqi 徐光啓, comp. *Nongzheng quanshu jiaozhu* 農政全書校注 (The anno-
    tated comprehensive manual of agricultural administration). 1639. Annotation
    by Shi Shenghan 石聲漢. Reprint. Taipei: Mingwen Shuju, 1981.

Yan Kejun 嚴可均, comp. *Quan Jin wen* 全晉文 (Complete prose of the Jin dy-
    nasty). In *Quan Shanggu Sandai Qin Han Liuchao wen* 全上古三代秦漢六朝文
    (Complete prose of high antiquity, three dynasties, Qin, Han, and Six dynas-
    ties). Beijing: Zhonghua Shuju, 1985.

Yang Shi 楊時. "Chunri" 春日 (Spring days). In *Yuxuan sichao shi: Songshi* 御選
    四朝詩.宋詩 (Imperially selected poetry from four dynasties: Song poetry),
    68:21a–b. SKQS ed.

Yang Wanli 楊萬里. *Chengzhai ji* 誠齋集 (Collected writings of [Yang] Cheng-
    zhai). SKQS ed.

Yi U-kyu, ed. *Chamsang ch'waryo* (Essence of sericulture). N.p.: Ch'ŏnghakkwan,
    1884. National Library of Korea exemplar.

Yokota Katsuzō. *Jinkō yōsan kagami: Ichimei Yokota yōsanki no Shiori* (A guidebook
    of artificial sericulture). Tokyo: Jinkō Yōsanhō Denshū Jimusho, 1898.

Yoshimoto Shizuo. "Chiku soshiki katsudō no yoru eisei gaichu kujō." *Kōshū Eisei*
    28, no. 7 (1964): 359–61.

Yu Yunwen 俞允文. "Feng" 蜂 (Bees). In *Yuding peiwenzhai yongwushi xuan* 御定
    佩文齋詠物詩選 (Imperially commissioned selected poetry on objects from
    the Peiwen Studio), 479:1a–1b. SKQS ed.

Yuan Kang 袁康. Compiled by Wu Ping 吳平. *Yuejue shu* 越絕書 (Lost histories
    of Yue). Shanghai: Shanghai Guji Chubanshe, 1985.

Yuan Zhen 元稹. "Luofeng" 蛞蜂 (Honeybees). In *Quan Tangshi* 全唐詩 (Com-
    plete Tang poetry), compiled by Peng Dingqiu 彭定求 et al., 399: 4484–85.
    Beijing: Zhonghua Shuju, 1999.

Yuzhi bencao pinhui jingyao 御製本草品匯精要 (Imperially commissioned essen-
    tial information, arranged in grades, on materia medica). 1505. Kangxi edition
    reproduced in Xuxiu Siku Quanshu 續修四庫全書 (Continued complete
    works of the four treasuries), vols. 990–91. Jinan: Qi Lu Shushe, 1994.

Yuzhi fanyi Shijing 御製繙譯詩經 (Imperially commissioned translation of *The
    Classic of Poetry*). SKQS, v. 185.

Yuzhi zengding Qingwen jian 御製增訂清文鑑／*Han-i araha nonggime toktobuha
    Manju gisun-i buleku bithe* (Imperially commissioned mirror of the Manchu
    language, expanded and emended). 1773. 1778 edition reproduced in *Qinding
    Siku quanshu huiyao* 欽定四庫全書會要. Reprint. Changchun: Jilin Chuban
    Jituan, 2005.

Zhang Daye 張大野. *Weichong shijie* 微蟲世界 (The world of a tiny insect). Beijing
    University Library exemplar. Digital facsimile through the China Academic
    Digital Associative Library database.

Zhang Pu 張溥. *Han Wei Liuchao baisanjia ji* 漢魏六朝百三家集 (Collected writings of one hundred three masters of the Han, Wei to six dynasties). Taipei: Taiwan Shangwu Yinshuguan, 1983.

Zhongguo Diyi Lishi Dang'an Guan 中國第一歷史檔案館. *Qianlong chao Manwen jixin dang yibian* 乾隆朝滿文寄信檔譯編 (The Manchu court letter archive of the Qianlong reign, edited and translated). Changsha: Yuelu Shushe, 2011.

———. *Qingdai Xinjiang Manwen dang'an huibian* 清代新疆滿文檔案匯編 (Compilation of the Manchu archives from Xinjiang in the Qing period). Guilin: Guangxi Shifan Daxue Chubanshe, 2012.

Zhou Bangyan 周邦彥. "Liu chou" 六醜 (Six uglies). In *Qingzhen ji jiaozhu* 清真集校注 (Collected writings of [Zhou] Qingzhen collated with a commentary), annotated by Sun Hong 孫虹, 81. Beijing: Zhonghua Shuju, 2002.

Zhou Tao 周燾. "Jing chou chunan miezi shu" 敬籌除蝻滅子疏 (Memorial respectfully deliberating the eradication of locust nymphs and eggs). 1752. In QJW, 2:1079a–b.

Zhouli zhushu 周禮注疏 (Commentary and subcommentary of *The Rites of Zhou*). Annotated by Zheng Xuan 鄭玄 and Jia Gongyan 賈公彥. In *Shisanjing zhushu* 十三經注疏 (Commentaries and subcommentaries of the Thirteen Classics), edited by Ruan Yuan 阮元. First published in 1797. Beijing: Beijing Daxue Chubanshe, 2000.

SECONDARY SOURCES

Abrol, Dharam Pal. "Defensive Behaviour of *Apis cerana* F. against Predatory Wasps." *Journal of Apicultural Science* 50, no. 2 (2006): 39–46.

Aldous, Christopher. "Transforming Public Health?: A Critical Review of Progress Made against Enteric Diseases during the American-Led Occupation of Japan (1945–52)." *Nihon ishigaku zasshi* 54, no. 1 (2008): 3–17.

Aldous, Christopher, and Akihito Suzuki. *Reforming Public Health in Occupied Japan, 1945–52: Alien Prescriptions*. New York: Routledge, 2012.

Amano, Tatsuya, et al. "Tapping into Non-English-Language Science for the Conservation of Global Biodiversity." *PLoS Biol* 19, no. 10 (2021): 1–29.

Anthropocene Working Group. "Working Group on the 'Anthropocene.'" http://quaternary.stratigraphy.org/working-groups/anthropocene.

Arunkumar, K. P., Muralidhar Metta, and J. Nagaraju. "Molecular Phylogeny of Silkmoths Reveals the Origin of Domesticated Silkmoth, *Bombyx mori* from Chinese *Bombyx mandarina* and Paternal Inheritance of *Antheraea proylei* Mitochondrial DNA." *Molecular Phylogenetics and Evolution* 40, no. 2 (2006): 419–27.

Bala, Arun, and Prasenjit Duara. "Introduction." In *The Bright Dark Ages: Comparative and Connective Perspectives*, edited by Arun Bala and Prasenjit Duara, 1–20. Boston: Brill, 2016.

Ball, George E. *The Art of Insect Illustration and Threads of Entomological History*. Edmonton: University of Alberta Libraries, 2005.

Barnes, Nicole Elizabeth. *Intimate Communities: Wartime Healthcare and the Birth of Modern China, 1937–1945*. Oakland: University of California Press, 2018.

Bartlett, Beatrice. *Monarchs and Ministers*. Berkeley: University of California Press, 1991.

Baxter, William H., and Laurent Sagart. *Old Chinese: A New Reconstruction*. New York: Oxford University Press, 2014.

Beetsma, J. "The Process of Queen-Worker Differentiation in the Honeybee." *Bee World* 60, no. 1 (1979): 24–39.

Behr, Wolfgang. "'Homosomatic Juxtaposition' and the Problem of 'Syssematic' (huìyì) Characters." In *Écriture Chinose: Données, usages et representations*, edited by Françoise Bottéro and Redouane Djamouri. Paris: École des Hautes Études en Sciences Sociales, Centre de Recherches Linguistiques sur l'Asie Orientale, 2006.

Beijing Shi Minzu Guji Zhengli Chuban Guihua Xiaozu 北京市民族古籍整理出版規劃小組, ed. *Beijing diqu Manwen tushu zongmu* 北京地區滿文圖書總目 (Union catalog of Manchu materials in the Beijing area). Shenyang: Liaoning Minzu Chubanshe, 2008.

Bello, David A. *Across Forest, Steppe and Mountain: Environment, Identity and Empire in Qing China's Borderlands*. Cambridge: Cambridge University Press, 2016.

———. "An Intermittent Order Contrived on Sand: Managing Water, Siltage, Locusts and Cultivators on the Lower Yangzi in the Early 1800s." *Resilience: A Journal of the Environmental Humanities*, no. 3 (2015–16): 14–33.

———. "Consider the Qing Locust." *East Asian Science, Technology and Medicine*, no. 48 (2018): 49–80.

Berenbaum, May. "Sons of Bees." *American Entomologist* 55, no. 4 (2009): 212–13.

Bernays, E. A., and R. F. Chapman. "Deterrent Chemicals as a Basis of Oligophagy in *Locusta migratoria* (L.)." *Ecological Entomology* 2, no. 1 (1977): 1–18.

Bian, He. *Know Your Remedies: Pharmacy and Culture in Early Modern China*. Princeton, NJ: Princeton University Press, 2020.

Biehler, Dawn. *Pests in the City: Flies, Bedbugs, Cockroaches, and Rats*. Seattle: University of Washington Press, 2013.

Biot, Édouard. *Le Tcheou-li ou Rites des Tcheou, traduit pour la première fois du chinois par feu Édouard Biot*. Edited by Jean-Baptiste Biot. First published 1851. Taipei: Ch'eng Wen, 1975.

Boltz, William G. "Liù shū 六書 (Six scripts)." In *Encyclopedia of Chinese Language and Linguistics*, edited by Rint P. E. Sybesma, 2:616–24. Leiden: Brill, 2017.

———. *The Origin and Early Development of the Chinese Writing System*. New Haven, CT: American Oriental Society, 1994.

Borgelt, Jan, Martin Dorber, Marthe Alnes Høiberg, and Francesca Verones. "More than Half of Data Deficient Species Predicted to Be Threatened by Extinction." *Communications Biology* 5, no. 679 (2022): 2–9.

Bottéro, Françoise. "Revisiting the *wén* 文 and the *zì* 字: The Great Chinese Characters Hoax." *Bulletin of the Museum of Far Eastern Antiquities*, no. 74 (2002): 14–33.

Bourque, Kevin. "'Tout est en desordre dans la ruche': Republican Discourse, Patriarchal Strategy, Gendered Labour and the Bees of the *Encyclopédie*." *Studies on Voltaire and the Eighteenth Century*, no. 12 (2006): 361–76.

Bray, Francesca. *Technology and Gender: Fabrics of Power in Late Imperial China*. Berkeley: University of California Press, 1997.

Bray, Francesca, Vera Dorofeeva-Lichtmann, and Georges Métailié, eds. *Graphics and Text in the Production of Technical Knowledge in China: The Warp and the Weft*. Boston: Brill, 2007.

Breed, Michael D., Terry A. Smith, and Armando Torres. "Role of the Guard Honey Bees (Hymenoptera: Apidae) in Nestmate Discrimination and Replacement of Removed Guards." *Annals of the Entomological Society of America* 85, no. 5 (1992): 633–37.

Buck, Peter. *American Science and Modern China, 1876–1936*. Cambridge: Cambridge University Press, 1980.

Bullock, Mary Brown. *An American Transplant: The Rockefeller Foundation and Peking Union Medical College*. Berkeley: University of California Press, 1980.

———. *The Oil Prince's Legacy: Rockefeller Philanthropy in China*. Washington, DC: Woodrow Wilson Center Press, 2011.

Burton-Rose, Daniel. "Towards a Sinophone Insect Humanities: A Review Essay." *Journal of the History of Biology* 53, no. 4 (2020): 667–78.

Cao Hui 曹暉, annot. *Bencao pinhui jingyao: Jiaozhu yanjiu ben* 本草品匯精要: 校註研究本 (Essential information, arranged in grades, on *materia medica*: Annotated critical edition). Beijing: Huaxia Chubanshe, 2004.

Cardoso, Pedro, et al. "Scientists' Warning to Humanity Scientists on Insect Extinctions." *Biological Conservation*, no. 242 (2020): 1–12.

Carr, Michael. "A Linguistic Study of the Flora and Fauna Sections of the 'Erh-ya.'" PhD diss., University of Arizona, 1979.

Carrington, Damian. "Insect Collapse: 'We Are Destroying Our Life Support Systems.'" *Guardian*, Jan 15, 2019. www.theguardian.com/environment/2019/jan/15/insect-collapse-we-are-destroying-our-life-support-systems.

Chambers, P. G., S. J. Simpson, and D. Raubenheimer. "Behavioural Mechanisms of Nutrient Balancing in *Locusta migratoria* Nymphs." *Animal Behavior*, no. 50 (1995): 1513–23.

Chapman, N. C., P. Nanork, M. S. Reddy, N. S. Bhat, M. Beekman, and B. P. Oldroyd. "Nestmate Recognition by Guards of the Asian Hive Bee *Apis cerana*." *Insectes Sociaux*, no. 55 (2008): 382–86.

Chen Gang 陳剛, ed. *Beijing fangyan cidian* 北京方言詞典 (Dictionary of the Beijing dialect). Beijing: Shangwu Yinshuguan, 1985.

Chen, Jianhui, et al., "Hydroclimatic Changes in China and Surroundings during the Medieval Climate Anomaly and Little Ice Age: Spatial Patterns and Possible Mechanisms." *Quaternary Science Reviews* 107, no. 1 (2015): 98–111.

Chiang, Yung-chen. "Social Engineering and the Social Sciences in China, 1898–1949 (Yenching, Nankai)." PhD diss., Harvard University, 1986.

Chinh, Tong X., Willem J. Boot, and Marinus J. Sommeijer. "Production of Reproductives in the Honey Bee Species *Apis cerana* in Northern Vietnam." *Journal of Apicultural Research* 44, no. 2 (2005): 41–48.

Chuang Chi-fa 莊吉發. "Qingchao qijuzhu ce de zuanxiu ji qi shiliao jiazhi" 清朝起居注冊的纂修及其史料價值 (Compilation of the Qing dynasty's *Record of Rising and Repose* books and their value as historical sources). In *Qingshi lunji* 清史論集, by Chuang Chi-fa, 19:157–84. Taipei: Wen Shi Zhe Chubanshe, 2008.

Clark, Hugh. "What's the Matter with 'China'? A Critique of Teleological History." *Journal of Asian Studies* 77, no. 2 (2018): 295–314.

Clark, J. F. M. *Bugs and the Victorians*. New Haven, CT: Yale University Press, 2009.

Claypool, Lisa. "Beggars, Black Bears, and Butterflies: The Scientific Gaze and Ink Painting in Modern China." *Cross-Currents: East Asian History and Culture Review*, E-Journal no. 14 (2015): 1–50.

Cockerell, T. D. A. [Theodore Dru Alison]. "Bees Obtained by Professor Claude R. Kellogg in the Foochow District, China, with New Records of Philippine Bombidae." *American Museum Novitates*, no. 480 (1931): 1–7.

Cook, Alexandra. "Linnaeus and Chinese Plants: A Test of the Linguistic Imperialism Thesis." *Notes and Records of the Royal Society*, no. 64 (2010): 121–38.

———. "Plant Technology and Science." In *A Cultural History of Plants in the Seventeenth and Eighteenth Centuries*, edited by Jennifer Milam, 85–109. London: Bloomsbury Academic, 2022.

Crosby, Alfred W. *Ecological Imperialism: The Biological Expansion of Europe, 900–1900*. Second edition. Cambridge: Cambridge University Press, 2004.

Dar, S. A., et al. "The Classic Taxonomy of Asian and European Honey Bees." In *Phylogenetics of Bees*, edited by Rustem Abuzarovich Ilyasov and Hyung Wook Kwon, 72–96. Boca Raton: CRC Press, 2019.

Davies, Malcolm, and Jeyaraney Kathirithamby. *Greek Insects*. New York: Oxford University Press, 1986.

Davis, Frederick Rowe. *Banned: A History of Pesticides and the Science of Toxicology*. New Haven: Yale University Press, 2014.

de Carvalho Cabral, Diogo. "Into the Bowels of Tropical Earth: Leaf-Cutting Ants and the Colonial Making of Agrarian Brazil." *Journal of Historical Geography*, no. 50 (2015): 92–105.

———. "Meaningful Clearings: Human-Ant Negotiated Landscapes in Nineteenth-Century Brazil." *Environmental History*, no. 26 (2021): 55–78.

Deb Roy, Rohan. "White Ants, Empire, and Entomo-politics in South Asia." *Historical Journal* 63, no. 2 (2019): 411–36.

Department of Systematic Biology, Entomology Section, National Museum of Natural History and Public Inquiry Services, Smithsonian Institution. "Numbers of Insects (Species and Individuals)." Information Sheet Number 18. Published online 1996. www.si.edu/spotlight/buginfo/bugnos.

Dirzo, Rodolfo, et al. "Defaunation in the Anthropocene." *Science* 345, no. 6195 (2014): 401–6.

Domańska, Ewa. "Animal History." *History and Theory* 56, no. 2 (2017): 267–87.

Easterby-Smith, Sarah. "Cross-Channel Commerce: The Circulation of Plants, People and Botanical Culture between France and Britain, c.1760–c.1789." In *Intellectual Journeys: The Translation of Ideas in Enlightenment England, France and Ireland*, edited by Lise Andriès, Frédéric Ogée, John Dunkley, and Darach Sanfey, 215–30. Oxford: Voltaire Foundation, 2013.

Egerton, Frank N. "History of Ecological Sciences, Part 45: Ecological Aspects of Entomology During the 1800s." *Bulletin of the Ecological Society of America* 94, no. 1 (2013): 36–88.

Elman, Benjamin A. "From Pre-modern Chinese Natural Studies to Modern Science in China." In *Mapping Meanings: The Field of New Learning in Late Qing China*, edited by Michael Lackner and Natascha Vittinghoff, 25–73. Boston: Brill, 2004.

Engel, Michael S. *Innumerable Insects: The Story of the Most Diverse and Myriad Animals on Earth*. New York: Sterling, 2018.

Estoup, Arnaud, Michel Solignac, and Jean-Marie Cornuet. "Precise Assessment of the Number of Patrilines and of Genetic Relatedness in Honeybee Colonies." *Proceedings of the Royal Society: Biological Sciences*, no. 258 (1994): 1–7.

Fan Cunxin 范存鑫 and Hu Fuliang 胡福良. "Qiantan Tangdai mifeng chanye yu mifeng wenhua de duofangwei fazhan" 淺談唐代蜜蜂產業與蜜蜂文化的多方位發展 (Discussion of the multifarious aspects of Tang dynasty beekeeping and bee culture). *Mifeng zazhi*, no. 3 (2020): 23–27.

Fan, Fa-ti. *British Naturalists in Qing China: Science, Empire, and Cultural Encounter*. Cambridge, MA: Harvard University Press, 2004.

Feng, Hong-Qiang, et al. "Nocturnal Migration of Dragonflies over the Bohai Sea in Northern China." *Ecological Entomology* 31, no. 5 (2006): 511–20.

Few, Martha. "Killing Locusts in Colonial Guatemala." In *Centering Animals in Latin American History*, edited by Martha Few and Zeb Tortorici, 62–92. Durham: Duke University Press, 2013.

Fujise Suehiko. "'Hae no inai machi' o tsukutta goro." In *Sengo fukkō kara kōdo seichō e: minshū kyōiku, Tōkyō Orinpikku, genshiryoku hatsuden* (Images of postwar Japan: from reconstruction to high growth), edited by Yoshiyuki Niwa, and Shun'ya Yoshimi, 17–31. Tokyo: Tokyo Daigaku Shuppankai, 2014.

Fu Rongshu 付榮恕. *Dongwuxue* 動物學 (Zoology). Shanghai: Fudan Daxue Chu-banshe, 2014.

Furth, Charlotte. *A Flourishing Yin: Gender in China's Medical History, 960–1665.* Berkeley: University of California Press, 1999.

———. *Ting Wen-Chiang: Science and China's New Culture.* Cambridge, MA: Harvard University Press, 1970.

Gao Lieguo 高列過. "Luo Yin 'Feng' shi Fo yuanliu bian kao" 羅隱 「蜂」 詩 佛源流變考 (Research on the Buddhist origins and development of Luo Yin's "Bee" poems). *Zhejiang shifan daxue xuebao (Shehui kexueban)*, no. 1 (2011): 50–56.

Gilley, David C. "The Behavior of Honey Bees (*Apis mellifera ligustica*) during Queen Duels." *Ethology* 107, no. 7 (2001): 601–22.

Gordon, Andrew. "Managing the Japanese Household: The New Life Movement in Postwar Japan." *Social Politics* (1997): 245–83.

Greenberg, Daniel. "Weird Science: European Origins of the Fantastic Creatures in the Qing Court Painting, the Manual of Sea Oddities." In *The Zoomorphic Imagination in Chinese Art and Culture*, edited by Jerome Silbergeld and Eugene Y. Wang, 379–400. Honolulu: University of Hawai'i Press, 2016.

Grimaldi, David, and Michael S. Engel. *Evolution of the Insects.* Cambridge: Cambridge University Press, 2005.

Gross, Miriam. *Farewell to the God of Plague: Chairman Mao's Campaign to Deworm China.* Oakland: University of California Press, 2016.

Gu Jianping 顧建平. *Hanzi tujie zidian* 漢字圖解字典 (Illustrated dictionary of Chinese characters). Shanghai: Dongfang Chuban Zhongxin, 2012.

Haas, William Joseph. "Gist Gee: A Life in Science and in China." PhD diss., Harvard University, 1991.

Hamdan, Khalil. "Natural Supersedure of Queens in Honey Bee Colonies." *Bee World* 87, no. 3 (2010): 52–54.

Hanyu da zidian Bianji Weiyuanhui 漢語大字典編輯委員會, eds. *Hanyu da zidian* 漢語大字典 (Great compendium of Chinese characters). Chengdu: Sichuan Cishu Chubanshe, 1991.

Harano, Ken-ichi, and Yoshiaki Obara. "The Role of Chemical and Acoustical Stimuli in Selective Queen Cell Destruction by Virgin Queens of the Honeybee *Apis mellifera*." *Applied Entomology and Zoology* 39, no. 2 (2004): 611–16.

Harbsmeier, Christoph. *Science and Civilisation in China. Volume 7: Part 1, Language and Logic.* Cambridge: Cambridge University Press, 1998.

Hasegawa, Saori. "Chosŏn hugi Han-Il ŭi hakkyo ryusa: T'ongyŏksadŭl ŭi kiyŏ wa pŏnyŏksŏ kŏmt'o rŭl chungsim ŭro" (History of Korean-Japanese exchange in medicine in the late Joseon dynasty: Focusing on the contribution of interpreters and translations). PhD diss., Inha University, 2021.

Heimpel, George E., and Jetske G. de Boer. "Sex Determination in the Hymenoptera." *Annual Review of Entomology*, no. 53 (2008): 209–30.

Henry, Todd A. *Assimilating Seoul: Japanese Rule and the Politics of Public Space in Colonial Korea, 1910–1945*. Berkeley: University of California Press, 2016.

Hepburn, H. Randall. *Honeybees and Wax: An Experimental Natural History*. Berlin: Springer-Verlag, 1986.

Hersy, Mark D., and Jeremy Vetter. "Shared Ground: Between Environmental History and the History of Science." *History of Science* 57, no. 4 (2019): 403–40.

Hirano, Kyoko. *Mr. Smith Goes to Tokyo: The Japanese Cinema under the American Occupation, 1945–1952*. Washington, DC: Smithsonian Institution Press, 1992.

Holmes, M. J., et al. "Genetic Reincarnation of Workers as Queens in the Eastern Honeybee *Apis cerana*." *Heredity*, no. 114 (2015): 65–68.

———. "Why Acquiesce? Worker Reproductive Parasitism in the Eastern Honeybee (*Apis cerana*)." *Journal of Evolutionary Biology* 27, no. 5 (2014): 939–49.

Hu Zonggang 胡宗剛. *Jingsheng shengwu diaochasuo shigao* 靜生生物調查所史稿 (Draft history of the Fan Memorial Institute of Biology). Jinan: Shandong Jiaoyu Chubanshe, 2005.

Huang Hsing-tsung. "Plants and Insects in Man's Service." In *Science and Civilisation in China. Volume 6, Biology and Biological Technology. Part I: Botany*, by Needham and Lu, 471–553. Cambridge University Press, 1986.

Huang, Qiang, and Zhijiang Zeng. "Nepotism in Swarming Honeybees (*Apis cerana cerana*)." *Chinese Bulletin of Entomology* 46, no. 1 (2009): 107–11.

Hunt, Michael H. "The American Remission of the Boxer Indemnity: A Reappraisal." *Journal of Asian Studies* 31, no. 3 (1972): 539–59.

Hutton, Eric L., trans. *Xunzi: The Complete Text*. Princeton, NJ: Princeton University Press, 2014.

Idema, Wilt. *Insects in Chinese Literature: A Study and Anthology*. Amherst: Cambria Press, 2019.

Igarashi Yoshikuni. *Bodies of Memory: Narratives of War in Postwar Japanese Culture, 1945–1970*. Princeton, NJ: Princeton University Press, 2000.

———. "Mothra's Gigantic Egg: Consuming the South Pacific in 1960s Japan." In *In Godzilla's Footsteps: Japanese Pop Culture Icons on the Global Stage*, edited by William M. Tsutsui and Michiko Itō, 83–102. New York: Palgrave Macmillan, 2006.

Ikeno Masafumi. "Sengo Nihon no Nōson kaihatsu ni okeru nōson shakaigakutekina shiya." In *Kaihatsu to nōson: Nōson kaihatsuron saikō*, edited by Masami Mizuno and Hiroshi Satō, 81–106. Chiba: Ajia Keizai Kenkyūjo, 2008.

Jacobs, Nancy Joy. *Birders of Africa: History of a Network*. New Haven, CT: Yale University Press, 2016.

Janku, Andrea. "'Heaven-Sent Disasters' in Late Imperial China: The Scope of the State and Beyond." In *Natural Disasters, Cultural Responses: Case Studies toward a Global Environmental History*, edited by Christof Mauch and Christian Pfister, 233–64. Lanham, MD: Lexington Books, 2009.

Ji Baozhong 嵇保中. "Kunchong shihua" 昆蟲詩話 (Notes on poetry about insects). *Nanjing linye daxue xuebao (Renwen shehui kexue ban)* 3, no. 1 (2003): 49–53.

Jiang, Lijing. "Retouching the Past with Living Things: Indigenous Species, Tradition, and Biological Research in Republican China, 1918–1937." *Historical Studies in the Natural Sciences* 46, no. 2 (2016): 154–206.

Karlgren, Bernhard. *Grammata Serica recensa.* Stockholm: Museum of Far Eastern Antiquities, 1957.

———. *The Book of Odes.* Stockholm: Museum of Far Eastern Antiquities, 1950.

Kendal, Jeremy, Jamshid J. Tehrani, and John Odling-Smee. "Introduction: Human Niche Construction in Interdisciplinary Focus." *Philosophical Transactions of the Royal Society B: Biological Sciences* 366, no. 1566 (2011): 785–92.

Kim, Chong-wŏn. "Chosŏn hugi tae-Ch'ŏng muyŏk e taehan ilgoch'al: Chamsang ŭi muyŏk hwaldong ŭl chungsim ŭro" (On the Sino-Korean trade in the late Chosŏn period). *Chungguk munje yŏn'gu*, no. 5 (1980): 1–49.

Kim Chu-wŏn, Ko Tong-ho, and Chŏng Che-mun. "Manmun *Sigyŏng* ŭ pŏnyŏk yangsang yŏn'gu" (Research on aspects of the Manchu translations of *The Classic of Poetry*). *Al'tai hakpo*, no. 19 (2009): 1–30.

Kim, Tae-ho. *Kŭnhyŏndae Han'guk ssal ŭi sahoesa* (Social history of rice in modern Korea). Seoul: Tŭlnyŏk, 2017.

Kim Yŏng-jin and Kim Sang-kyŏng. "Han'guk nongsa sihŏm yŏn'gu ŭi yŏksajŏk koch'al: Kwŏnŏp mobŏmjang ŭl chungsim ŭro" (Historical approach of Korean agricultural experimental research: About Kwonup Mobeomjang [Model Farm]). *Nongŏpsa yŏn'gu* 9, no. 1 (2010): 1–33.

Kirschner, Marc W., and John C. Gerhart. *The Plausibility of Life: Resolving Darwin's Dilemma.* New Haven, CT: Yale University Press, 2005.

Kluge, Nikita Julievich. "Circumscriptional Names of Higher Taxa in Hexapoda." *Bionomina*, no. 1 (2010): 15–55.

Knapp, Keith Nathaniel. *Selfless Offspring: Filial Children and Social Order in Early Medieval China.* Honolulu: University of Hawai'i Press, 2005.

Knoblock, John, trans. *Xunzi: A Translation and Study of the Complete Works.* Stanford, CA: Stanford University Press, 1990.

Koeniger, N., and G. Koeniger. "An Evolutionary Approach to Mating Behaviour and Drone Copulatory Organs in *Apis.*" *Apidologie* 22 (1991): 581–90.

Koerner, Lisbet. *Linnaeus: Nature and Nation.* Cambridge, MA: Harvard University Press, 1999.

Kohler, Robert E. *Lords of the Fly: Drosophila Genetics and the Experimental Life.* Chicago: University of Chicago Press, 1994.

Kolbert, Elizabeth. *The Sixth Extinction: An Unnatural History.* London: Bloomsbury, 2014.

Kornicki, Peter F. *Languages, Scripts, and Chinese Texts in East Asia.* Oxford: Oxford University Press, 2018.

Koyama, S., T. Takagi, S. J. Martin, T. Yoshida, and J. Takahashi. "Absence of

Reproductive Conflict during Queen Rearing in *Apis cerana*." *Insects Sociaux*, no. 56 (2009): 171–75.

Krementsov, Nikolai L. "Dobzhansky and Russian Entomology: The Origin of His Ideas on Species and Speciation." In *The Evolution of Theodosius Dobzhansky*, edited by Mark B. Adams, 31–48. Princeton: Princeton University Press, 2014 [1994].

Ku Cha-ok. "Sŏdunbŏl ŭi kŭndae nonghak kyoyuk kwa kwahakkisul chŏn'gae" (Modern agricultural education and research in Suwŏn). *Nongŏpsa yŏn'gu 9*, no. 1 (2010): 97–135.

Ku To-yŏng. "16-segi Chosŏn tae-Myŏng sahaeng muyŏk ŭi suibp'um kwa kŭ chŏn'gae yangsang" (Chinese goods in sixteenth-century Korea, coming through the envoy trades between Korea and China). *Kukhagyŏn'gu*, no. 34 (2017): 709–65.

"Kwŏn Chung-hyŏn." *Han'guk minjok munhwa taebaekkwa* (Encyclopedia of Korean culture). http://encyclopedia.aks.ac.kr.

Kwon, Soo Jin et al. "Urinara chaeraebyŏ ŭi yujŏnjŏk tayangsŏng" (Genetic diversity of Korean native rice varieties). *Han'guk yukchonghak hoeji 32*, no. 2 (2000): 186–93.

Le Grand Ricci Online. Database by Brill.

LeCain, Timothy J. *The Matter of History: How Things Create the Past*. Cambridge: Cambridge University Press, 2017.

Lee, Tsui-hua Yang. "Geological Sciences in Republican China, 1912–1937." PhD diss., State University of New York at Buffalo, 1985.

Legge, James. *The Sacred Books of China. The Texts of Confucianism. The Lî Kî, I–X*. Oxford: Clarendon Press, 1885.

Legge, James, trans. *The Chinese Classics*. 1893. Facsimile reproduction. Taipei: SMC Publishing, 1991.

Lei, Hsiang-lin. *Neither Donkey nor Horse: Medicine in the Struggle over China's Modernity*. Chicago: University of Chicago Press, 2014.

Lei Mingxia 雷明霞. "Wei shei xinku wei shei tian: Yong feng shi shangxi" 爲誰辛苦爲誰甜: 詠蜂詩賞析 (Who has labored and who enjoyed the sweets?: Examining poetry about bees). *Mifeng zazhi*, no. 7 (2017): 46.

Li Lu 李璐. "Fengmi shici yu Songdai jingji shehui" 蜂蜜詩詞與宋代經濟社會 (Poetry and song lyrics about honeybees and Song dynasty socioeconomic conditions). *Xiangtan daxue xuebao (Zhexue shehui kexueban) 37*, no. 3 (2013): 150–52.

———. "Tangshi de chunji kunchong yixiang yanjiu" 唐詩的春季昆蟲意象研究 (Research into the image of springtime insects in Tang poetry). *Xiangnan xueyuan xuebao 35*, no. 3 (2014): 75–78.

Li, Ming, and Le Kang. "Bing Zhi: Pioneer of Modern Biology in China." *Protein and Cell 1*, no. 7 (2010): 613–15.

Li Peishan 李佩珊 et al. *Baijia zhengming: Fazhan kexue de biyou zhi lu* 百家爭鳴：

發展科學的必由之路 (Hundred schools contended: The destined path for developing science). Shanghai: Shangwu Chubanshe, 1985.

Li Sugen 李夙根. "Jin Guo Pu 'Mifeng fu' jiaoyi" 晉郭璞蜜蜂賦校譯 (Guo Pu's Jin dynasty "Rhapsody on Honeybees" collated and translated). *Yangfeng keji*, no. 1 (1994): 34.

Li Xiangjun 李向军. *Qingdai huangzheng yanjiu* 清代荒政研究 (A study of Qing administration of natural disasters). Beijing: Zhongguo Nongye Chubanshe, 1995.

Li Xiaoyu 李晓愚. "Cong Huangjia yaodian dao 'zhenqi zhi chu': *Jinshikunchong-caomu zhuang* yu Mingdai guji yishuhua gaizao" 從皇家藥典到「珍奇之櫥」：《金石昆蟲草木狀》與明代古籍藝術化改造 (From Imperial Pharmacopeia to "Cabinet of Curiosities": *Forms of the Natural World* and the fine art transformation of Ming dynasty works). *Wenyi yanjiu*, no. 2 (2022): 117–33.

Li Xueqin 李學勤. *Ziyuan* 字源 (Etymology of characters). Tianjin: Tianjin Guji Chubanshe, 2012.

Liu, Michael Shiyung. *Prescribing Colonization: The Role of Medical Practices and Policies in Japan-Ruled Taiwan, 1895–1945.* Ann Arbor, MI: Association for Asian Studies, 2009.

Lu Keliang 鲁克亮 and Liu Qiongfang 刘琼芳. "Guangxi de huangshenmiao yu huangzai" 广西的蝗神庙与蝗灾 (Locust plagues and Guangxi's locust spirit temples). *Guizhou minzu yanjiu* 26, no. 108 (2006): 145–52.

Lurie, David. B. "Orientomology: The Insect Literature of Lafcadio Hearn (1850–1904)." In *JAPANimals: History and Culture in Japan's Animal Life*, edited by Gregory M. Pflugfelder and Brett L. Walker, 244–70. Ann Arbor: Center for Japanese Studies, University of Michigan, 2005.

Ma, Saiping, Marcos Martinón-Torres, and Zebin Li. "Identification of Beeswax Excavated from the Han Period Mausoleum M1 of the King of Jiangdu, Jiangsu, China." *Journal of Archaeological Science: Reports*, no. 4 (2015): 552–58.

Magee, Judith. *Chinese Art and the Reeves Collection.* London: The Natural History Museum, 2011.

Major, John S., Sarah A. Queen, Andrew S. Meyer, and Harold D. Roth, eds. and trans. *The Huainanzi: A Guide to the Theory and Practice of Government in Early Han China.* New York: Columbia University Press, 2010.

Marcon, Federico. *The Knowledge of Nature and the Nature of Knowledge in Early Modern Japan.* Chicago, IL: University of Chicago Press, 2015.

Mayhew, Robert. "King-Bees and Mother-Wasps: A Note on Ideology and Gender in Aristotle's Entomology." *Phronesis* 44, no. 2 (1999): 127–34.

Mayr, Ernst. *Systematics and the Origin of Species.* New York: Columbia University Press, 1982.

McHam, Sarah Blake. *Pliny and the Artistic Culture of the Italian Renaissance: The Legacy of the Natural History.* New Haven, CT: Yale University Press, 2013.

Meir, Paul Penera, and Stephen J. Simpson. *Advances in Insect Physiology, Volume 36:*

Locust Phase Polyphenism: An Update. Cambridge, MA: Academic Press, 2009.

Merrick, Jeffrey. "Royal Bees: The Gender Politics of the Beehive in Early Modern Europe." *Studies in Eighteenth Century Culture*, no. 18 (1988): 7–37.

Mervart, David. "The Point of the Centre: Present and Past Discourses of 'China'-hood." *Araucaria: Revista Iberoamericana de Filosofía, Política y Humanidades*, no. 35 (2016): 127–50.

Métailié, Georges. "Aperçu de l'entomophagie en Chine." In *Savoureux insectes—De l'aliment traditionnel à l'innovation gastronomique*, edited by Elisabeth Motte-Florac and Philippe Le Gall, 73–88. Tours: Presses Universitaires François Rabelais, 2016.

———. "Le *Bencao gangmu* de Li Shizhen et l'histoire naturelle au Japon durant la période d'Edo (1600–1868)." *Etudes Chinoises*, no. 25 (2006): 41–68.

———. "The *Bencao gangmu* of Li Shizhen: An Innovation in Natural History?" In *Innovation in Chinese Medicine*, edited by Elisabeth Hsu, 221–61. Cambridge: Cambridge University Press, 2001.

Mikulak, Maxim W. "Darwinism, Soviet Genetics, and Marxism-Leninism." *Journal of the History of Ideas* 31, no. 3 (1970): 359–76.

Milburn, Olivia. "A Taste of Honey: Early Medieval Chinese Writings about Sweeteners." *Early Medieval China*, no. 26 (2020): 43–66.

———. "Bodily Transformations: Responses to Intersex Individuals in Pre-Imperial and Imperial-Era China." *Nan Nü* 16, no. 1 (2014): 1–28.

———. "The Chinese Mosquito: A Literary Theme." *Sino-Platonic Papers*, no. 270 (2017): 1–50.

Miller, Owen. "The Myŏnjujŏn: A Silk Merchants' Guild in Late Chosŏn Korea," *Papers of the British Association for Korean Studies* 10 (2005): 185–210.

Mizutani Kiyoshi. "Nihon no eisei chūgai bōjoshi." *Eisei dōbotsu* 44, no. 1 (1993): 53–62.

Moon, Manyong. "Becoming a Biologist in Colonial Korea: Cultural Nationalism in a Teacher-cum-Biologist." *East Asian Science, Technology and Society: An International Journal*, no. 6 (2012): 65–82.

Muller, A. Charles. "The Diamond Sutra." Resources for East Asian Language and Thought. October 26, 2013. www.acmuller.net/bud-canon/diamond_sutra.html.

Munz, Tania. *The Dancing Bees: Karl von Frisch and the Discovery of the Honeybee Language*. Chicago: University of Chicago Press, 2016.

Nakamura Hideyuki. "Mieru mono kara Mienai mono e." In *Sengo fukkō kara kōdo seichō e: Minshu kyōiku, Tōkyō Orinpikku, genshiryoku hatsuden* (Images of postwar Japan: From reconstruction to high growth), edited by Yoshiyuki Niwa and Shun'ya Yoshimi, 61–98. Tokyo: Tokyo Daigakku Shuppankai, 2014.

Nam, Mi-hye. "17-segi yangjam chŏngch'aek ŭi ch'ui wa yangjamŏp ŭi sŏngjang" (Korean sericultural policies and the growth of sericulture in the seventeenth century). *Sahak yŏn'gu*, no. 88 (2007): 653–83.

———. "18-segi Yŏngjodae yangjam chŏngch'aek kwa yangjamŏp" (A study of sericulture and the policy during the reign of King Yŏngjo in the eighteenth century). *Han'guk munhwa yŏn'gu*, no. 16 (2009): 233–65.

Nappi, Carla. *The Monkey and the Inkpot: Natural History and Its Transformations in Early Modern China*. Cambridge, MA: Harvard University Press, 2009.

Needham, Joseph, and Lu Gwei-Djen. *Science and Civilisation in China. Volume 6, Biology and Biological Technology. Part I: Botany*. Cambridge: Cambridge University Press, 1986.

Neitzel, Laura L. *The Life We Longed For: Danchi Housing and the Middle Class Dream in Postwar Japan*. New York: Columbia University Press, 2016.

New England Complex Systems Institute. "Concepts: Emergence." Published online 2011. https://necsi.edu/emergence.

Nho Si-Kab and Jae Man Lee. "Hyŏnjon hanŭn Han'guk chaeraejong champ'umjong ŭi hyŏngjil t'ŭksŏng" (Characteristics of Korean native strains in the domesticated silkworm, *B. mori*). *Han'guk chamsa kongch'ung hakhoeji* 42, no. 1 (2000): 10–13.

———. "Tongwi hyoso mit RAPD punsŏk ae ŭihan Han'guk chaeraejong nuaegyet'ong ŭi kyet'onghakjŏk t'ŭksŏng" (Phylogenetic relationships and characterization of Korean native silkworm strains based on RAPDs and isozyme analysis, *B. mori*). *Han'guk chamsa kongch'ung hakhoeji* 43, no. 2 (2001): 59–66.

Ni Genjin 倪根金. "Zhongguo lishi shang de huangzai ji zhihuang" 中國歷史上的蝗災及治蝗 (Locust plagues and their control in Chinese history). *Lishi jiaoxue*, no. 6 (1998): 48–51.

Nornes, Markus. *Forest of Pressure: Ogawa Shinsuke and Postwar Japanese Documentary*. Minneapolis: University of Minnesota Press, 2007.

Nowak, Martin A., Corina E. Tarnita, Edward O. Wilson. "The Evolution of Eusociality." *Nature* 466, no. 7130 (August 26, 2010): 1057–62.

Odling-Smee, John, et al. "Niche Construction Theory: A Practical Guide for Ecologists." *Quarterly Review of Biology* 88, no. 1 (2013): 4–28.

Oh Chin-sŏk. "Tae-Han chegukki in'gong yangjam hoesa wa chamŏpkwa sihŏmjang" (Sericultural enterprises and sericultural experiment stations in 1900s Korea). *Sŏul kwa yŏksa*, no. 85 (2013): 121–76.

Oldroyd, Benjamin P., and Siriwat Wongsiri. *Asian Honey Bees: Biology, Conservation, and Human Interactions*. Cambridge, MA: Harvard University Press, 2006.

Oldroyd, Benjamin P., et al. "Worker Policing and Worker Reproduction in *Apis cerana*." *Behavioral Ecology and Sociobiology*, no. 50 (2001): 371–77.

Onaga, Lisa Aiko. "Silkworms, Science, and Nation: A Sericultural History of Genetics in Modern Japan." PhD diss., Cornell University, 2012.

Ota Hiroki. "Historical Development of Pesticides in Japan." *Survey Reports on the Systemization of Technologies*, no. 18. Tokyo: National Museum of Nature and Science, 2013.

Overmeire, S. Van. "The Perfect King Bee: Visions of Kingship in Classical Antiquity." *Akroterion* 56, no. 1 (2011): 31–46.

Oyama Kanjirō. "Tokyoto ni okeru chiku eisei sōshiki no ka to hae kujo." *Kōshū Eisei* 28, no. 7 (1964): 363–66.

Pak, Kyŏng-ja, and Ko Pu-ja. "Chosŏn wangjo sillok e kiroktoen 15-segi chungban esŏ 17-segi chungban ŭi poksikkŭmje" (Regulations on dress and its ornaments in *Veritable Records of Chosŏn Dynasty* from the mid-fifteenth century to the mid-seventeenth century). *Poksing munhwa yŏn'gu* 16, no. 4 (2008): 748–61.

Palladino, Paolo. *Entomology, Ecology and Agriculture: The Making of Scientific Careers in North America, 1885–1985.* Amsterdam: Harwood Academic Publisher, 1996.

Pang, Tatiana A., and M. P. Volkova. *Descriptive Catalogue of Manchu Manuscripts and Blockprints in the St. Petersburg Branch of the Institute of Oriental Studies, Russian Academy of Sciences: Issue 2.* Wiesbaden: Harrassowitz, 2001.

Pattinson, David. "Bees in China: A Brief Cultural History." In *Animals Through Chinese History: Earliest Times to 1911,* edited by Roel Sterckx, Martina Siebert, and Dagmar Schäfer, 99–117. Cambridge: Cambridge University Press, 2019.

———. "Pre-modern Beekeeping in China: A Short History." *Agricultural History* 86, no. 4 (2012): 235–55.

Pines, Yuri, ed. and trans. *The Book of Lord Shang: Apologetics of State Power in Early China.* New York: Columbia University Press, 2017.

Pline l'Ancien. *Histoire naturelle. Livre XI (Des Insectes. Des Parties du corps).* Edited and translated by Alfred Ernout and R. Pépin. Paris: Les Belles Lettres, 1948.

Pliny. *Natural History, Volume III: Books 8–11.* Translated by H. Rackham. Cambridge, MA: Harvard University Press, 1940.

Prete, Frederick R. "Can Females Rule the Hive? The Controversy over Honey Bee Gender Roles in British Beekeeping Texts of the Sixteenth-Eighteenth Centuries." *Journal of the History of Biology* 24, no. 1 (1991): 113–44.

Qin Jie 秦杰. "Yingguang shanshuo hua zhutai" 熒光閃爍話燭臺 (A glittering, flickering lamp). *Rongbaozhai,* no. 4 (2008): 22–31.

Ratnieks, Francis L. W., Kevin R. Foster, and Tom Wenseleers. "Conflict Resolution in Insect Societies." *Annual Review of Entomology* 51 (2006): 581–608.

Reardon-Anderson, James. *The Study of Change: Chemistry in China, 1840–1949.* Cambridge: Cambridge University Press, 1991.

Richards, Richard A. *The Species Problem: A Philosophical Analysis.* Cambridge: Cambridge University Press, 2010.

Ro, Sang-ho. *Neo-Confucianism and Science in Korea: Humanity and Nature, 1706–1814.* Oxon: Routledge, 2021.

———. "Shifting Perceptions of Insects in the Late Chosŏn Period." *International Journal of Korean History* 25, no. 1 (2020): 41–83.

Rogers, Naomi. "Germs with Legs: Flies, Disease, and the New Public Health." *Bulletin of the History of Medicine* 63, no. 4 (1989): 599–617.

Rogers, Stephen M. and Swidbert R. Ott. "Differential Activation of Serotonergic Neurons During Short- and Long-Term Gregarization of Desert Locusts." *Proceedings of the Royal Society B: Biological Sciences* 282, no. 1800 (2015): 1–10.

Rothschild, N. Harry. "Sovereignty, Virtue, and Disaster Management: Chief Minister Yao Chong's Proactive Handling of the Locust Plague of 715–16." *Environmental History* 17, no. 4 (2012): 783–812.

Rozycki, William. *Mongol Elements in Manchu.* Bloomington: Indiana University Research Institute for Inner Asian Studies, 1994.

Russell, Edmund. *War and Nature: Fighting Humans and Insects with Chemicals from World War I to Silent Spring.* Cambridge: Cambridge University Press, 2001.

Samways, Michael J., et al. "Solutions for Humanity on How to Conserve Insects." *Biological Conservation*, no. 242 (2020): 1–15.

Sawada Rui. "Sengo Nihon ni okeru 'Ka to hae no inai seikatsu' jissen undō no tenkai: Kyōiku eiga 'Hyakunin no yōki na nyōbō tachi' no bunseki kara." *Bunka shigengaku*, no. 13 (2015): 31–44.

Schlesinger, Jonathan. *A World Trimmed with Fur: Wild Things, Pristine Places, and the Natural Fringes of Qing Rule.* Stanford: Stanford University Press, 2017.

Schmalzer, Sigrid. *Red Revolution, Green Revolution: Scientific Farming in Socialist China.* Chicago: University of Chicago Press, 2016.

Schmid, Andre. *Korea between Empires, 1895–1919.* New York: Columbia University Press, 2002.

Schneider, Laurence A. *Biology and Revolution in Twentieth-Century China.* Lanham, MD: Rowman and Littlefield, 2003.

———. "Michurinist Biology in the People's Republic of China, 1948–1956." *Journal of the History of Biology*, no. 45 (2012): 525–56.

Schuessler, Axel. *Minimal Old Chinese and Later Han Chinese: A Companion to Grammata Serica Recensa.* Honolulu: University of Hawai'i Press, 2009.

Scott-Phillips, Thomas C., et al. "The Niche Construction Perspective: A Critical Appraisal." *Evolution* 68, no. 5 (2014): 1231–43.

Screech, Timon. *The Lens within the Heart: The Western Scientific Gaze and Popular Imagery in Later Edo Japan.* Second edition. Honolulu: University of Hawai'i Press, 2002.

Seaman, Louis Livingston. *The Real Triumph of Japan: The Conquest of the Silent Foe.* New York: D. Appleton, 1908.

Seeley, Joseph, and Aaron Skabelund. "Tigers—Real and Imagined—in Korea's Physical and Cultural Landscape." *Environmental History* 20, no. 3 (2015): 475–503.

Seki Naomi. "Sengo Nihon no 'ka to hae no inai seikatsu undō': Minshū sanka to kokusai kyōryoku no shiten kara." *Kokusai hoken iryō* 24, no. 1 (2009): 1–11.

Setoguchi Akihisa. "Control of Insect Vectors in the Japanese Empire: Transformation of the Colonial/Metropolitan Environment, 1920–1945." *East Asian Science, Technology and Society: An International Journal* 1, no. 2 (2007): 167–81.

———. *Gaichū no tanjō: Mushi kara Mita Nihon Shi*. Tokyo: Chikuma Shobō, 2009.

Sheng, Jia. "The Origins of the Science Society of China, 1914–1937." PhD diss., Cornell University, 1995.

Sherman, Paul W., et al. "The Eusociality Continuum." *Behavioral Ecology* 6, no. 1 (1995): 102–8.

Sin Yong-ha. "Pak Che-ga ŭi sanggongŏp kaeballon kwa kaeguk t'ongsangnon." (Pak Che-ga's thought on economic development and foreign trade). *Kyŏngje nonch'ong* 36, no. 3 (1997): 307–21.

Siniawer, Eiko Maruko. *Waste: Consuming Postwar Japan*. Ithaca, NY: Cornell University Press, 2018.

Sleigh, Charlotte. *The Paper Zoo: 500 Years of Animals in Art*. Chicago: University of Chicago Press, 2017.

Smocovitis, Vassiliki Betty. *Unifying Biology: The Evolutionary Synthesis and Evolutionary Biology*. Princeton, NJ: Princeton University Press, 1996.

Sŏ Yŏng-hŭi. "Kwŏn Chung-hyŏn, Yi Chi-yong, kaehwaronja, Han-Il tongmaengnonja ŭi pyŏnsin kwa haengno" (Kwŏn Chung-hyŏn and Yi Chi-yong: The life and choices of a reformist and supporter of Korea-Japan alliance). *Naeil ŭl yŏnŭn yŏksa*, no. 19 (2005): 52–66.

Söderblom Saarela, Mårten. "Manchu and the Study of Language in China (1607–1911)." PhD diss., Princeton University, 2015.

Spence, Jonathan D. *To Change China: Western Advisers in China, 1620–1960*. Harmondsworth, England: Penguin Books, 1980.

Sriskantharajah, Srimathy. "Malaria Elimination: Are We Nearly There Yet?" Bug-Bitten. April 25, 2019. http://blogs.biomedcentral.com/bugbitten/2019/04/25/malaria-elimination-are-we-nearly-there-yet.

Standaert, Nicolas. "Jesuit Accounts of Chinese History and Chronology and Their Chinese Sources." *East Asian Science Technology and Medicine*, no. 35 (2012): 11–87.

Stephens, Holly. "Agriculture and Development in an Age of Empire: Institutions, Associations, and Market Networks in Korea, 1876–1945." PhD diss., University of Pennsylvania, 2017.

Sterckx, Roel. "Ritual, Mimesis, and the Nonhuman Animal World in Early China." *Society & Animals*, no. 24 (2016): 269–88.

———. *The Animal and the Daemon in Early China*. Albany: SUNY Press, 2002.

Stige, Leif C., et al. "Thousand-Year-Long Chinese Time Series Reveals Climatic Forcing of Decadal Locust Dynamics." *PNAS* 104, no. 41 (2007): 16188–93.

Suh, Soyoung. "Herbs of Our Own Kingdom: Layers of the 'Local' in the Materia Medica of Choson Korea." *Asian Medicine: Tradition and Modernity* 4, no. 2 (2008): 395–422.

Suzuki Takeshi and Ogata Kazuki. *Nihon no Eisei Gaichū*. Tokyo: Shinshichōsha, 1968.

Tarpy, D. R., and M. K. Mayer. "The Effects of Size and Reproductive Quality on the Outcomes of Duels between Honey Bee Queens (*Apis mellifera* L.)." *Ethology Ecology and Evolution* 21, no. 2 (2009): 147–53.

Taylor, Nik. "Anthropomorphism and the Animal Subject." In *Anthropocentrism: Humans, Animals, Environments*, edited by Rob Boddice, 265–79. Leiden: Brill, 2011.

Tian, Huidong, et al. "Reconstruction of a 1,910-Y-Long Locust Series Reveals Consistent Associations with Climate Fluctuations in China." *PNAS* 108, no. 35 (2011): 14521–26.

Tjan Tjoe Som (Zeng Zhusen 曾珠森). *Po Hu T'ung: The Comprehensive Discussions in the White Tiger Hall*. E. J. Brill: Leiden, 1949.

Tojo, Koji, et al. "Species Diversity of Insects in Japan: Their Origins and Diversification Processes." *Entomological Science* 20, no. 1 (2017): 357–81.

Tomizawa Kazuhori and Esaki Satoshi. "Sanshu kensahō shikōki ni okeru chihōchō no sanshu kensa ni tsuite" (The inspection of silkworm eggs conducted by municipal intendances during the period enforcing the inspection law: The study focusing on the efforts in Gunma Prefecture). *Takasaki Keizai daigaku ronshū* 48, no. 4 (2006): 53–71.

Trueman, John W. H. "A Brief History of the Classification and Nomenclature of Odonata." *Zootaxa*, no. 1668 (2007): 381–94.

Tsintsius, V. I., ed. *Sravnitel'nyĭ slovar' tunguso-man'chzhurskikh iazykov: Materialy k ėtimologicheskomu slovariu* (Comparative dictionary of the Manchu-Tungus languages: Materials toward an etymological dictionary). Leningrad: Nauka, 1975–77.

Tu, Chenyu. "On the Source Text of Ši Ging Ni Bithe (1654)." Manchu Studies Group (blog). April 22, 2021. www.manchustudiesgroup.org/2021/04/22/on-the -source-text-of-si-ging-ni-bithe-1654.

Tu, Xiongbing, et al. "Growth, Development and Daily Change in Body Weight of *Locusta migratoria manilensis* (Orthoptera: Acrididae) Nymphs at Different Temperatures." *Journal of Orthoptera Research* 21, no. 2 (2012): 133–40.

Tuchikane (Doi), Kazuko. "Meiji ki no Nihon yōsangyo to yōsansho: Shuppan jōkyō no kentō" (Japanese sericulture and sericulture manuals in the Meiji period: An investigation of the state of printing). *Nihon jōshi daigaku daigakuin bungaku kenkyūjo kiyō*, no. 26 (2020): 41–55.

Uchida, Katsuyoshi. "Kaikaki ni okeru Nippon no seiyō nōgaku no juyō: Tsuda Sen (1873–1908) wo chūsin ni" (Japanese adoption of Western agricultural studies: The case of Tsuda Sen). *Nongŏpsa yŏn'gu* 1, no. 1 (2002): 99–108.

Unschuld, Paul U., annot. and trans. *Ben Cao Gang Mu, Volume VIII: Clothes, Utensils, Worms, Insects, Amphibians, Animals with Scales, Animals with Shells*. Oakland: University of California Press, 2021.

Valenti, Federico. "Biological Classification in Early Chinese Dictionaries and Glossaries: From Fish to Invertebrates and Vice Versa." PhD diss., Università degli Studi di Sassari, 2017.

Vogel, Gretchen. "Where Have All the Insects Gone?" *Science*. May 10, 2017. www
.sciencemag.org/news/2017/05/where-have-all-insects-gone.

Von Zach, Erwin Ritter. "Ueber Wortzusammensetzungen im Mandschu." *Wiener
Zeitschrift für die Kunde des Morgenlandes*, no. 11 (1897): 242–48.

Wagner, David L., et al. "Insect Decline in the Anthropocene: Death by a Thousand Cuts." *PNAS* 118, no. 2 (2021): 1–10.

Walker, Brett L. "Sanemori's Revenge: Insects, Eco-system Accidents, and Policy
Decisions in Japan's Environmental History." *Journal of Policy History* 19, no. 1
(2007): 113–44.

Wang Hui 王暉. "'Chong,' 'chong' zi chuyi yu yifu 'chong' pang leishu fanchou
yanbian kao" 「虫」、「蟲」字初義與意符「虫」旁類屬範疇演
變考 (Examination of the original meaning of *chong* 虫 and *chong* 蟲 and
the changes in classification of characters with the *chong* semantic component). *Shaanxi Shifan Daxue xuebao (Zhexue shehui kexue ban)* 41, no. 6 (2012):
163–69.

Wang Ling 王令. "I Dreamed of Locusts." Introduced and translated by Jonathan
Pease. *Comparative Criticism*, no. 15 (1993): 215–22.

Wang Yonghou 王永厚. "Yong feng shi hua" 詠蜂詩話 (Notes on poetry about
bees). *Mifeng zazhi*, no. 4 (1998): 32.

Wang, Yuanchong. "Manchu-Chosŏn Relations and the Making of the Qing's
'Zhongguo' Identity, 1616–43." *Chinese Historical Review* 22, no. 2 (2015): 95–119.

Wang, Zuoyue. "Saving China through Science: The Science Society of China,
Scientific Nationalism, and Civil Society in Republican China." *Osiris* Second
Series, no. 17 (2002): 291–322.

———. "The Chinese Developmental State during the Cold War: The Making of
the 1956 Twelve-Year Science and Technology Plan." *History and Technology*, no.
31 (2015): 3, 180–205.

Whipple, George Chandler. *Typhoid Fever: Its Causation, Transmission and Prevention*. New York: John Wiley & Sons, 1908.

White, N. J., et al. "Averting a Malaria Disaster." *Lancet*, no. 135 (1999): 1965–67.

Wieger, Léon. *Chinese Characters*. Translated by Leo Davrout. New York: Dover,
1965.

Winston, Mark L. *The Biology of the Honey Bee*. Cambridge, MA: Harvard University
Press, 1991.

Wongsiri, Siriwat, Lai You-sheng, and H. Allen Sylvester. "Queen Rearing with
Apis cerana." *American Bee Journal* 130, no. 1 (1990): 32–35.

World Health Organization. "This Year's World Malaria Report at a Glance." November 2018. www.who.int/malaria/media/world-malaria-report-2018/en.

Xin Jiaoyu She 新教育社, ed. *Zhongxue shengwu jiaoxue de gaizao* 中学生物教学
的改造 (The reform of biological education in middle schools). Beijing: Renmin Jiaoyu Chubanshe, 1951.

Yamamo'to Chyoho. "Tae-Han chegukki Kwangju e issŏsŏŭi Okumura nammae chinjong p'ogyo sirŏp hakkyo sŏllib ŭl tullŏssago" (The Buddhist missionary activities of Okumura family and the foundation of the Kwangju Vocational School in the 1900s). *Minjok munhwa yŏn'gu*, no. 57 (2012): 213–65.

Yamanaka Kenta. "Sengo nanyo ni okeru 'Ka to Hae no inai seikatsu' no tenkai." *Nichijō to bunka*, no. 5 (2018): 39–48.

Yang Chin-Lung 楊晉龍. "*Shi zhuan daquan* yu Qingdai qianqi *Shijing* xue guan-lianxing tanlun: Yi *Siku quanshu zongmu* zhulu zhi zhuanzhu wei duixiang de kaocha" 《詩傳大全》與清代前期《詩經》學關聯性探論—以《四庫全書總目》著錄之專著為對象的考察 (On the relationship between [*The Classic of*] *Poetry, Complete Tradition* and research on *The Classic of Poetry* in the early Qing period as seen from *Contents of the Complete Writings of the Four Trea-suries*). *Zhongguo wenzhe yanjiu jikan*, no. 48 (2016): 97–138.

Yang Fengmou 楊豐陌 and Zhang Benyi 張本義. *Dalian Tushuguan cang shaoshu minzu guji tushu zonglu* 大連圖書館藏少數民族古籍圖書總錄 (General cat-alog of historical materials in national minority languages held by the Dalian Library). Shenyang: Liaoning Minzu Chubanshe, 2004.

Yang Shupei 楊淑培. "Zhongguo gudai dui mifeng de renshi he yangfeng jishu" 中國古代對蜜蜂的認識和養蜂技術 (Knowledge about bees and beekeeping techniques in ancient China). *Nongye kaogu* 1 (1988): 242–51.

———. "Zhongguo yangfengshi zhi guanjian" 中國養蜂史之管見 (Observations on the history of beekeeping in China). *Zhongguo nongshi*, no. 2 (1988): 82–90.

Yang, Tsui-hua. *Patronage of Science: The China Foundation for the Promotion of Education and Culture*. Translated by Chi-Chu Chen and Yu-wen Su. Second Edition. Taipei: China Foundation for the Promotion of Education and Cul-ture, 2015.

Ye Gaoshu 葉高樹. "Man-Han hebi *Qinding fanyi wujing sishu* de wenhua yihan: Cong 'yin guoshu yi tong jingyi' dao 'yin jingyi yi tong guoshu'" 滿漢合璧《欽定繙譯五經四書》的文化意涵：從「因國書以通經義」到「因經義以通國書」 (The cultural import of the Manchu-Chinese bilingual *Imperi-ally authorized translations of the Five Classics and Four Books*: From "Grasping the meaning of the classics through the dynastic language" to "Grasping the dynas-tic language through the meaning of the classics"). In *Jingxue yanjiu luncong* 經學研究論叢, 13:1–42. Taipei: Taiwan Xuesheng Shuju, 2006.

———. "*Shijing* Manwen yiben bijiao yanjiu: Yi 'Zhou nan,' 'Zhao nan' wei li" 《詩經》滿文譯本比較研究——以〈周南〉、〈召南〉為例 (A com-parative study on the Manchu translations of *The Classic of Poetry* using the examples of the "Odes of Zhou and South" and "Odes of Shao and South"). *Guoli Taiwan Shifan Daxue lishi xuebao*, no. 20 (1992): 219–34.

Yi Sŏn-a. "19-segi kaehwap'a ŭi nongsŏ kanhaeng kwa pogŭp ŭi ŭiŭi." (The histor-ical meaning of agricultural books published and distributed by the Enlighten-ment Party in the nineteenth century). *Nongŏpsa yŏn'gu* 8, no. 2 (2009): 57–75.

Yi Yŏng-hak. "1920-nyŏndae Chosŏn chongdokbu ŭi nongŏp chŏngch'aek" (The agricultural policies of government-general of Korea in the 1920s). *Han'guk minjok munhwa*, no. 69 (2018): 303–36.

Yu, Ge, Huadong Shen, and Jian Liu. "Impacts of Climate Change on Historical Locust Outbreaks in China." *Journal of Geophysical Research* 114, no. D18 (2009): 1–11.

Zanasi, Margherita. "Exporting Development: The League of Nations and Republican China." *Comparative Studies in Society and History* 49, no. 1 (2007): 143–69.

Zenkoku Chiiki Fujin Dantai Renraku Kyōgikai. *Zenchifuren 30-nen no ayumi.* Tokyo: Zenkoku Chiiki Fujin Dantai Renraku Kyōgikai, 1986.

Zha Jinping 查金萍. "Han Wei Liuchao niaoshouchong fu santi" 漢魏六朝鳥獸蟲賦三題 (Three topics on rhapsodies about birds, beasts, and insects in the Han, Wei, and Six dynasties). *Anhui Daxue Xuebao* (*Zhexue Shehui Kexue ban*), no. 1 (2006): 56–59.

Zhang Chenliang 張辰亮. *Hai cuo tu biji* 海錯圖筆記 (Jottings on *Oceanic Complexities, Illustrated*). Beijing: Zhongxin Chubanshe, 2017.

Zhang Daye. *The World of a Tiny Insect: A Memoir of the Taiping Rebellion and Its Aftermath.* Translated by Xiaofei Tian. Seattle: University of Washington Press, 2013.

Zhang Hong 張虹, Cheng Dakun 程大鯤, and Tong Yonggong 佟永功, eds. "Qianlong chao 'Qinding Xin Qingyu' (wu)" 乾隆朝「欽定新清語」（五）. *Manyu yanjiu*, no. 2 (1997): 37–44, 59.

Zhang, Jie, et al. "Decadal Variability of Droughts and Floods in the Yellow River Basin during the Last Five Centuries and Relations with the North Atlantic SST." *International Journal of Climatology* 33, no. 15 (2013): 3217–28.

Zhang Lei 張磊. "Zhongguo gudai dengju xingzhi he zhaomingliao yanbian guanxi kao" 中國古代燈具形制和照明料演變關係考 (Research on the relationship between the design of ancient Chinese lamps and the development of lighting fuels). *Nanjing yishu xueyuan xuebao*, no. 6 (2009): 190–94.

Zhang, Qiang, Marco Gemmer, and Jiaqi Chen. "Climate Changes and Flood/Drought Risk in the Yangtze Delta, China during the Past Millennium." *Quaternary International*, nos. 176–77 (2008): 62–69.

Zhang, Qiang, et al. "Fatal Honey Poisoning Caused by *Tripterygium wilfordii* Hook F in Southwest China: A Case Series." *Wilderness and Environmental Medicine* 27, no. 2 (2016): 271–73.

Zhang, Qiang, et al. "Fatal Honey Poisoning in Southwest China: A Case Series of 31 Cases." *Southeast Asian Journal of Tropical Medicine and Public Health* 48, no. 1 (2017): 189–96.

Zhang, Qiong. *Making the New World Their Own: Chinese Encounters with Jesuit Science in the Age of Discovery.* Leiden: Brill, 2015.

Zhang Yihe 章義和. *Zhongguo huangzai shi* 中國蝗災史 (A history of locust plagues in China). Hefei: Anhui Renmin Chubanshe, 2008.

Zhang, Zhibin, and Dianmo Li. "A Possible Relationship between Outbreaks of the Oriental Migratory Locust (*Locusta migratoria manilensis* Meyen) in China and the El Niño Episodes." *Ecological Research* 14, no. 3 (1999): 267–70.

Zhou Yao 周堯, Wang Siming 王思明, and Xia Rubing 夏如兵. *Ershi shiji Zhongguo de kunchong xue* 二十世紀中國的昆蟲學 (A history of entomology in modern China). Xi'an: Shijie Tushu Chuban Gongsi, 2004.

Zou Shuwen 鄒樹文. "Guanyu woguo gudai dongwu fenleixue de taolun" 關於我國古代動物分類學的討論 (A discussion on the zoological systems of ancient China). *Kunchong xuebao* (*Acta Entomologica Sinica*) 19, no. 3 (1976): 325–34.

CONTRIBUTORS

DAVID A. BELLO is the E. L. Otey Professor of East Asian Studies at Washington and Lee University. He is the author of *Across Forest, Steppe and Mountain: Environment, Identity and Empire in Qing China's Borderlands* (Cambridge University Press, 2016) and *Opium and the Limits of Empire: Drug Prohibition in the Chinese Interior, 1729–1850* (Harvard Council on East Asian Studies, 2005).

DANIEL BURTON-ROSE is a visiting assistant professor of History of Science, Technology, and the Environment, Department of History at Wake Forest University. He has published in the journals *Asian Medicine* (for which he also serves as editor for East Asia), *Daoism: Religion, History and Society, Journal of the History of Biology, Journal on Religion and Violence,* and *T'oung Pao,* among others, and has contributed to the anthologies *Communicating with the Gods: Spirit-Writing in Chinese History* (Brill, 2023) and *Transgender China* (Palgrave-Macmillan, 2012).

LIJING JIANG 姜儷婧 is an assistant professor in the Department of History of Science and Technology at Johns Hopkins University. She is the book review editor of the *Journal of the History of Biology,* to which she has also contributed.

OLIVIA MILBURN is a professor at the School of Chinese, Hong Kong University. Her books include *The Empress in the Pepper Chamber: Zhao Feiyan in History and Fiction* (University of Washington Press, 2021), *The Spring and Autumn Annals of Master Yan* (Brill, 2016), and *Cherishing Antiquity: The Cultural Construction of an Ancient Chinese Kingdom* (Harvard University Asia Center, 2013).

SANG-HO RO is associate professor of Korean Studies and East Asian Studies, Ewha Womans University. He is the author of *Neo-Confucianism and Science in Korea, 1706–1814* (Oxon: Routledge, 2021).

KERRY SMITH is an associate professor in the History and East Asian Studies Departments at Brown University. He is the author of *A Time of Crisis: Japan, the Great Depression, and Rural Revitalization* (Harvard University Press, 2001).

MÅRTEN SÖDERBLOM SAARELA is an assistant research fellow of the Institute of Modern History at Academia Sinica. He is the author of *The Early Modern Travels of Manchu: A Script and Its Study in East Asia and Europe* (University of Pennsylvania Press, 2020).

FEDERICO VALENTI received his PhD in classical Chinese culture from the University of Venice and received the Jing Brand Scholarship at the Needham Research Institute at the University of Cambridge.

INDEX

Page numbers in *italics* refer to figures.

Liu Meng shrines, 84, 93n43

locusts: and administrative responsibility, 84–85, 86, 90; as agricultural pests, xxvi, 42, 50–51, 58, 67, 69–71, 86; associated with crickets and grasshoppers, 44–46, 51, 52, 61n29; in Beijing dialect, 47, 57, 61n35; as *chong*, xxiii–xxiv; in *The Classic of Poetry*, 45–46, 52, 56–57, 60n19; climate and habitat, 67, 73–77, 81–82, 88; control measures, 69, 71–73, 80–81, 82–89, 92n34; feeding behavior, 79, 83, 92n32, 93n42; as food, 73, 81; historical and environmental analysis, 68–70, 90–91n1; immature, 50, 51, 52, 54, 55, 58, 67, 74, 82, 92n34; lifecycle of, 51–52, 83; in Manchu and Chinese, 41, 42, 44, 45, 47–51, 53–59, 77–78; in Manchu memorials, 50–51, 52; as metaphor, xviii, xxixn6; metaphysics and rituals, 71–72, 73, 83; outbreaks, 72, 73–75, 81, 82, 84–89, 90, 91n19, 92n22; peasant beliefs about, 81, 82; phenotypic plasticity, 69–70, 88; Qing management of, xxv, xxvi, 67–69, 71, 80, 84–89, 90; records of disasters, 175; reproduction, 67, 73–74, 75, 76–77, 88; shrines to repel, 84, 93n43; swarming, xxixn6, 74, 78–79, 82, 83, 84, 85, 88–89; in wetland reed stands, 82, 86, 88–89

loyal subjects (*liangmin*), 70, 71

Lu Shiyi, essay on locust eradication, 83–84

Lu Yudao, 188

Lunheng (Doctrines weighed; Wang Chong), 24, 169

Lyle, Clay, 126

Lysenko, Trofim, 187, 193–94; "New Developments in the Science of Biological Species," 193

MacArthur, Douglas, 123

Madeira, 167, 171

Maeil Sinbo, 106

Mainichi newspaper, 120, 128, 137, 146, 155n66

malaria, xxii, xxiii, 124, 151n2, 152n15; depicted in public health calendar, xvi

Manchu and Chinese, Divided into Sections (Man-Han leishu), 48

Manchu-Chinese dictionaries, 46–48, 57

Manchu language: avoidance of polysemy, 59; borrowings from Chinese, xviii, 42, 52–53, 58; coining of words, 54–55, 56, 57, 58, 62n54; insect names, 41–46, 47–49, 54–55, 78; plant and animal names, 62n54; Qianlong reform of the lexicon, 52–53, 58; translations of *The Classic of Poetry*, xxv, 42, 43–47, 52, 53, 56, 57, 60n17

Manchu memorials, 50–51, 53

Manual of the Mustard Seed Garden (Jieziyuan huapu), 174

Mao Zedong, 184; Mao Zedong Thought, 199; "On Contradiction," 197, 198

Marcon, Federico, 170

Marxism-Leninism, 187–88, 195, 199

materia medica, 169, 201n40; *Comprehensive Materia Medica* (Li Shizhen), xx, 6, 169–71, 173, 175

materialism in environmental history, xvii

Matsumura Shōnen, 166; *6000 Illustrated Insects of Japan-Empire*, 166, 179n31; *Memoiren Matsumuras*, 179n31

Mayr, Ernst, 189, 192–93, 195–96, 201n37; *Systematics and the Origin of the Species*, 192–93

McLachlan, Robert, 167, 170–71

Mendel, Gregor, 191

173, 182n70; political and biological nomenclature, 165–66, 167–68, 179n42; specimens treated by, 162, 163, 178n18; and transmission of scientific knowledge to China, 161, 165; women as collaborators, 178n13

Neitzel, Laura, 118

Neuroptera (lacewings), 166, 179n28; chronicled by McLachlan, 170–71, 176; "pseudo-neuroptera," 181n62. See also Odonata

New Life Movement (Japan, 1955), 118–19, 143, 151n8

Nho, Si-Kab, 108

niche construction theory (NCT), 69, 70

Nie Huang, Oceanic Complexities, Illustrated, 171–73

Nōgyō sekai (Agriculture world), 133

nonhuman agency, xvii

Odonata, 161–62, 166; Calopterygidae, 182n70; included in Neuroptera, 166, 179n28; as pseudo-neuroptera, 181n62. See also dragonflies; Neuroptera

Okumura Enshin, 101, 114n24

Okumura Ioko, 101, 111

Okumura Mitsuko, 101

100 Merry Wives, The (Hyakunin no yōki na nyōbō tachi), 136, 137–41, 154n61, 155nn71–72; women sweeping in front of their homes, 141

Oracle Bone Script, 5, 10, 18n6; zhi graph, 10, 19n36. See also pictographs

organophosphates, 153n33

Pak Che-ga, 98

parasites, xxii–xxiii, xxxn11, 134; elites as, 28

peasants and locust control, 80–84

Peking Medical Union, 175

Peking Natural History Bulletin, 170

pest control: aluminum screening, 149; entomology and, 186, 187, 191; flypaper, 121, 134, 149, 150; incineration as, 150; industry, 136, 149; legislation, 146; mosquito netting, xviii, 124, 142, 145; in the Science and Civilisation in China series, 177n5; United States, 126, 151n6, 152n20. See also insect eradication campaigns; pesticides

pesticides, 128, 151n9; benzene hexachloride (BHC), 125–26, 153n32; DDT (dichloro-diphenyl-trichloroethane), 124–26, 153nn31–32; diazinon, 153n33; malathion, 153n33; methyl parathion, 153n33; parathion, 153n33; organophosphates, 153n33; pyrethroids, xxii, xxxn24, 121, 125, 152n17; Varsan, 125–26, 136, 139, 140–41

pharmacopeias, 169–70, 172, 201n40; Comprehensive Materia Medica (Li Shizhen), xx, 6, 169–71, 173, 175

phonetic reconstructions, 10, 19n35; dong wu, 20n65

pictographs, 4, 5; animal depictions, 8, 10, 18nn5–6, 19nn35–36; fish, 10

Pliny the Elder, Naturalis historia, 169, 180n45

pollination, xxi

"portmanteau biota" (Crosby), 109

Project to Establish Hygienic Cities, Towns, and Villages (Nagasaki), 128

Pu Zhelong, 185

public health: under American occupation of Japan, 123–27; China, xix, xxvii; infrastructure, xxiii, 146–47, 147–48; Japan, xxvi–xxvii, 117–18, 120, 121, 128, 132, 134–35, 137; parasites, xxix–xxxn11, 134. See also environmental sanitation; insect eradication campaigns; Ministry of Health and Welfare (Japan)

pyrethroids, xxii, xxxn24, 121, 125, 152n17

9780295751801